W9-BRD-199

EFFECTIVE DATA BASE DESIGN

WILLIAM H. INMON

PRENTICE-HALL INC.
Englewood Cliffs, New Jersey 07632

Library of Congress Cataloging in Publication Data

INMON, WILLIAM H
Effective data base design.

Bibliography: p.
Includes index.
1. Data base management. I. Title.
QA76.9.D3154 001.64 80-15025
ISBN 0-13-241489-9

PRENTICE HALL SERIES IN DATA PROCESSING MANAGEMENT
Leonard Krauss, editor

Printed in the United States of America
10 9 8 7 6 5 4 3 2 1

Editorial Production/Supervision by Theodore Pastrick
Manufacturing Buyer: Anthony Caruso

For my dad, Garland Inmon

PRENTICE-HALL INTERNATIONAL, INC., *London*
PRENTICE-HALL OF AUSTRALIA PTY. LIMITED, *Sydney*
PRENTICE-HALL OF CANADA, LTD., *Toronto*
PRENTICE-HALL OF INDIA PRIVATE LIMITED, *New Delhi*
PRENTICE-HALL OF JAPAN, INC., *Tokyo*
PRENTICE-HALL OF SOUTHEAST ASIA PTE. LTD., *Singapore*
WHITEHALL BOOKS LIMITED, *Wellington, New Zealand*

CONTENTS

SIX

COMBINING CONSIDERATIONS OF FLEXIBILITY AND PERFORMANCE 81

SEVEN

LARGE DATA BASE DESIGN 95

EIGHT

RESTRUCTURING DATA BASES 105

PREFACE

The motivation for writing *Effective Data Base Design* stems from the curious phenomenon of consulting with many data base users and observing over a period of time a recurring pattern of the very serious problems encountered in the building of data base applications. The discussions with various data base users ranged from in-depth to superficial. In the vast majority of cases, the problems of their systems could be directly traced to design: system design, data design, and in some cases program design. In the case where program design alone was the problem (a rare phenomenon) other books on programming, modularity, structured walk-throughs, and so on, apply. In the more usual case, a poor design of data structures, data bases, and interrelationships of data, was at least a contributing factor in the building of unsatisfactory systems and was usually a large part of the problem. It became apparent that solving the major problems of data design would be a significant step toward the larger problem of building satisfactory data base applications.

It is a sad fact of life that when a person learns the mechanics of data base design, he or she often feels equipped to design an application with no further study. Perhaps the architects of today's data base management systems have done a disservice by making it too *easy* to construct data bases. The freedom the beginner has in constructing data bases usually results in a poor design, which in turn triggers all sorts of other problems. The purpose of this book is to explore many of those problems and to discuss how they can be prevented.

In many respects, the most critical moment in the life of the development of a system is its design. Once the designer casts the form of the data "in concrete," it becomes increasingly expensive (in terms of labor, money, machine resources, etc.) to change the design. The longer the system development process goes, the more expensive and distasteful change becomes, however the system is designed. This hard fact of life is usually learned by management after one (sometimes two) really expensive failures. The philosophy of "build it now, make it run later" has proven over and over again to be an open invitation to all types of failure.

This book attempts to do two things: to identify the major problems of data base design in today's production systems, and to discuss solutions to those problems that are appropriate at the design level and, in some cases, at the implementation level. The problems identified (in one form or the other) are typical of nearly all production data base applications. The author does not assume an understanding of IMS by the reader in the identification of data base problems. In discussing the solution to data base design problems at the design level, some discussions are relevant to IMS, others are not. In discussions of problems at their lowest level, the implementation level, some knowledge of IMS is quite useful.

The important points to be made that are couched in terms of IMS have equal validity in one form or the other in most other data base management systems. The interested reader should have little difficulty in translating those points when appropriate. The intent of this book is not to teach the reader IMS. The intent is to alert the reader to data base design concepts and problems and to discuss solutions.

The book attempts to address both the academic and the industrial reader. Different types of readers from industry will find parts that will interest them. Management will be interested in concepts of data base design. Data administration personnel will be interested in such topics as design review methodology and auditing of data bases. Data analysts will be interested in the performance of the application. Application personnel will be interested in the review checklist for data structures.

In addition to data base design discussed at the conceptual level, the academic community will be interested in such topics as data elasticity and the achievement of flexibility in data base design. There is a rather direct relationship between the analytical tools for flexibility and canonical data structures, for example.

Chapter 1, which deals with the evolution of data base design, is of particular interest. Because many of us deal with data bases and data base design on a day-to-day basis, we are too close to our work to perceive the nearly universal evolution that is occurring. Often, stepping back and viewing data base design and development from a different perspective leads to powerful new insights.

Chapter 5 addresses flexibility in the structuring of data. A careful reading of this chapter will arm the reader with analytical tools that will allow him or her to assess the degree of flexibility of a data structure early in the design phase of the system, at the point where change can be made to the data structure without severely impacting the system.

Chapter 7 addresses problems associated with large data bases. It is likely that new data base management systems (and new releases of existing systems) will have features that will ease some of the problems that exist today. With today's software, the designer is on shaky ground when the size of the data bases he or she is working with becomes unwieldy.

Chapter 8 discusses the restructuring of data bases. By means of introducing the user to some untraditional techniques of design, the author attempts to free the reader from some of the concepts of "classical" data base design. Often, elegance at this level pays dividends in many other places.

Chapter 10 discusses the structural analysis of data by means of a checklist. The list is a start toward tying down design review criteria diagnostics in a formal manner.

The exercises at the ends of some of the chapters are intended to be their own reward. For the most part there are no "right" or "wrong" answers. Instead, the benefit of the exercise will come to the reader in pursuing the activity suggested. It has been the author's experience that nothing replaces active participation.

The main thrust of this book is toward problems associated with the design and construction of production data base systems. Experimental or research-oriented data base management systems are not emphasized. In the future it is likely that relational data base management systems will make their presence felt in the world of production data base systems. When they do, they will inevitably carry with them their own set of problems (which may not be very different from those presented in this book). When that time arrives, it will be appropriate to address them in the same way that we address the data models that comprise the majority of production systems today.

ACKNOWLEDGMENTS

This book has been influenced technically by two people, Mark Sherman and Jim Sheetz. Mark's influence is found throughout the book. His contributions come mainly from conversations and work experiences. Jim's influence has come mostly through his presentations on such subjects as design review methodology and the development of on-line systems.

Also, Jeanne Friedman has been invaluable in her editing and commentary, both of which have helped to produce a better final product.

For these reasons I am grateful to Mark, Jim, and Jeanne.

W. H. Inmon

ONE

EVOLUTION OF DATA DESIGN

As a data processing installation matures, its needs for and priorities of design evolve. There is a rather predictable course of evolution that typifies most (not all) shops as they grow over time. Generally speaking there are four recognizable stages of evolution: design by default, design for the introduction of the data base concept, design for performance, and design for flexibility (Fig. 1.1).

DESIGN BY DEFAULT

The first level of design, *design by default*, is typified by processing flat files. The media associated with this level of design are sequential tapes, paper tapes, sorted cards, and some direct-access usage, such as ISAM (indexed sequential access method). Data is processed in batch mode almost exclusively. The designers at this level are faced with problems of large sorts and merges, multifile match programs, card editing and process-

Figure 1.1 Evolution of Data Design: Data design has evolved through four stages within a mature organization.

ing, and voluminous reports. Figure 1.2 depicts the environment of the designer.

Some of the major problems with design by default are redundancy of storage, redundancy of processing, an exponential increase in complexity as systems grow in volume and as they age, and inability to change the system as its real-world representation changes. The availability of data to the user is an issue because as new systems are created or changes to old systems are made, the cost of change and new development is high and programs often take a long time to implement. Data processing departments at this level of design often have the reputation of being sluggish and unresponsive to the user. Users learn not to expect expedient results. Often, by the time a new system or major changes to a system are

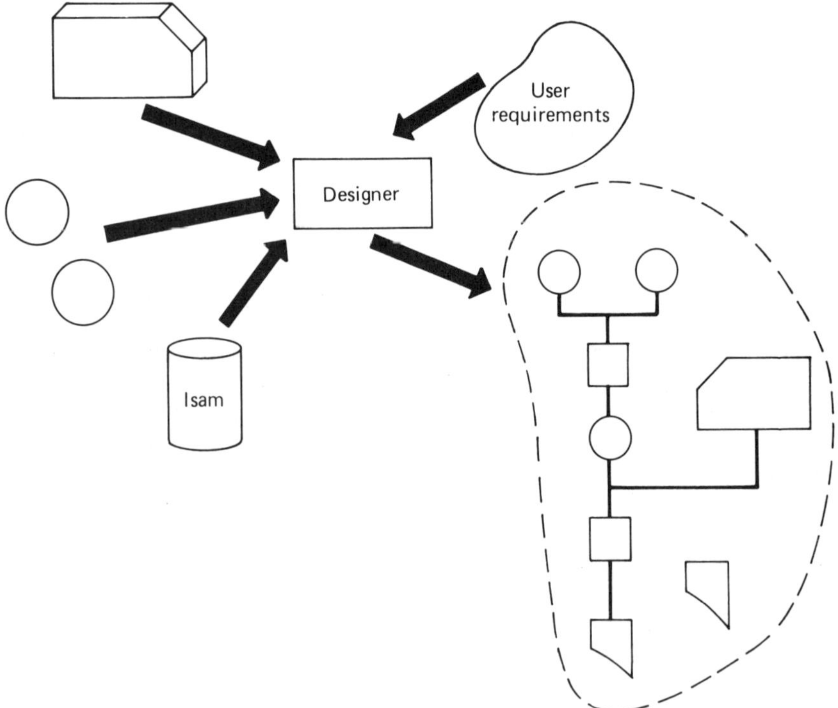

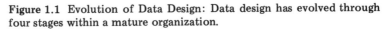

Figure 1.2 Evolution of Data Design: Design by Default. System development is usually a long and tedious process. Design is dominated by flat file concept.

implemented, the users' needs have changed so that the system as initially designed no longer fits the users' requirements. The exponential demand for new systems and the corresponding growth in system size leads to the next step of evolution—the data base concept.

DATA BASE CONCEPT

The *data base concept* evolved as an answer to the problems of design by default. Shops implementing the data base concept did so to reduce wasteful processing, reduce wasteful storage, centralize data and increase user availability, enhance control of data (physically and conceptually), and allow the development of systems to continue in an orderly fashion. Ultimately the concept of data base achieved some, but certainly not all of the goals the original enthusiasts had envisioned. Going "data base" did not prove to be the panacea it was originally advertised to be.

To achieve the data base concept, it is necessary to have a *data base management system* (DBMS). Most shops purchased the software; a few shops built their own. It is through the DBMS that the user can access data and derive the benefits of the data base concept. A major selling point of the data base concept is the ability to share data (or integrate it) and the freedom it allows the designer.

The designer can usually choose from many options of the DBMS to implement the same functional result. DBMSs are necessarily complex because they have to take into account many diverse and complex features, such as the teleprocessing network that used the DBMS, the physical storage of data, the logical views of data superimposed on the physical data, the needs of application programs to process the users' requests, the vagaries of the SCP (system control program) under which the DBMS runs, and operational aspects of the running of the system. In short, the greater the function of the DBMS, the more complex it becomes. Furthermore, the environment it manages is constantly changing. This makes the job of the DBMS even more difficult. Figure 1.3 depicts some of the complexities the DBMS must deal with.

The initial thrust of data base designers was to learn what tools were available within the DBMS and how to use them. In doing so, some of the potential of the data base concept was unlocked. There was a problem, however, in building data base systems knowing only what tools the DBMS offered and the mechanics of using them. The vast majority of the systems designed and built in this mode are terribly inefficient. In the case of batch systems, inefficiency may be tolerable or manageable. In the case of on-line systems, the inefficiencies of poor design are usually unacceptable for no other reason than high visibility. In fairness, as data

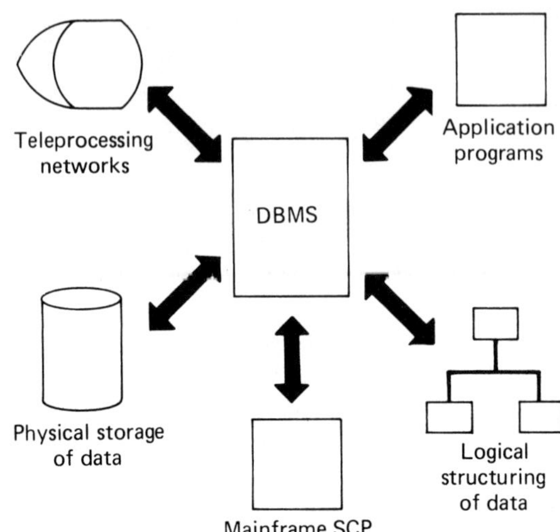

Figure 1.3 Evolution of Data Design: Data Base Concept. Data base management systems are complex because they manage many loosely related aspects of a computer system and a company's loosely related information requirements. Typically, the DBMS gives the designer many ways of achieving the same functional result.

base designers are taught the tools of using the DBMS, they are not usually taught the economies underlying use of the tools. It is a normal occurrence to have two very similar options perform in drastically different ways.

As shown in Fig. 1.4, the designer in the data base environment must

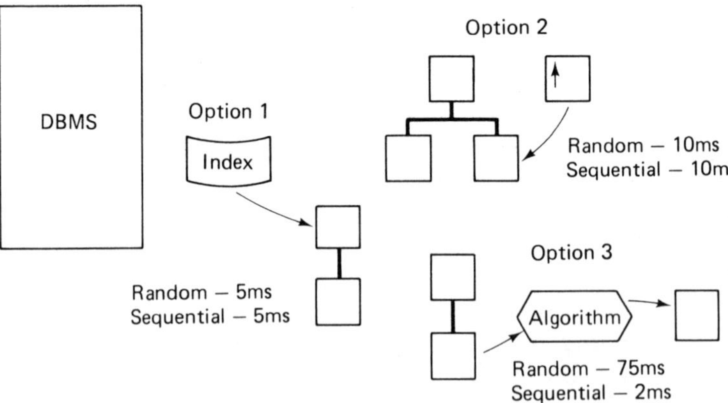

Figure 1.4 Evolution of Data Design: Design for Performance. To design for performance, the designer had to understand the economies involved in the selection of options available within the DBMS. Understanding the options allowed the designer to make quantifiably justified trade-offs. More sophistication on the part of the designer was required.

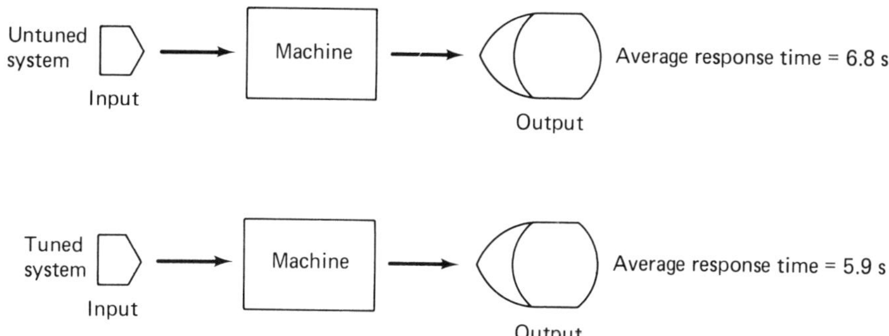

Figure 1.5 Evolution of Data Design: Design for Performance. Shops that did not design for performance found that tuning a system helped, but was not the secret to performance.

understand the significance of his or her choice of design options. Unless the designers have been forewarned about certain practices, the result is an innocently designed failure. With all the options that are available, the designer has to cope with some very complex and tedious problems based upon scanty, cryptic, or nonexistent information. It is then no wonder that systems designed at this level typically perform poorly.

Managers found that buying bigger and faster hardware was not a solution to performance as it improved performance only marginally. This was a surprise because in the era of design by default, buying upgraded hardware was always an alternative to greater throughput. Managers also found that tuning their systems produced only marginal results. In short, if the design had not been done with performance objectives understood from the very start, there was not a lot the manager could do except to rebuild the system.

Figure 1.5 illustrates the fact that marginal performance can be obtained by tuning the system. Tuning is a constant effort, since the size of data bases, the transaction volume and mix, the degree of organization of data, and many other relevant factors are constantly growing.

Figure 1.6 shows that adding machine speed and capacity is not the solution to achieving satisfactory on-line systems.

DESIGN FOR PERFORMANCE

The first step in *designing for performance* is to understand the underlying economies involved in choosing DBMS options. Because of the complexities of the DBMS, this is not always an easy thing to do. Once the economies are understood, there are several steps that can be taken. The

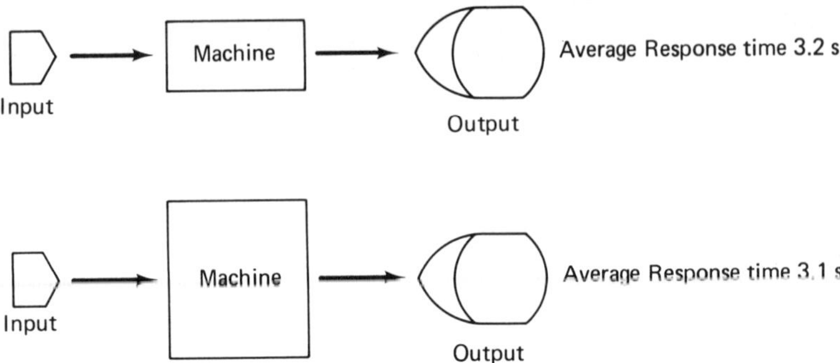

Figure 1.6 Evolution of Data Design: Design for Performance. Shops that did not design for performance found that going to larger and faster hardware did not necessarily appreciably improve performance.

first is to create quantifiable standards that enhance successful performance. The second is to create guidelines for the designer should he or she not have any other indication of what is expensive and what is not expensive to use. The third is to ensure that priorities in the design process are clearly established. This guarantees that important aspects of design are not overlooked while focusing on some trivial detail. It is very easy to get lost in the details of a DBMS and optimize some small aspect of design while one or more major considerations are overlooked. The fourth step (for some shops) for on-line system development is the concept of the standard work unit at all levels of design. The standard work unit concept quantifies the amount of resources used by any execution of a transaction and produces a uniform distribution of the profiles of transaction executed. Finally, design review methodology is introduced to try to identify and correct bottlenecks before they are programmed into the application and thus expensive to correct.

It was a shock when managers found they could not tune their way to performance or buy hardware to achieve it. They had no real option to the achievement of satisfactory performance except to design it correctly from the start. This took discipline and a more-than-cursory understanding of the DBMS. It also had political overtones far removed from the technical world.

Once systems were built that performed well, designers relaxed in the comfort that they had finally mastered the art of data base design. Time passed and systems aged. The users' environment changed and designers were called upon to make the corresponding changes in their data bases. In some cases the changes were easy to make and could be done quickly and cheaply. In many other cases, the changes greatly affected the structure of the data base (and thus the programs that supported the structure) and were costly and lengthy to effect. Managers became irritated because of this effort. It became clear that data designed with flexibility in mind was highly desirable.

DESIGN FOR FLEXIBILITY

As a general rule, data base design that is optimized for performance directly conflicts with *design considerations for flexibility*. Thus, it is not surprising that a highly efficient system is usually highly inelastic. Data designers found that the ingredients necessary to the construction of flexibility were understanding the data as it exists in the users' environment, understanding the structures of the DBMS and their limitations, and understanding the relation of elements to their boundary and the corresponding implications. Figure 1.7 depicts the environment of the designer at this level of sophistication.

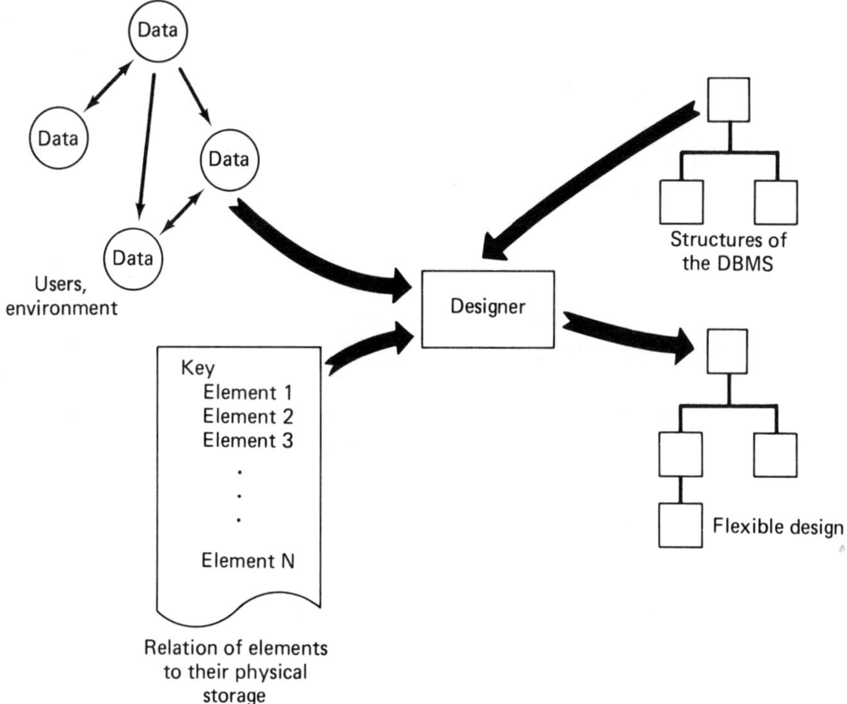

Figure 1.7 Evolution of Data Design: Design for Flexibility. The ingredients necessary to the construction of flexible structures are a thorough understanding of the user's environment, the structure of the DBMS, and the relation of elements to their physical storage.

Once a designer grasps the importance of those concepts, he or she is able to intelligently balance them against the considerations of performance. What results is a calculated trade-off based upon the requirements and goals of the system versus the risk of change in the users' environment and a minimization of impact of change. The designer has to understand what the major risks are and how to best prepare for them.

The final result is a state-of-the-art design. At last, the original promise of the data base concept was being fulfilled, but not without much effort and many mistakes.

DATA INTEGRATION

As a related issue, how has the goal of *data integration* (or *data sharing*) been met through the various stages of evolution? One of the justifications of moving from design by default to the data base concept was data integration. Initially, there was some consolidation of data, but as data base design progressed through its stages of evolution, data did not become significantly more integrated. The degree of data integration over the course of evolution is shown by Fig. 1.8.

To a limited extent, there were some technical reasons why data integration was not achieved, principally the problems of large data bases and conflicts of interest when data was used in an exclusive mode. These problems were applicable in only a few instances. The main reason data was not shared was a reluctance by management to loosen the reins of control at whatever cost. Generally speaking, where data was shared, management understood and supported the data base concept. Conversely, when data was not shared, management was not aware of the advantages and economies that could be derived. In a few cases management had been educated to the data base concept but did not trust the day-to-day operation of their system to another group when the data involved was crucial to the business of their department (Fig. 1.9).

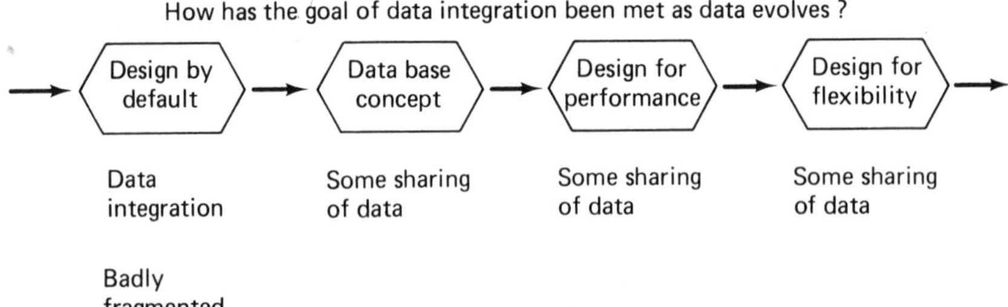

Figure 1.8 Evolution of Data Design: Data Integration. How has the goal of data integration been met as data evolves? In short, the goal of data integration has been only marginally accomplished.

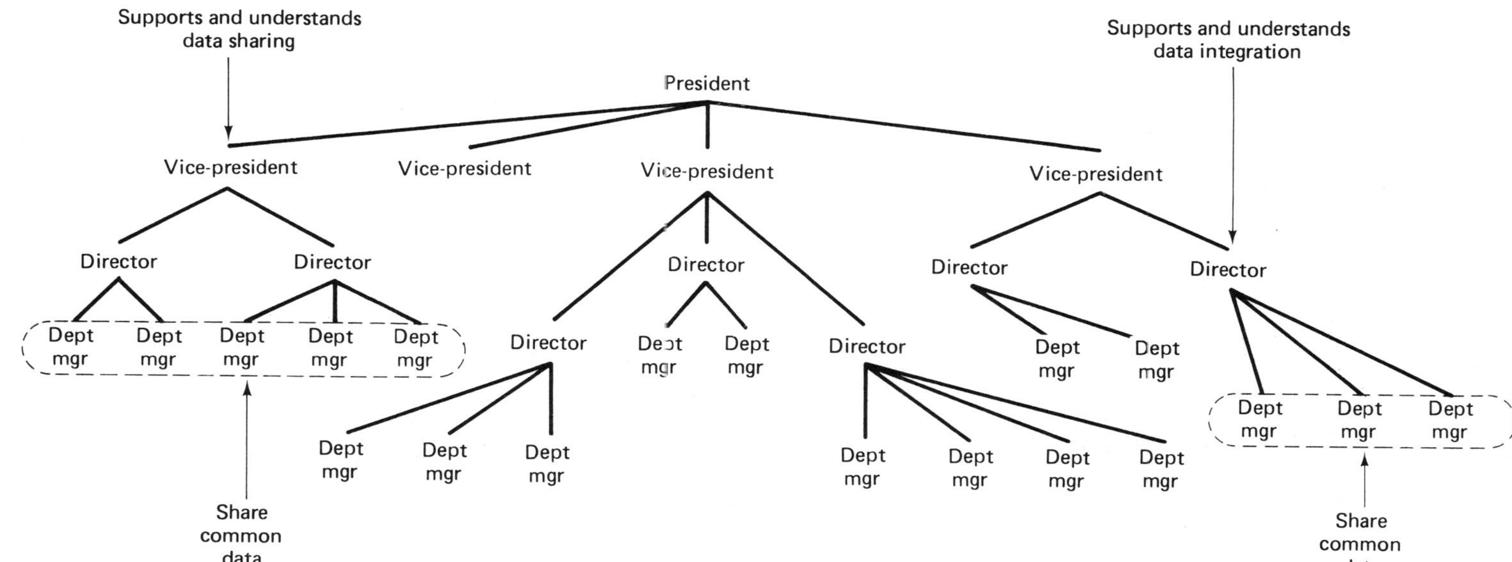

Figure 1.9 **Evolution of Data Design: Data Integration. The technical tools for sharing data have been in place for a long time. The reason for the lack of shared data is political.**

SUMMARY

The phases of data base design evolved (and are still evolving) in response to some basic need or pressing problem with the current mode of operation. The data processing organizations that suffered the least from the impact were those that recognized the evolution that was occurring, recognized what the next phase would be, and sought answers before the problems that were pressing became acute. The less successful organizations allowed problems to become acute before being forced to seek a new direction. As the stages of evolution are viewed from a broad perspective, it becomes clear that the design process is the key to achieving flexible and efficient systems.

TWO

DATA BASE ENVIRONMENT

A data base exists as a physical collection of data organized to reflect the needs of the user. The difficulty in building effective data base systems is not in the mechanics of construction, but in the intelligent design and purposeful use of the data base.

The world of data base design is one of selecting options where there are few absolute rights and wrongs and surprisingly few general guidelines. The specifics of the problem at hand determine what is a good choice or a bad choice. A practice that is impractical in one environment may be optimal in another environment. The major factors that determine the quality of a decision are the end user's application, the characteristics of the hardware on which the data base system exists, and the software that is used to handle the data.

There are two important components in the development of a data base system that must be successfully implemented:

1. Data base design.
2. Program design.

If either of these components has significant flaws, the system will be something less than a success. It is quite possible to develop one component quite satisfactorily and the other poorly. The best data base design, coupled with an unsatisfactory program design, will be as unsuccessful as a poor data base design coupled with a good program design. It can be stated, however, that if the data base design is poor and must be reworked, well-designed programs will be adversely affected, whereas when program design is poor and data base design is adequate, the impact of correcting faults is somewhat less severe.

Since there are no hard-and-fast rules to guide the designer, other criteria must be used to produce a sound design. This book attempts to explore those criteria. To understand them it is necessary to be aware of the environment in which data bases are created and used.

PROGRAMMING ENVIRONMENT

A data base exists through its programs. It is loaded, retrieved, updated, and deleted by programs. Most DBMS (IMS, TOTAL, ADABAS, etc.) operate in a mode of executing precompiled programs, but some (such as QBE) operate in an interpretive mode. Even in the case of QBE, the data is defined to the DBMS and is operated on by programs generated by QBE. Since data bases have a very close relationship to the programs that support them, decisions concerning the structuring of data must be filtered through programming considerations. Figure 2.1 shows that data bases closely relate to programs that support them.

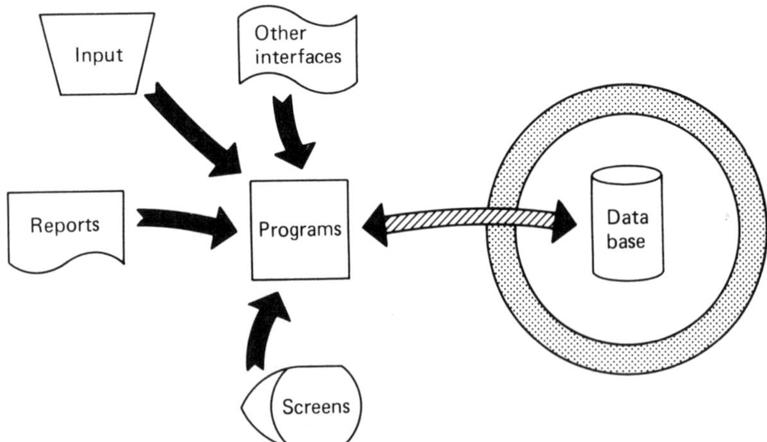

Figure 2.1 Data bases are created, updated, and scanned by programs. The DBMS isolates data bases from general use by formatting the data according to the system's own conventions.

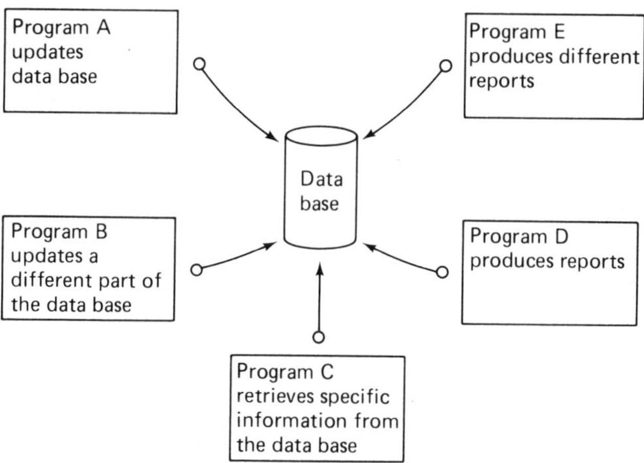

Figure 2.2 The activity of the data base is performed by several programs, each of which has a separate function.

A standard practice is to group programs by function as they relate to the data base. Some programs update all or portions of a data base, other programs retrieve data and produce reports, and still other programs scan the data base collecting selective data. It is usually beneficial to impose a limit on the scope of function of a program and separate it from other programs that serve other functions. This separation allows certain functions of the system to remain operational when other functions may be inoperable. This philosophy is reflected by Fig. 2.2.

Programs that support data bases should be designed with certain characteristics in mind. The following is a very minimal set of those characteristics:

1. *Performance*—The purpose of the program should be accomplished with a minimum of executable code and, especially, a minimum number of calls to the data base.
2. *Flexibility*—A program should be able to be modified by a competent programmer with a minimum amount of effort.
3. *Simplicity*—The program should be as straightforward as the specifications will allow.

STORAGE MEDIA OF DATA BASES

Although data bases usually reside in direct-access devices, they may exist on sequential storage (tape) as well. Tapes typically are used to back up copies of data bases. Sometimes archival data or audit data is stored on tape. There are severe limitations to data that reside on purely sequential storage media, and it may be stretching a point to call data in that form a data base. Some of the limitations of sequentially stored data are:

1. No random usage of data.
2. Complex interfaces between sequential sets of data.
3. Usage is limited to one environment at a time.
4. Redundancy of processing and storage.

The data base concept is aimed at unlocking the full potential of data and does so best by accessing data both sequentially and randomly. For this reason, data bases normally reside in direct-access storage. To grasp some of the concepts of data base design, it is necessary to know a few basic facts about direct-access organizations. The following discussion is at a very general level. It is necessary to go beyond this level when working in the environment of a specific DBMS, machine, and storage device. The discussion should, however, give the reader a general flavor of some of the pertinent issues.

DIRECT ACCESS

The most useful data organization for on-line processing is *direct access* (for HDAM in IMS). It allows limited amounts of data to be accessed quickly and with little overhead. Space on a disk(s) is allocated for the data base. This space is then divided by the DBMS into two subareas: the primary data area and overflow (e.g., IMS's HDAM—Root Addressable Area and overflow). Initially, the DBMS attempts to map data into the primary area by means of a randomizer (Fig. 2.3).

When a user requests specific data, the application program that is servicing the request goes through the DBMS to reach the required data. The randomizer (which is part of the DBMS) is a subroutine that translates the key of the data to an address that lies within the primary data area. If that particular space is already occupied by other data (synonym collision), the DBMS searches elsewhere in the prime data area or into overflow.

When a record is to be accessed, the randomizer is used. Given the value of the key to be located (in IMS, the key of the root), the randomizer translates the value into some area in the primary data area. The location is calculated and is accessed. The values obtained are analyzed by the DBMS. If the desired record is found or if no record exists at that location, the search is over. If, however, a different record is found, other locations in the prime area or overflow must be searched. Only then can it be determined if the data is in the data base.

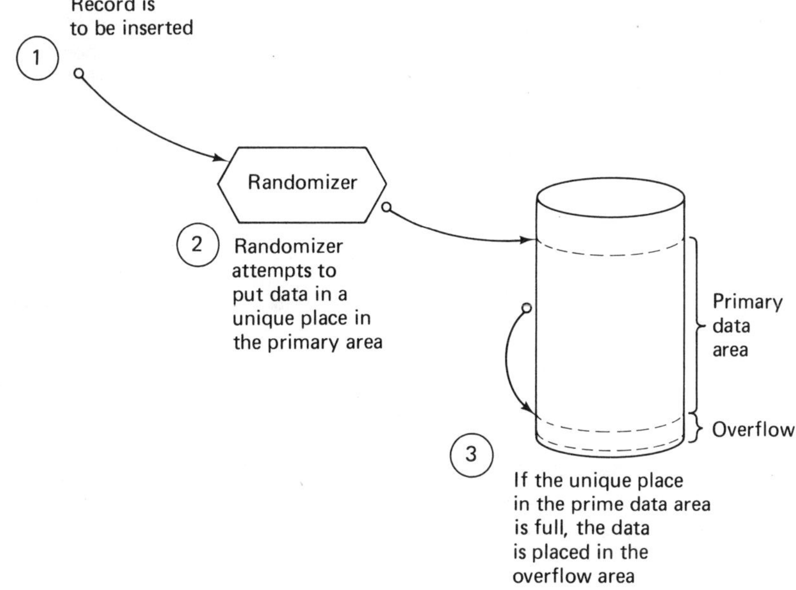

Figure 2.3 How data is loaded into direct-access storage.

INDEXED DATA

Access to data through an *index* is another useful organization of data. As in direct access, an amount of space in direct-access storage is allocated for the prime data area. In addition, an index and overflow are allocated. There may be more than one level of indexing (it may be advantageous to put one or more levels of index in main storage at execution time). These indices do not have to reside in or near the prime data area.

The index consists of a set of values of keys of records (in IMS, the key of the root) and an address where the key can be found. The index may point to every record or every *n*th record, depending on the designer's arrangement.

Initially, data is loaded in sequence into the primary data area. The index is created while the load is occurring. During update, when a record is inserted, first the index and then the sequential ordering of data are used to determine where the record is to be placed. If space is available, the record is written; otherwise, it is written into overflow. Figure 2.4 illustrates loading of data into an indexed data base.

In an indexed environment, data can be accessed directly or sequentially (in IMS in sequence by the key of the root segment). *Direct* retrieval uses the index to randomly locate a record while *sequential* access proceeds along the physical order of the data base (interrupted occasionally by a pointer from the prime data area to overflow). Sequential

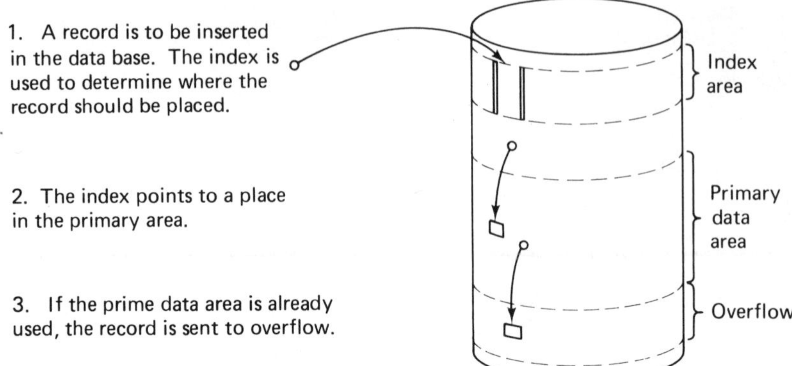

1. A record is to be inserted in the data base. The index is used to determine where the record should be placed.
2. The index points to a place in the primary area.
3. If the prime data area is already used, the record is sent to overflow.
Index area
Primary data area
Overflow

Figure 2.4 How data is loaded into an indexed data base.

searches can be expensive (in terms of input/output) when many records are in overflow, since the sequential order of data is preserved by means of pointers, regardless of the actual physical placement of data.

COMBINED DIRECT AND INDEXED DATA

It is possible to achieve the effect of *combined direct and indexed* sequential organization of data by randomizing data into the primary data area (Fig. 2.5) and building a separate index that points to each root.

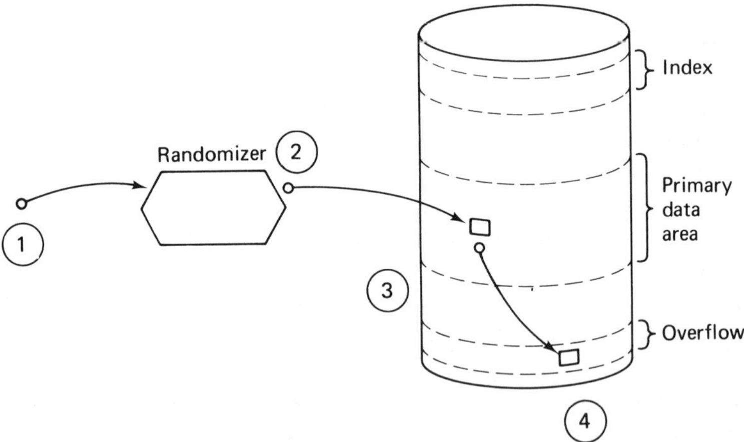

Figure 2.5 How a direct indexed data base is built: 1. A record is to be inserted. 2. Its key is randomized and the proper location in the primary data area is determined. 3. The record is inserted in the primary data area unless it is already occupied, at which point it is inserted into the overflow area. 4. After insertion into either the primary data area or the overflow area, an index is built pointing to the location of insertion.

Since the root segments are physically stored in a random order, sequential access is done through the index. Usually, it is a good practice to read only a few records using the index, since each access using the index goes to a new location in the data base.

Although the physical organization of data is a prime factor in data base design, it is certainly not the only one. The complexity of the data base, the different uses of the data that are possible, the total space requirements, and many other factors must be considered. Small and simple data bases that serve a limited function usually present no problems in adapting them to their media. It is when data bases are large and complex that problems associated with their physical existence manifest themselves. As a data base grows in size, it becomes increasingly challenging to keep it functioning in an acceptable fashion.

DATA BASE MANAGEMENT SYSTEM

Even though there are legitimate design considerations that deal with the physical media of a data base, far and away the most influential factor in data base design is the DBMS. The function of the DBMS is complex and varied because it must actively participate in several widely dissimilar environments that are constantly changing. The DBMS provides an interface between the machine, the data, and application programs. Through the application program, the DBMS handles the activity of the user of the system. The DBMS manages data activity with the native data organization. It interfaces with the operating system and hardware on which the data base exists and if a network monitor is being used, interfaces application requests to and from the monitor. The DBMS is necessarily a complex function and changes continually as different aspects of its environment change. Figure 2.6 is a representation of the relationship of the DBMS to its environment.

DBMS—ON-LINE, BATCH

The DBMS normally provides capability for handling data in the *batch* mode and may offer the facility for *on-line* function. The impact on application design decisions is large, depending on which (or both) of these basic modes of operation the system will operate. The reason that there is such a difference between design decisions for batch and on-line operation is that in a batch mode it is relatively easy to isolate data and its associated processes if performance or availability becomes a problem. In the batch mode it is usually possible to solve throughput problems by buying more system (hardware) capacity.

Such is not the case with on-line processing. As a general rule, a pro-

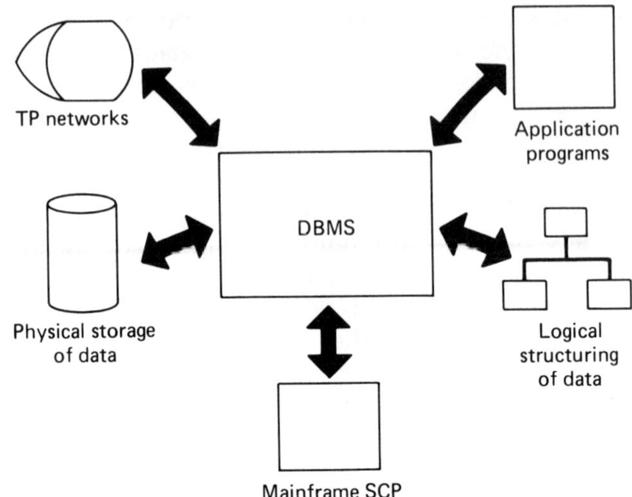

Figure 2.6 The DBMS must interface with and integrate many widely diverse functions. Not only are these functions complex in their own right, they are constantly being changed.

gram in batch can be insulated from other programs so that if there is a problem, it will not affect other programs or data in the system. In an extreme case, a batch program (or programs) can be moved to any entirely different machine to solve throughput problems. However, in the on-line environment, the opportunities for isolation are limited. Of necessity, programs and data must coexist together and share a common resource other than the hardware—the on-line controller. The exposure of an on-line system that malfunctions is much greater than that of a batch program problem. Independence of batch programs and the close relationship of on-line programs is shown in Fig. 2.7.

Because of this basic difference between batch and on-line, programs and data bases that are used in one or the other mode reflect different philosophies. It is an accepted practice to design data bases to fit well within their own mode of operation. Complications can occur when data is to be used in both modes.

Batch Mode Characteristically a batch environment is best suited for sequential processing, although the data base concept allows the batch designer to take advantage of random access of data. Usually, activity to be transacted is collected, and at some point all of the activity is transacted against the data base. Batch runs tend to be long-running (relative to on-line activity). In IMS, for example, data bases designed for batch mode tend to have more levels of hierarchy with more siblings. The time spent by IMS interpreting the structure of data is generally not im-

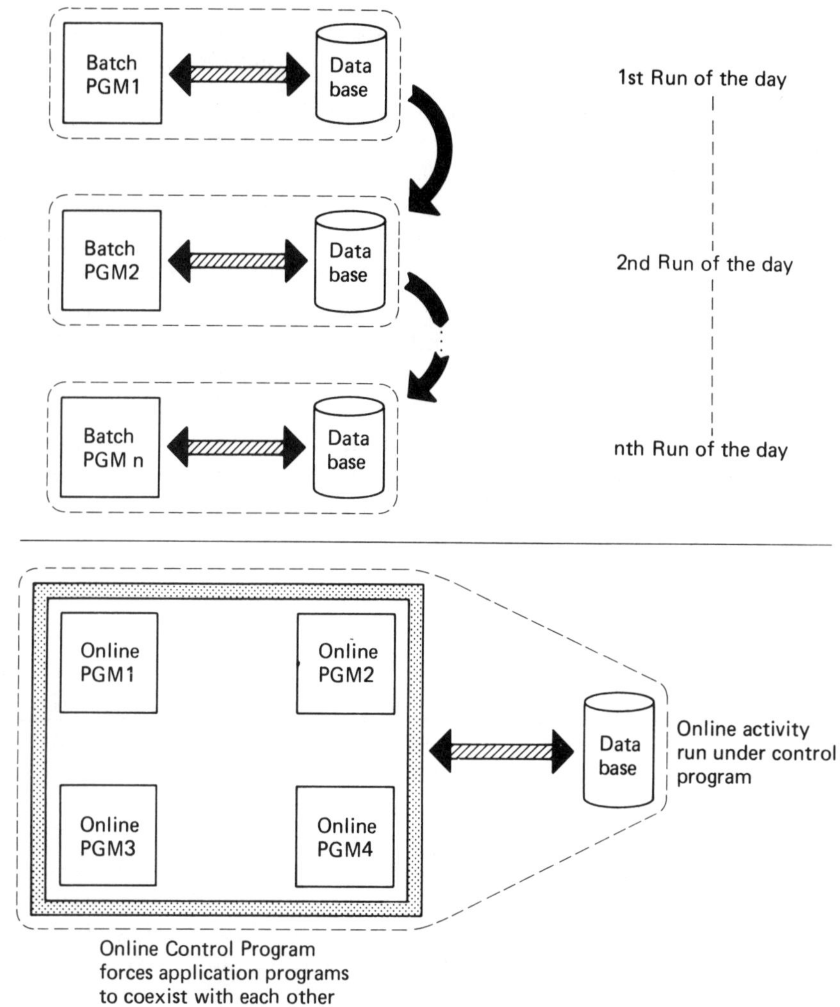

Figure 2.7 Programs in batch mode exist relatively independently from each other, whereas in the on-line mode, application programs necessarily exist together. This difference in the two modes of processing has profound implications in the design of the data and programs for an application.

portant. In batch, activity tends to occur in large clusters, not in fine pieces. It is not uncommon to scan an entire data base, manipulating data or examining and extracting data according to some criterion.

On-Line Mode On-line systems are "up" for a certain number of hours a day (up to 24 hours). When they are not up or when the operator takes a data base off-line, the data base is available for batch activity. This time is referred to as a *window*. When the on-line system is up, good design practices dictate that the system display the following characteristics:

1. Each transaction (or program) should be limited in scope. It should use a minimum amount of resources. This allows other transactions an opportunity to compete for the same resources.
2. The data bases are streamlined for on-line processing. They are designed to minimize I/O activity to satisfy most requests. In IMS, this amounts to a data base of few hierarchical levels and few segment types.
3. The units of work that the end user can do are broken into basic functions. (This is rather subjective; what may be basic to one user may be sophisticated to another.)
4. Data bases are available across transaction types in the on-line system. If a transaction ties up a data base (or part of a data base) for a significant amount of time, other significant parts of the on-line system may suffer.

DATA BASE RECOVERY

An essential part of every DBMS is how it handles data base integrity and recovery. The elements of data base recovery impact the design of data base applications. Incorrect data (and occasional inoperable conditions) caused by application program error should be corrected by the programmer, but other errors are usually handled external to application programming. Errors (through operations, hardware, or software malfunction) will occur over the life of a system in the most perfect of environments, so data base recovery is a fact of life. A DBMS should allow the designer to adopt one of several recovery philosophies, depending upon the nature of the system and the error.

1. *Postponed recovery*—Users can be warned and prevented from accessing data that should not be accessed, but in all other respects the system is unimpaired.
2. *Limited data recovery*—A specific unit or units of data can be restored without disturbing the remaining data in the data base.
3. *Partial recovery*—A certain type of data or sections of data can be recovered without disturbing the remaining data in the data base.
4. *Data base recovery*—The entire data base can be recovered to:
   a) A selected point in time
   b) A previous version of the data base, or
   c) The execution of a given transaction.

5. *External recovery of data bases*—Data can be recovered external to the DBMS. This type of recovery is done using utilities not integrated with the DBMS or by directly changing data in the data base without using facilities of the DBMS. This option is usually the least desirable because of the exposure in manipulating the internals of a DBMS externally.

The time required to recover a data base is critical. In an on-line environment, when the process of recovery is occurring, the data (or parts of the data) are unavailable on-line. If a single data base is used by many transactions and then becomes unavailable, its loss will have a major impact (which is one rationale for keeping data bases simple and small). Good design practices and effective operating procedures minimize the occurrence of wholesale data base recovery.

DBMS AND SYSTEM THROUGHPUT

The DBMS and the supporting software and hardware on which the DBMS operates have a certain capacity for work to fulfill the needs of the system. Can the DBMS handle the volume of activity and yield an acceptable response time? Is there enough capacity to handle the projected workload? Is there sufficient time in the batch window? Can the DBMS handle system resources adequately?

To build a successful data base application, these questions must be considered. Application design—both program design and data design—is the key to the effective use of the DBMS. Attempting to build data base systems without understanding the importance and impact of good design usually leads to unsatisfactory results.

STRUCTURAL CAPABILITIES OF A DBMS

When data is defined to the DBMS, it is stored and transported according to some structure. What is of importance are (1) what structures cannot be represented by the DBMS and (2) of the structures it can represent, which are expensive to implement.

The inability of a DBMS to represent a type of data structure is a constraint on the designer, as is the inability of a DBMS to handle efficiently all representations of data that can be defined. If an application is best represented structurally in a certain way and the structure can be defined to the DBMS, there is no problem. But if the DBMS must be awkwardly shaped to handle a structural type that it is not designed to handle, there will probably be a problem.

Of the structures that are available within the DBMS, some will be implemented quite naturally and others will be awkward. Of great importance to the designer are the costs (in terms of machine resources and storage) associated with different structural representations.

From a broad perspective, it is comfortable to have a DBMS that handles many structural types (i.e., a degree of generality associated with the structural capabilities of the DBMS). What may not be apparent is that there is a price to pay for generality. This fact is usually not stressed by the software vendor.

DATA BASE AND THE USER

The data base application as a whole (programs, data, networks, etc.) performs some function (hopefully useful) for an end user. It would be nice to demonstrate the following traits at the user level.

1. *Effectivity*—Does the system produce accurate, reliable, timely, and complete information?
2. *Simplicity*—Is the system easy to use and understand?
3. *Cost effectiveness*—Is the function being performed worth the expense of development and operation of the system?
4. *Flexibility*—As the user's environment changes, can the system change as well (in a timely and inexpensive manner)?
5. *Development*—Can the system be built in a reasonable amount of time?

Building a data base system that exhibits all of the foregoing features is quite a challenge. There are many factors that work at cross purposes to each other. Furthermore, in the current state of the art, no DBMS has an entirely satisfactory set of tools to satisfy all users' needs.

PITFALLS OF DATA BASE DESIGN

The environment of data base systems has many complex parts. Organizing and controlling a data base project is technically and administratively challenging. When a designer sets out to accomplish a task, the options available and the requirements of the task may be overwhelming. To make intelligent decisions, the designer must be aware of *all* the costs associated with a given decision in relation to other options available. This is difficult to do. The worst possible result of not understanding all the implications of a decision to discover the real costs after the system has been constructed.

EXERCISES

1. Briefly describe each of the following. Identify the relation between each entry in the list and the entire development process. Identify the responsible departments within a company.
   a) User function.
   b) System development time.
   c) Processing time.
   d) Structural complexity of data.
   e) Storage space (for data).
   f) Algorithmic complexity.
   g) Tailor-made DBMS.
   h) Generalized DBMS.
2. Based upon your discussion of Exercise 1, give specific examples of trade-offs of the following:
   a) Processing time vs. storage space.
   b) Processing time vs. system development time.
   c) System development time vs. algorithmic complexity.
   d) Processing time vs. structural complexity of data.
   e) Structural complexity of data vs. system development time.
   f) User function vs. development time.
   g) User function vs. processing time.
   h) User function vs. structural complexity of data.
   i) Structural complexity of data vs. storage space.
   j) Tailor-made DBMS vs. generalized DBMS.
3. Select a large, complex program for analysis. From the data structures in the program, select one data element representative of:
   a) An element that is used extensively in the program.
   b) An element that is used in three or four places.
   c) An element that is not used at all.

   Determine the impact on the program for each type of data element when:
   i. The element is physically enlarged.
   ii. The element is deleted from the structure (and hence from the program).
   iii. The element is repositioned in the structure.
   iv. Another element must be added to the structure and referenced in every case where the original element is used.

Suggest some strategies to reduce the impact of changing data elements within a program.

4. In an existing system, select data elements that represent:
   a) A key of a widely used segment (or record).
   b) An element that contains information directly from the user's environment.
   c) An element that contains information internal to the system (pointers, counters, cross references, etc.).
   d) An element that appears on multiple outputs (screens, reports, etc.).

   For each type of element:
   i. Identify the source of input.
   ii. Identify where it is changed.
   iii. Determine when the data will leave the system.
   iv. Determine all places where the data is accessed for purposes of output.
   v. Locate any other type of data element that contains the same values. Examine the rationale for not having combined the data elements.

   Based upon the foregoing analysis, suggest some guidelines for documentation, organization of the functions of creation, update, and deletion of data, and redundancy.
5. Select a program that randomly accesses two or more physically distinct sets of data. Suppose that the program was changed so that it could only access tape. Analyze the impact on the program. Suggest processing alternatives for working in the strictly sequential mode of operation.
6. Select two programs, one of which:
   a) Accesses data directly through a randomizer.
   b) Accesses data directly through an index.

   Then:
   i. For each type of program, trace the flow of control from the application program through the operating system to the data, then back to the application program for a single retrieval of a unit of data (segment, record, etc.). Pay particular attention to buffers used, I/Os, seek time, rotational delay, and overflow processing.
   ii. Based upon information derived in part i, analyze the performance characteristics of:
      1) Twenty consecutive random calls for data in a randomized environment.
      2) Twenty consecutive random calls for data in an indexed environment.

3) Twenty consecutive sequential calls for data in a randomized environment.

4) Twenty consecutive sequential calls for data in an indexed environment.

iii. Based upon information derived in part ii, make some generalizations about direct and indexed retrievals.

iv. Repeat parts i to iii, but for insertion of new segments rather than retrievals.

7. In a batch environment (without the use of a DBMS), design a control program that will:
   a) Allow data to be accessed directly.
   b) Allow data to be accessed sequentially.
   c) Allow concurrent access in both direct and sequential modes.
   d) Allow different parts of the same data set to be updated and retrieved at the same time.
   e) Allow different programs multiple views of the same data.
   f) Provide for recovery of data when normal processing is interrupted.
   g) Protect data that is being updated by one program from update or retrieval by other programs. Discuss implications on performance.
8. Repeat a) through g) for an on-line environment for an existing data base application, outline the necessary steps to implement the following recovery philosophies:
   a) Postponed recovery.
   b) Unit recovery.
   c) Partial recovery.
   d) Data base recovery.
   e) Recovery external to the DBMS.

   For each philosophy:
   i. Identify the exposures and trade-offs.
   ii. Discuss the impact on:
      1) Operations.
      2) The user.
      3) Data administration.
   iii. Determine which philosophy is currently being used in your shop and evaluate that decision.
9. For an existing data base application that has both batch and on-line processing:
   a) Determine the average, previous maximum, and projected maximum number of transactions processed in a day.
   b) Determine the average, previous maximum, and projected maximum of batch processing for a day.
   c) Determine the unused capacity of the machine on which the application is running.

d) Roughly project when the current resources will not be able to meet the requirements of the application.

10. For a small data base application to be developed, translate the users requirements into:
    a) Conceptual processes.
    b) Conceptual structures of data.

    Relate the processes to each other where appropriate. Identify all relationships between data structures.

    Roughly project the data into its physical form.

    Simulate one full cycle of operation of the system from the users' standpoint. Determine problems such as:
    i. Wasted work.
    ii. Unnecessary repetition.
    iii. Critical response times.
    iv. Throughput bottlenecks.
    v. Stability of the data.
    vi. Unanticipated usage of the system.

THREE

DATA STRUCTURES AND DATA DESIGN

The entire process of design, from the feasibility study to the point at which program specifications are to be written, can be considered to be data base design. The early phases of data base design involve the identification and organization of conceptual data elements, an analysis of their relationship to each other, and a conceptual understanding of the processing requirements that will use the data elements. At that time, very little consideration is made of the physical representation of the data. The final output of this phase of design is an *information model* (or *conceptual model*) of the data.

The next phase of design (which is absolutely crucial to the success of the system) is the transformation of the information model into a *storage model*. In this phase the designer takes the conceptual data of the information model and creates tangible data structures that are defined to the DBMS (see Fig. 3.1).

The criticality of translating conceptual data into a storage model can be stated in this way: Some degree of error can be tolerated in defining

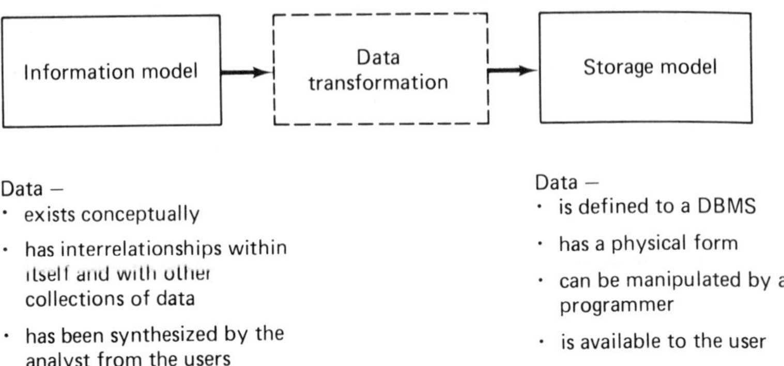

Figure 3.1

the information model without severely impacting the data base system, but a mistake of any consequence in transforming conceptual data to a storage model will surely result in serious consequences. In the case of IMS, the designer translates the information model into a hierarchical structure(s). In doing so, he or she must be thoroughly familiar with the implications of choosing design options in a hierarchical environment.

DATA STRUCTURES WITHIN A DBMS

DBMS software available today generally supports three major ways of building data structures. Structuring data with inverted lists (which ADABAS supports) is quite efficient for the purpose of data retrieval. Networking of data structures (supported by IDMS) allows the designer many possibilities in representing interrelated data types. The other major mode of structuring data is hierarchical (supported by IMS). Most of the general concepts discussed in this book apply in one form or the other to most DBMS (to some extent), although specific considerations and examples directly apply to IBM's IMS.

HIERARCHICAL DATA STRUCTURES

It is necessary to understand what the components of a hierarchical data base are, how they relate to each other, and their limitations in understanding the implications of design in a hierarchical environment. Good design practices are based on more than a knowledge of the mechanics of construction of a hierarchical data base. The components of hierarchical data structures are deceptively simple, so that it is a temptation to trust intuition rather than going through the rigors of discipline necessary to grasp the implications of design. Three basic components form an IMS hierarchic data structure: data elements, segments, and relationships between segments.

DATA ELEMENTS

A *data element* may be descriptive or structural. A *descriptive* data element describes some property or quantity of data related to the user's environment, whereas a *structural* data element is used to describe something about the structuring of the data.

A descriptive data element has some physical form: binary, character, packed decimal, and so on. It is an abstraction of some entity in the user's environment, such as a balance in a savings account, the number of subassemblies of a given assembly, or the number of dependents of an employee. Figure 3.2 shows descriptive data elements as they physically exist in direct-access storage.

A data element has two properties that are the chief concern of the designer: volatility and the propensity for environmental change (semantic change).

1. *Volatility*—refers to the rate at which the contents of a data element change. A highly volatile data element might be the Dow Jones average; a low-volatility data element might be the marital status of a person.

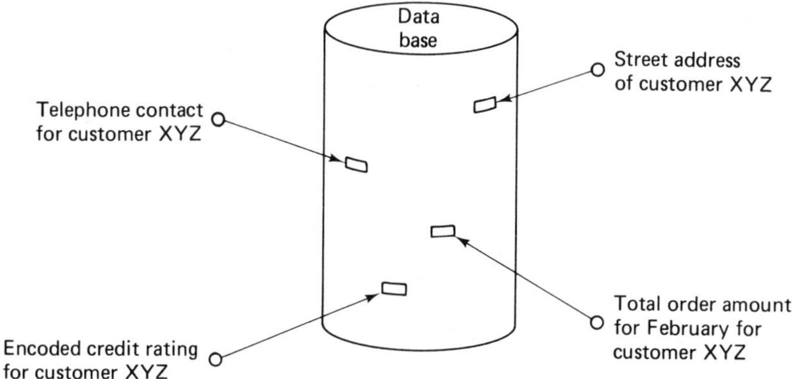

Figure 3.2 Descriptive data elements.

2. *Environmental change* (hereafter this term will be used to refer specifically to the phenomenon described)—refers to a change in the way the data is stored and transported within the DBMS. A simple example might be altering the physical size of the element (from 9 to 10 bytes), moving the element to another segment, or having to associate new elements with an existing element (e.g., adding the ZIP code to an address). An environmental change normally occurs because of a change in the user's environment. As an example of environmental change versus volatility, see Fig. 3.3.

As far as design is concerned, the issues related to volatility are update frequency, reliability and integrity of data, storage considerations, and others. Problems associated with volatility are usually visible. The problems associated with environmental change are not so obvious. In IMS, the designer simply physically shapes the data one way and hopes that changes in the user's environment do not necessitate frequent physical

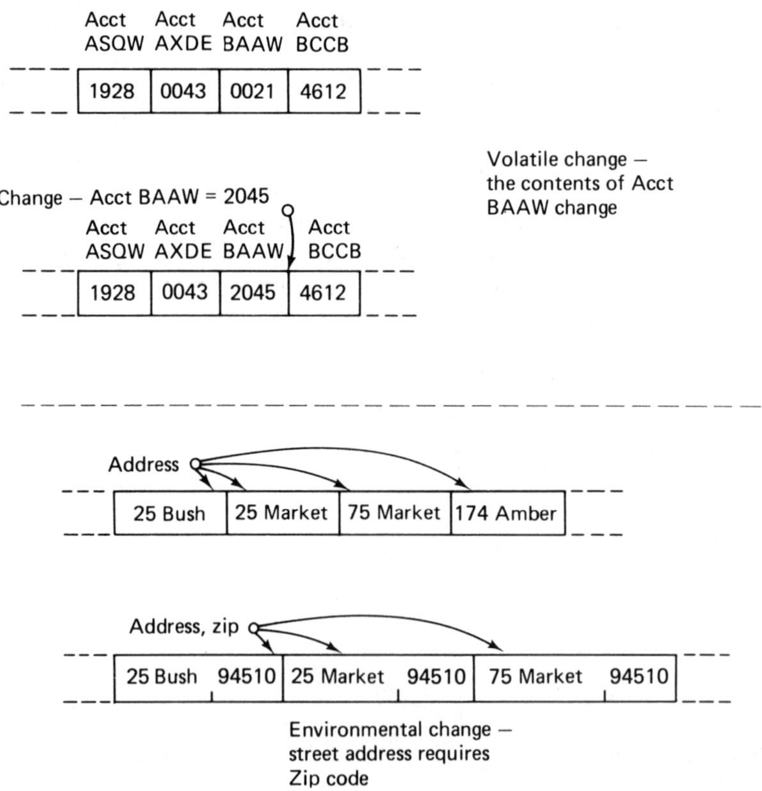

Figure 3.3 A change in volatility requires a change of data values. An environmental change requires a change in data structuring.

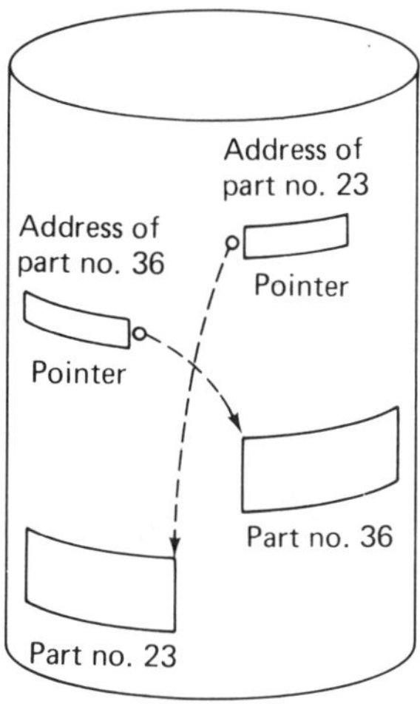

Figure 3.4 Pointer elements are a reference to some other location in a data base.

restructuring of the data. The designer is put in a vulnerable position when he or she ignores or underestimates the chances and impact of environmental change.

An example of a structural data element is a *pointer*. It is used to explicitly relate two elements or segments (in the same or different data bases). A pointer can refer to the specific address of a location in a data base or be a symbolic reference that can be translated by a randomizer or index to uniquely locate another piece of data in some data base. A simple pointer is shown by Fig. 3.4.

A pointer is used for structural information, not descriptive information. It does not say anything about itself or the location to which it refers. Instead, it makes a statement concerning the relationship between parts of the system.

SEGMENTS

A *segment* is a grouping of data elements that is usually (not necessarily) ordered into a predefined format (see the Appendix). Other standard data base terminology for a segment is a record or node. In IMS, segment length is fixed or variable (the more common case is fixed). Like a data element, it is an abstraction of some entity in the user's environment. The elements in an IMS segment may be thought of as being connected by a "boundary"; that is, the data elements that exist within the segment are bound together by the fact that they are stored together and transported together. The unit of storage then forms the boundary of

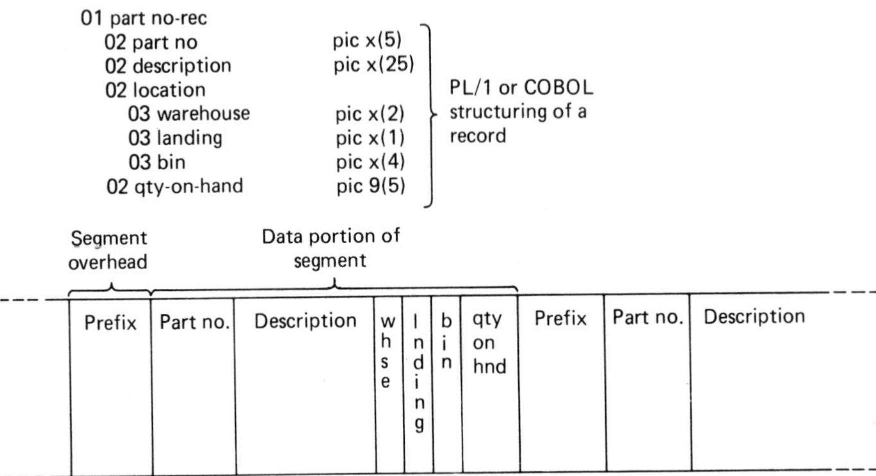
01 part no-rec
02 part no pic x(5)
02 description pic x(25)
02 location
03 warehouse pic x(2)
03 landing pic x(1)
03 bin pic x(4)
02 qty-on-hand pic 9(5)
PL/1 or COBOL structuring of a record
Segment overhead
Data portion of segment
Prefix
Part no.
Description
whse
lnding
bin
qty on hnd
Prefix
Part no.
Description

Figure 3.5 Data base segment.

the segment. Because of this physical binding, one of the fundamental decisions that a designer makes relates to the segmentation of data.

An IMS segment may or may not have a key. The usual case is for keyed segments, but there are plenty of valid cases where the segment is unkeyed. The elements that a segment contains may be descriptive or structural, or both. Every segment has some overhead (or *prefix space*) associated with it. Prefix data is primarily used by the DBMS to interpret and maintain the hierarchic structure of segments. Typically, the prefix contains such information as pointers, segment codes, delete bytes, counters, and other information necessary to the functioning of the DBMS. A segment necessarily contains at least a key or a data element; otherwise, there is no reason for its existence. When a segment does contain a single key or data element, very often the data structure should be redesigned, because a segment of very short length (relative to its prefix) may be a waste of space and processing time.

The most common arrangement of an IMS segment is one that contains a key and several data elements. This arrangement corresponds roughly to a data structure that might be found as a record layout of COBOL or PL/1 (Fig. 3.5).

RELATIONSHIPS BETWEEN SEGMENTS

Hierarchical data bases are made up of different segment types, each of which has a relationship with other segment types. Each segment in a data base, except the root, has at least one relationship with some other segment. That relationship is referred to as a *parent/child relationship*.

For every occurrence of the parent, there may be zero or more occurrences of the child, the child may have only one physical parent, and a child may not exist if the physical parent does not exist. The parent/child relationship may be descriptive or structural. (*Note:* In the case where descriptive and structural data elements exist in the same child segment, the relationship is normally thought of as structural.) A *descriptive* relationship between segments is one in which the child reflects some characteristic belonging to the parent. A *structural* relationship is one in which the child connects the parent to some other segment. Figure 3.6 is an example of these relationships.

One way of viewing a hierarchical data base is to consider it a tree structure, where each segment is a node of the tree and the relationships between segments form the branches of the tree.

There can exist multiple segments beneath any parent. If the segments are the same type and on the same level, they are called *twins*. If they are on the same level and are a different type, they are called *siblings* (Fig. 3.7).

The size of a segment, the number of twins, and the number of segment types depend upon how the designer interprets the user's environment. There are useful data base systems with both small and large amounts of data. In its most effective form, the *hierarchical structuring* of data is a vehicle to efficient and convenient usage by both programmer and end user.

To achieve the greatest benefits of hierarchical structuring, the designer needs to have a grasp of the motivation for segmentation. Well-organized data is easy to use, operationally efficient in the management of space, and capable of undergoing physical redefinition with a minimum of effort.

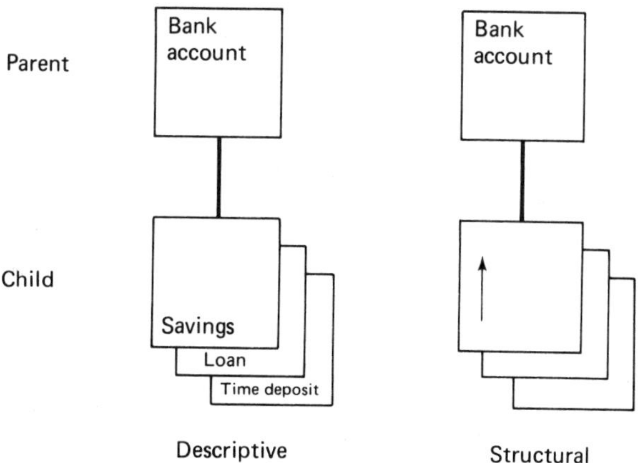

Figure 3.6 Parent/child (P/C) relationship may be either descriptive or structural.

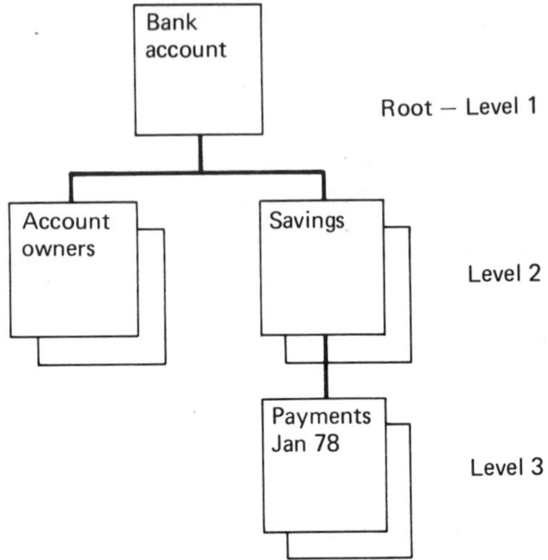

Figure 3.7 Typical hierarchical data base structure.

Using segmentation correctly as a tool enhances the chances of achieving these goals. Following are some of the fundamental motivations for segmentation:

1. *Segmentation as an abstraction*—it is used to separate data into units that conform with the way data are viewed and used in the real world (Fig. 3.8). The ability to separate data into discernable, disassociated units forces organization in a data base application.
2. *Reduction of redundancy by segmentation*—it allows a given ele-

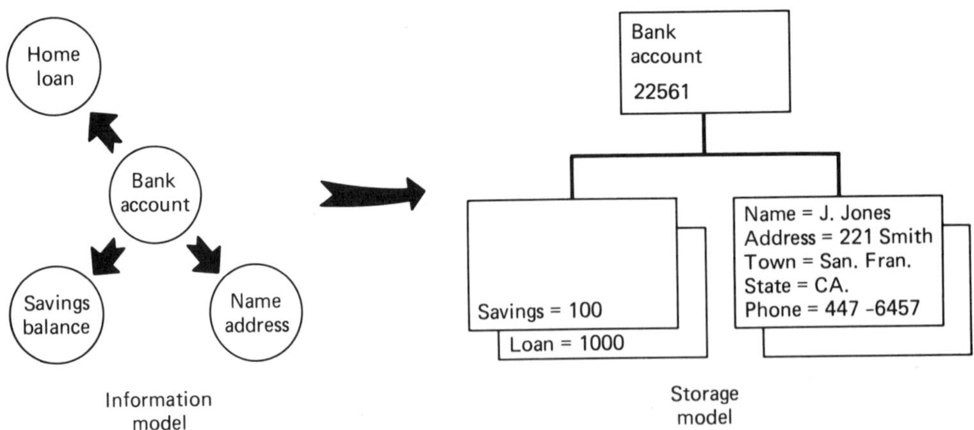

Figure 3.8 Data is segmented to represent a meaningful unit of information in the user's environment.

Bank account = 94012
Owner = J. Jones
Address = 221 Smith
Savings = 100

Bank account = 94012
Owner = J. Jones
Address = 221 Smith
Loan = 200

Bank account = 94012
Owner = J. Jones
Address = 221 Smith
Cert. deposit = 650

Redundant structuring of data

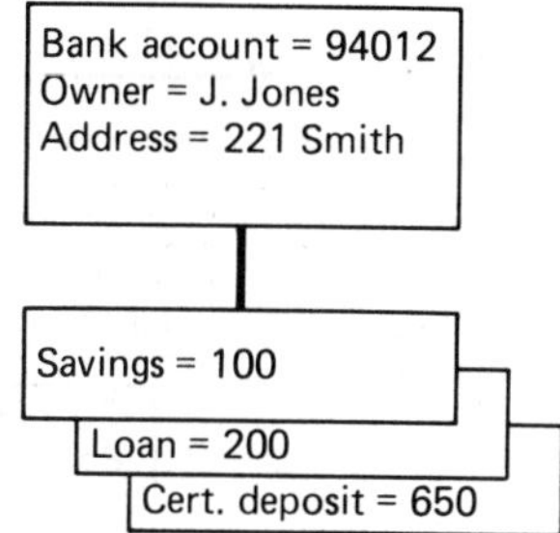

Figure 3.9 Segmentation can be used to reduce redundancy.

ment the chance to exist a minimum number of times in the data base (Fig. 3.9). Removing redundancy has many advantages, such as not wasting space and eliminating unnecessary processing time.

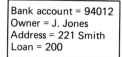

3. *Simplification of processing*—by breaking data into meaningful units, the content and function of the data become clear (Fig. 3.10). Such may not be the case where data are conglomerated.
4. *Separation of data elements according to their volatility*—data elements whose volatility is greatly different probably have differing operational requirements (Fig. 3.11). Separating elements according to their volatility can result in less total work done by the system.
5. *Separation of large units of data into smaller, more manageable units*—in some cases the size of a unit of data can be a constraint in a system (Fig. 3.12). Breaking the large unit into finer pieces may save much processing time.
6. *Iterations of data*—there are several problems with data structures that contain space for iterated values, such as tables. When the table is not full, space is wasted, and when the table needs more space than is originally allocated, extra processing and wasted space are the result. Only when a table is exactly full are iterated values optimal. Segmentation allows an iterated structure to be represented with a high degree of generality (Fig. 3.13).
7. *Separation of data elements according to propensity for environmental change*—when a designer segregates data elements according

Bank account = 94012
Name = J. Jones
Address = 221 Smith
Loan = 100
Savings = 200
Cert. deposit = 550
Credit rating = 1000
Master charge = 75
Bank amer. = 100
Home loan = 52,250
2nd lien = 1st Fed Savings
Wife = K. Jones
Car loan = 2,200
Salary = 12,000
Employer = Water Works
Phone = 221 - 4212
Last payment = Dec. 76

Bank account = 94012
Name = J. Jones
Address = 221 Smith
Credit rating = 1000
Wife = K. Jones
Salary = 12,000
Employer = Water Works
Phone = 221 - 4212
2nd lien = 1st Fed Savings

Loan = 100
Last payment = Jan 77

Savings = 200
Last payment = Feb 76

Cert. deposit = 550
Bought = May 75

Master charge = 75
Last payment = Dec 76

Bank Amer. = 100
Last payment = Mar. 78

Home loan = 52,250
Last payment = Apr. 78

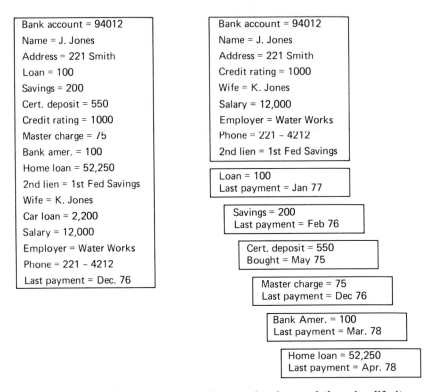

Figure 3.10 Segmentation can help organize data and thus simplify its intent and usage. In this case, "last payment" may refer to any one of several types of payments as it stands in the unsegmented case. When the data is segmented, it becomes clear what "last payment" applies to.

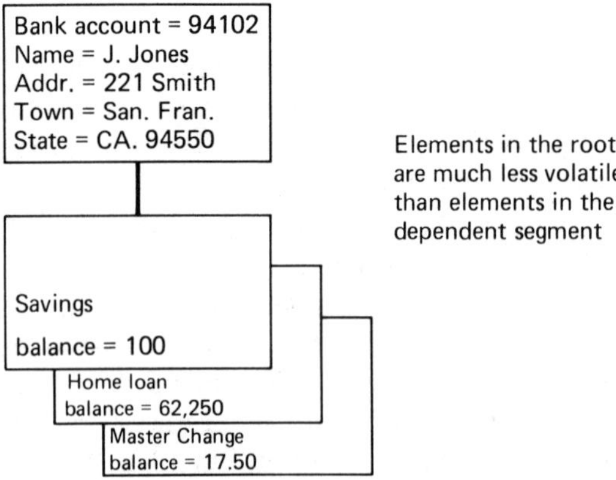

Figure 3.11 Segmentation can be used to separate elements with different levels of volatility.

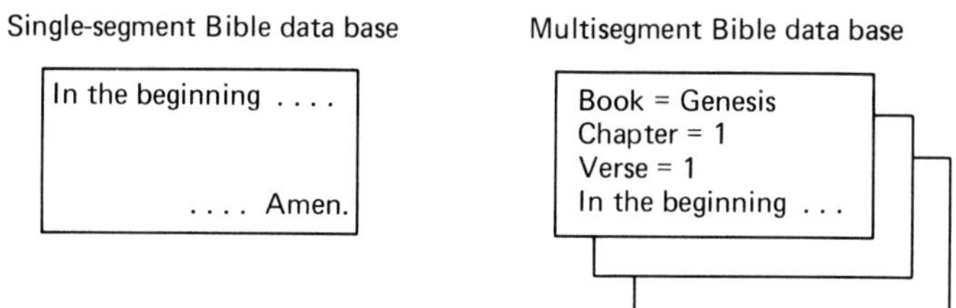

Figure 3.12 Segmentation can be used to break data into reasonably sized units.

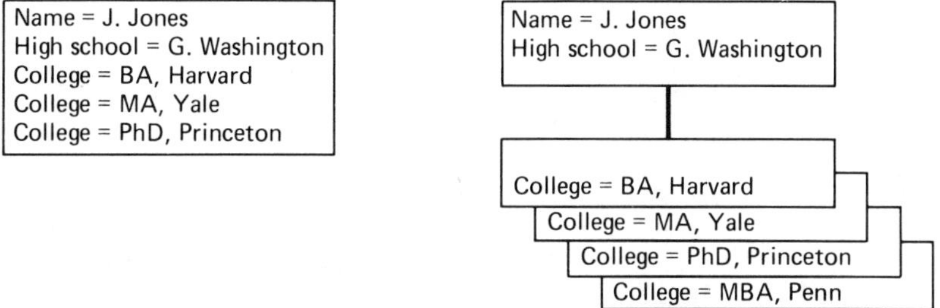

Figure 3.13 Segmentation can be used to add a degree of generality to data base.

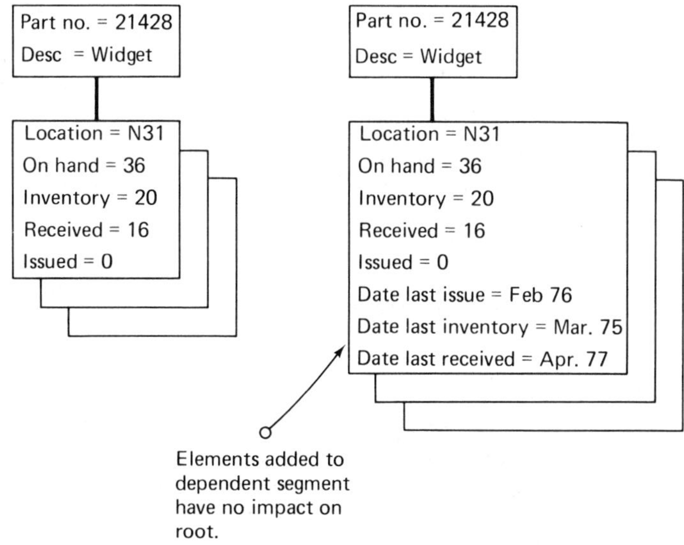

Figure 3.14 Data elements with a high propensity for environmental change can be separated by segmentation.

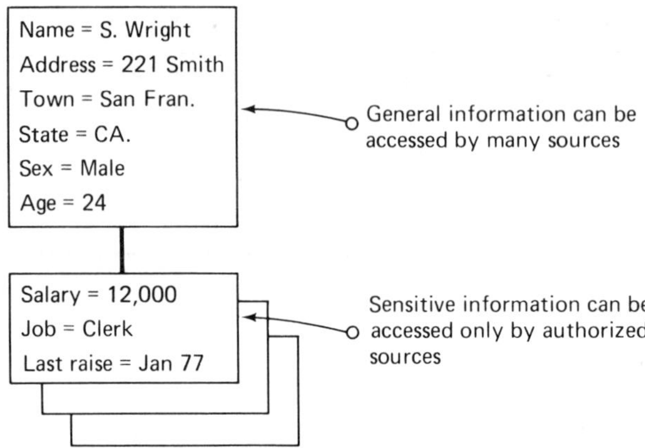

Figure 3.15 Segmentation can provide some security features.

to their propensity for environmental change, he or she minimizes the impact of future change in the user's environment (Fig. 3.14). This ability to segregate data is especially effective where data are predictably unstable.

8. *Security*—separation of data elements because of sensitivity of the contents of the data can be used in conjunction with other security features to achieve a level of security (Fig. 3.15).
9. *Ability to view the same data in multiple ways*—segmentation allows data to be grouped so that different users see the same data in a different way (Fig. 3.16).

There are more motivations for segmentation than the ones presented here. In deciding how data is to be segmented, the designer is rarely influenced by a single factor; more likely several motivations will be brought to bear.

DATA BASE RELATIONSHIPS

There are two ways that data bases can relate to their data bases—through explicit relationships or implicit relationships. An *explicit relationship* connects two data bases by the explicit physical existence of a pointer. An *implicit relationship* between data elements or data bases is one that is entirely supported by application program logic where there is no other tangible connection between the entities that are involved. An example of an implicit relationship would be a personnel

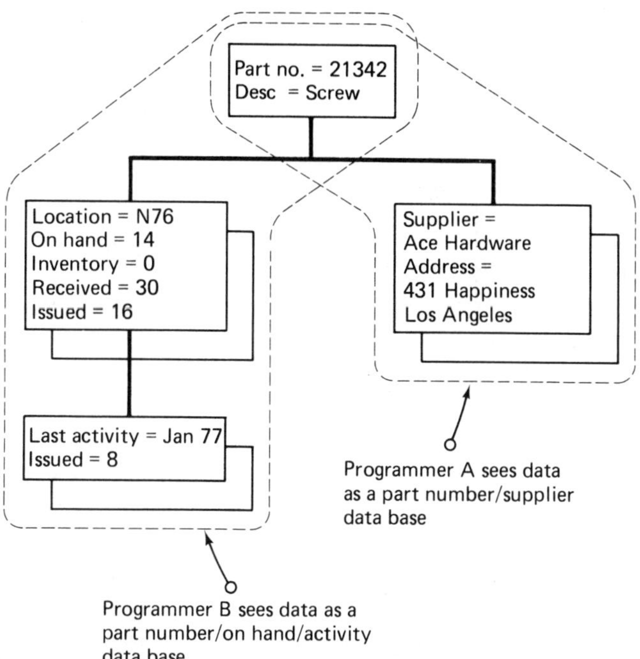

Figure 3.16 Segmentation allows different people to see the same data differently.

data base that contains the rate of pay for an employee and a payroll data base that contains the hours worked and cumulative wages. To calculate the amount of cumulative wages to be added for a given pay period, the personnel data base must be accessed to determine the rate of pay. Figure 3.17 addresses two ways of relating data bases. In one case, data bases are validated by pointers explicitly within the confines of the DBMS. In the other case, an application program summarizes all a and b in data base B to a total Σ a and Σ b in data base A.

Explicit relationships are implemented in two modes: through the *facility of the DBMS* (in IMS, logical relations) or through *application programs* (Fig. 3.18). Each philosophy has its advantages and disadvantages. Implementing pointers within the facility of the DBMS limits the types of structures that can be built. Pointers in the DBMS may be operationally more efficient to use than those implemented through application programs. Also, the DBMS has utilities that support necessary maintenance functions for the pointers, which is not the case with pointers maintained by application programs. However, there are times when these very same utilities will present a technical barrier to solution of problems.

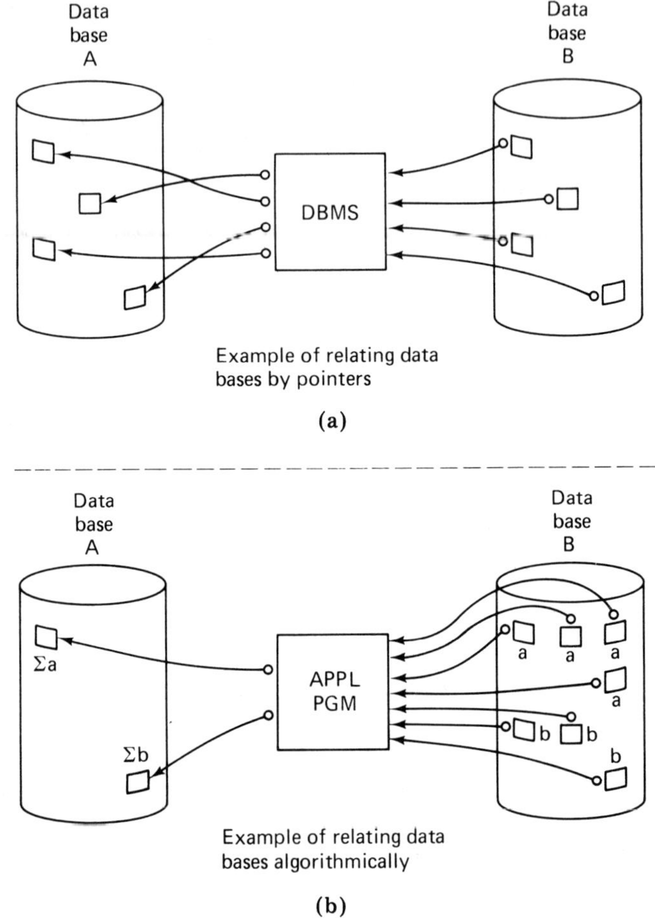

Figure 3.17 (a) Pointers in data base A point to data in data base B through the facilities of the DBMS. (b) Data in data base B sums to values contained in data base A.

Following are some of the trade-offs associated with the different ways of building pointer relationships:

DBMS-supported Pointers

1. Limited structural capability.
2. Operational efficiency.
3. Existing support utilities.
4. Locked into facilities of DBMS.

Application-supported Pointers

1. Unlimited structural capability.
2. Overhead in data base calls.
3. Must write tailored utilities.
4. Capability of dealing with exceptions.

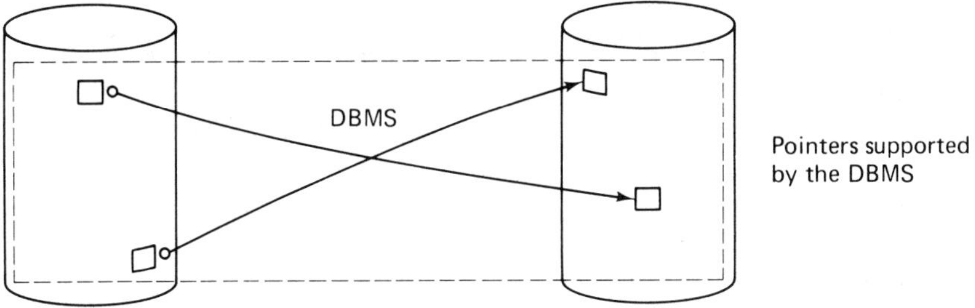

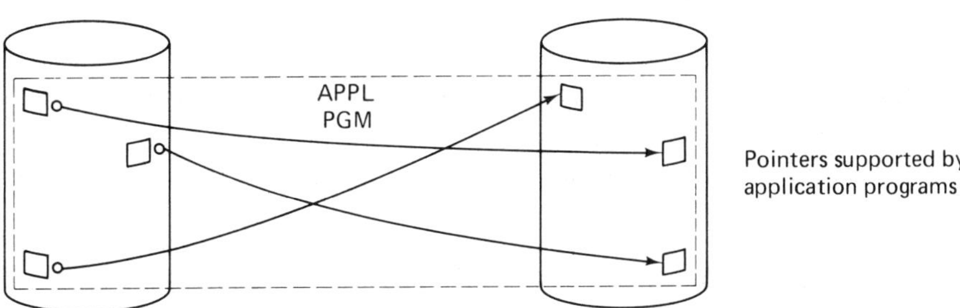

Figure 3.18 Pointer segments can be implemented within the scope of the DBMS or as a part of an application.

EXERCISES

1. Select an existing data base application. In terms of data elements, trace the flow of data from the point of origin to their entry into the system, through update, and finally to output. Analyze the grouping of data elements and propose alternative arrangements. Locate any redundant elements and investigate the rationale for redundancy. Identify and justify any data elements with unusual characteristics (such as size, brevity of existence, volatility, volume, etc.).
2. Select an application that uses pointers. Classify the types of pointers as:
   a) Symbolic.
   b) Direct.
   c) Explicit relationships.
   d) Implicit relationships.

Then:

i. Discuss the impact of changing symbolic pointers to direct, and vice versa.

ii. For all explicit relationships, discuss the advantages and disadvantages of a segment containing both symbolic and direct pointers.

iii. Discuss the possibility of changing any explicit relationship to an implicit relationship, and vice versa.

iv. Can any implicit relationship be changed to an explicit one? Any explicit relationship to an implicit one?

3. How does the DBMS delineate a segment internally (i.e., how does the DBMS know how to determine the beginning and end of a segment when it is stored as raw data)?

   What is the exact format of the segment after the DBMS returns it to the program? What data can or cannot be accessed by the application program? Is there a way to access data in a segment that is not to be shown to the programmer?

   How does the DBMS know if any two segments (twins, dependents, parents, siblings, etc.) are related? How does the DBMS relate that information to the program?

   Does the DBMS necessarily know all the relationships between segments? If not, why not?

4. For an existing data base application, identify each segment type in relation to other segment types (twin, parent, etc.). Determine what entity in the user's environment is represented by a segment. Are any segments redundant? Can any two segments be consolidated? Should any segment be separated into more than one segment type? If you would change the structure of the data base, what would you change, and why?

5. What advantages (and disadvantages) does building an explicit relationship within the confines of a DBMS have over a relationship built external to the DBMS, in regard to:

   a) Data reorganization.
   b) Initial loading of data base.
   c) Segment insertion.
   d) Segment update.
   e) Segment deletion.
   f) Maintenance utilities.
   g) Future system enhancement.
   h) Data integrity.

FOUR

DATA BASE DESIGN AND OPTIMIZATION

There are several parameters on which data base design can be optimized. It may be appropriate to emphasize one aspect at the cost of the others, depending upon the application and general nature of the project. That decision is a philosophical one which must be made and supported by management. Usually, each parameter of system optimization should be considered so that trade-offs can be planned. The basic criteria by which data base design can be optimized are:

1. Application development time.
2. Execution time.
3. Data storage.
4. User level of expectation.
5. Data flexibility.

OPTIMIZATION OF DEVELOPMENT TIME

Optimizing system development time entails making the system as simple to code and construct in as short an amount of time as is possible. It usually means that the time spent designing the data structures that will support the system is kept at a minimum. The less time spent in data and program design, the more time is available for other aspects of development. In a large project some parts of the system may be in the process of design while other, interrelated parts of the system are being programmed or implemented. Such a risky plan of action should be embarked upon only when management is absolutely committed to a minimization of development time and is willing to assume the amount of risk being taken.

Almost inevitably, overoptimization of development time results in disaster once the system approaches implementation. In case after case, the disaster occurs because the proper focus on data and program design has been done haphazardly and the result is a system that must be reprogrammed constantly. This course of action is recommended only in a posture of extreme duress, and then only when personnel intimately familiar with the DBMS, the application, and the construction of rapidly written programs are available.

The reason optimization of development time is a temptation is that between the DBMSs and the available programming languages, there are enough options to accommodate almost any design, regardless of how inflexible or inefficient the design may be. Indeed, one of the real weaknesses of many DBMSs is that they have too many options. It is not difficult to produce a design that has data structures and programs that will do the job for a particular concept. What is difficult is to propose the best data and program design that will do the job and that can be done only by carefully matching the requirements of the system with the strengths and weaknesses of the DBMS. For best long-term results, such a job should not be done in a panic.

Unfortunately, the pitfalls of overoptimization of fast development time may not be obvious until well into the life of the project. The dangers of this approach are not apparent until testing or implementation of the systems points out flaws, which by then are expensive to correct. Typically, flaws occur in system performance, inflexible data, or in unnecessarily complicated processes.

OPTIMIZATION OF EXECUTION TIME

Optimization of execution time within a data base system is usually associated with an on-line system, but not necessarily. In certain cases in a batch environment it will be important to optimize the total amount of time necessary to the running of the system. In an on-line system, optimization of response time can be done for transactions that update or transactions that retrieve. There will be a difference in design philosophy depending upon the mode of operation to be optimized.

Optimizing execution time requires a carefully designed and (usually) complex set of programs and a well-planned organization of data. A finely tuned system is sensitive to change and as such is subject to many variables that affect performance. The well-tuned system requires regular monitoring. When major changes in the system profile occur, care must be taken to maintain the level of performance. As a general rule, a change to a well-tuned system will adversely affect performance.

OPTIMIZATION OF STORAGE

To some degree, optimizing the space used by the data within the system is a good practice. However, because storage is cheap relative to other resources in the computing environment, storage considerations are usually not as important as other considerations at design time. There are systems large enough, however, to warrant more than a casual analysis of their space requirements. Techniques that save space inevitably trade the savings for CPU utilization. As an example, complex data compression techniques require CPU cycles in the storage and retrieval of data. As a rule the more complex the algorithm, the more CPU is used and the more space is saved. This trade-off should be carefully considered.

Optimization of space usually involves creating sophisticated structures and, in doing so, an additional level of programming complexity is introduced. Future changes to the system are subject to the inherent complexities. For data to be optimized to use space effectively, the structure of the data should be static in nature (i.e., the chance of environmental change should be very low). When the basic structure of the data changes, maintenance can only be done by personnel familiar with the complexities of the system.

OPTIMIZATION OF USER'S LEVEL OF EXPECTATION

The system, as viewed by the user, may be very elegant or rather simple. Usually, elegance at the user level translates into complex processes and complex data structures. What the user may view as a simple convenience may translate into an operational and developmental monstrosity. There is a real danger in finalizing the list of user specifications until it has been reviewed by the data and programming designer. It is their job to alert management to any major difficulties. The result of not allowing the designers a chance for reviewal at a sufficiently early point in the design process may result in the construction of a system that will not work at all (or work improperly). Mistakes are not uncovered until sometime during implementation in the worst case. This is the most expensive and embarrassing way to ferret out mistakes. It is always costly. Unfortunately, it is not a rarely occurring phenomenon.

OPTIMIZATION OF DATA FLEXIBILITY

DBMSs go the first step toward data independence, but they only go so far. If the user's environment is likely to change or historically has been unstable, it may be advantageous to optimize the degree of data independence for a particular application. This means that future unseen changes can be absorbed by the system with a minimum of impact. However, this usually requires careful planning, which negatively impacts system development time. Also, data structures that are highly flexible do not lend themselves to operational efficiency.

Not optimizing data flexibility to the right degree may enhance other aspects of the system, but may prove to be very costly when parts of the system must be reprogrammed.

OPTIMIZATION TRADE-OFFS

There is always a price to pay for overoptimizing any aspect of a system at the expense of others, because all other aspects of the system will be negatively impacted. However, when done judiciously, optimization of system design parameters can produce a useful and cost-effective system. If there is one particularly dangerous set of parameters that should not be overoptimized, it would be optimization of development time and the user's level of expectation. Mistakes here eventually are magnified, whereas mistakes elsewhere are more manageable.

Ignoring any aspect of design has the same effect as making bad decisions. The effective data designer will be aware of the alternatives and of the impact of his or her decisions in all cases.

IMPACT OF DBMS ON DESIGN DECISIONS

The considerations of efficiency of data design occur on two levels: the macro level and micro level. If design at the gross level is done poorly, a very good design at the detail level will have little impact. Figure 4.1

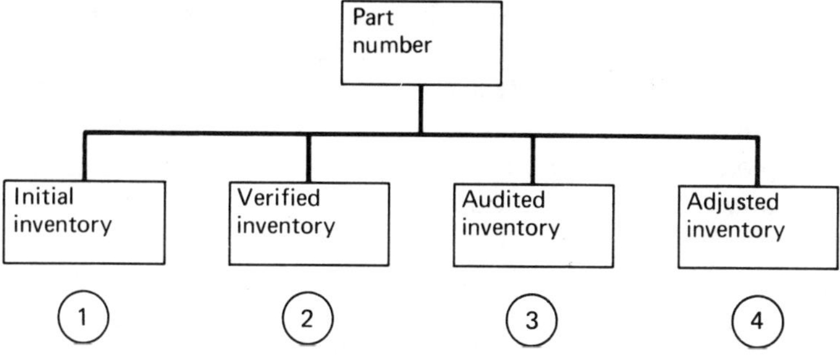

Example of poor macro design–

1 Initially, all inventory data is entered here

2 When it is verified by the foreman, it is removed from (1). and entered into (2)

3 When it is audited, either (1) or (2) is deleted and is entered into (3).

4 When faulty parts are discovered, they are entered individually into (4).

Figure 4.1 **The most effective microtuning of this system could only marginally improve its performance. The application is required to shift data en masse when the data changes from one state to another. Much I/O activity will be required by this shifting of data, when in fact the content of the data changes very little, if at all. The design is inefficient at a gross level for these reasons, and tuning this application will have little long-range impact. If the data was not moved about en masse as its status changed, the design would be acceptable at the macro level.**

shows one way of structuring data so that even the best program design is bound to be less than sufficient.

The capabilities of the DBMS—its strengths and weaknesses—play a big role in design decisions. The specifics of how the DBMS organizes and handles data are significant factors in determining what are "right" and "wrong" decisions. There are surprisingly few "good" principles at the macro level of design that are independent of a given DBMS. There are a few more principles that are dependent upon characteristics that typify most DBMSs. To understand what "good" and "bad" mean in terms of the DBMS, the designer must understand what is "expensive" and "inexpensive" to do. The list of generally expensive features of a DBMS are:

1. Calls to the DBMS—they cause I/Os. Minimizing the number of calls is useful.

2. I/O activity in relation to other processes. Other processes might be subroutine calls, calls to the DBMS (not requiring I/O), and so on. Arranging data structure and call flow to minimize I/O is advantageous.
3. Complex structures tend to be more expensive to manipulate than do simple structures. Complex structures involve overhead that simpler structures do not have.
4. Insertion and deletion is more expensive than replacing or modifying a segment. Insertions and deletions normally cause space management activity in direct-access devices that does not occur for replacement activity. Also, much insertion and deletion may necessitate frequent data base reorganization.
5. Large data bases have problems that small and medium-size data bases do not have (see Chapter 7).

There are other criteria that could be listed given a specific DBMS. However, using just these simple criteria, it is possible to construct a checklist of sound design practices.

OPTIMIZATION OF PERFORMANCE IN A DATA BASE APPLICATION

The strategy of optimization of performance is simply stated thus: Reduce the total amount of energy expended within the system along all critical paths to achieve maximum performance. Any part of the design that uses or waits for critical system resources is subject to review and alteration when optimizing execution time. A cogent analysis of execution time bottlenecks depends upon foreknowledge of what processes are critical to the operation of the designed system and what resources are critical within the DBMS and host SCP.

One of the simplest techniques to achieve operational efficiency is to organize the key sequence of segments to allow fast access for the most used or critical processes. If the processing is done randomly, a direct ordering of root segments through a randomizer is beneficial. If the major amount of processing is to be done in a sequential fashion, a sequential ordering of data is advantageous. Figure 4.2 shows how data can be matched to their processing requirements.

Not only will a given access be efficient if this guideline is followed, but the total amount of work done by the system will be less. In the case (the usual one) where root segments are accessed both randomly and sequentially, intuitively it seems that a combination of data organizations (indexed and randomized) will be most useful. This may not be the case at all because of the high system overhead involved in maintaining the index

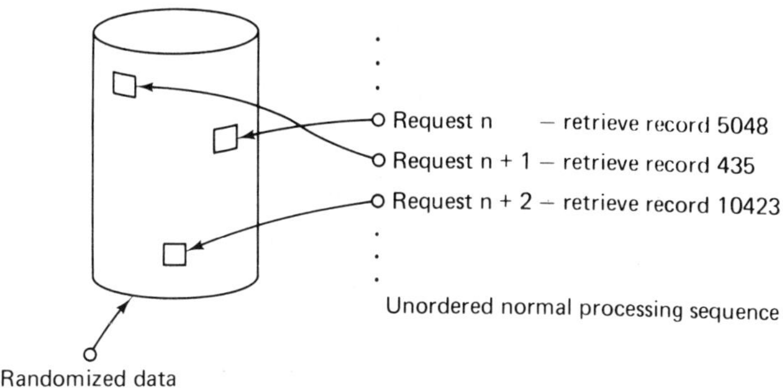

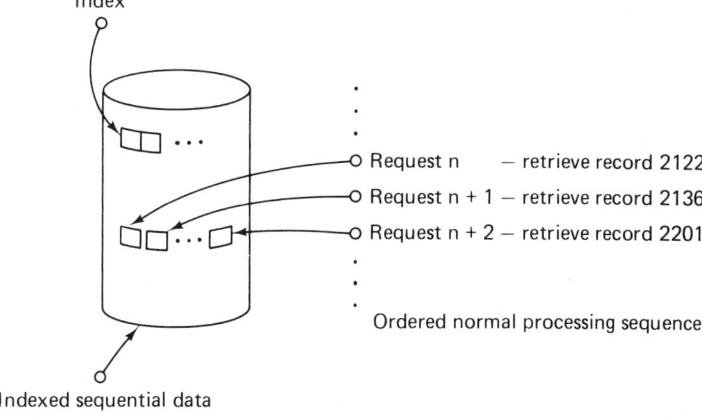

Figure 4.2 Fitting the order of the data to the normal processing sequence reduces system overhead.

(each insertion or deletion of a root requires index maintenance). Maintaining an index on a randomized data base is expensive, since each root requires an index and it is likely that no two consecutive index entries will point to two roots that are physically adjacent. The cost of index maintenance should be weighed against alternative processing modes.

Organizing data for expedient use by the DBMS is another technique for performance. As an example, in IMS, arranging the sibling segments below the root in the order most frequently processed can reduce access time. This technique depends entirely upon the DBMS and how it physically stores segments, how it traverses its structure, and what internal structure options the DBMS supports. If (as in IMS) the order of traversal is top to bottom, left to right, and the DBMS examines the dependent segments in the order in which they are stored, it is important to keep the most accessed segments to the top and left of the structure (Fig. 4.3).

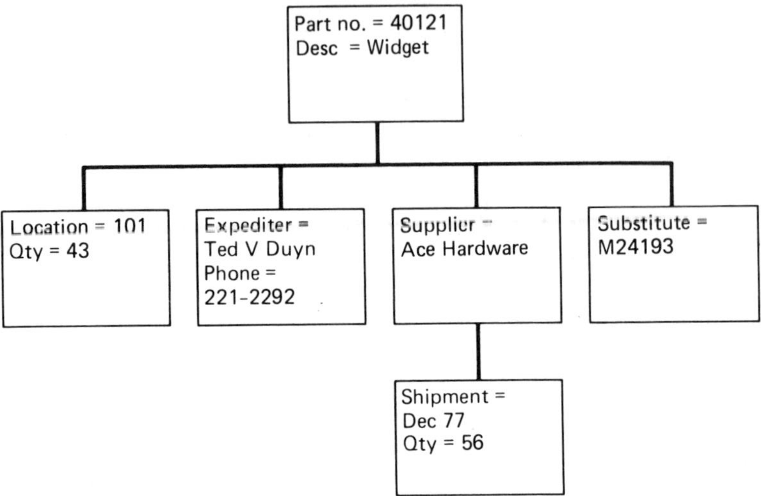

Figure 4.3 Segments to the top and left of the structure should be more likely to be accessed when the data base is scanned top to bottom, left to right (as in IMS).

By extending the idea of ordering segments according to mode of traversal and frequency of access, the idea of separating segments that have widely variant frequencies of access into separate data bases comes to mind. The same split may be done for data that is used exclusively on-line and data that is exclusively used off-line. However, carrying this idea to the extreme may lead to an undesirable proliferation of data bases. Splitting data bases by key will introduce a certain amount of redundancy at the root level, but it means that processes sensitive to execution time have to manipulate a minimum amount of data (see Fig. 4.4).

Creating data bases whose content is closely related and allowing some redundancy to creep into the system at the root level produces data structures with a minimum of siblings and levels. This means, as a general rule, that narrower data bases are more efficient as far as execution time is concerned than are "fat" structures. By the same token, the shallower the structure, the more efficient it is to process. Consider the call sequence necessary to process a data base that is five levels deep as opposed to a data base that is two levels deep. A fewer number of calls are used to process the shallower structure. Figure 4.5 illustrates this.

Structures that are narrow and shallow not only minimize the amount of energy it takes to service them, but normally the structures are less prone to programmer error since they are simpler. The fewer choices presented to the programmer, the fewer opportunities he or she has to err. The ultimate in shallow and narrow data base structures is the *root-only* data base. Because of its simplicity, it can keep certain types of system activity to a

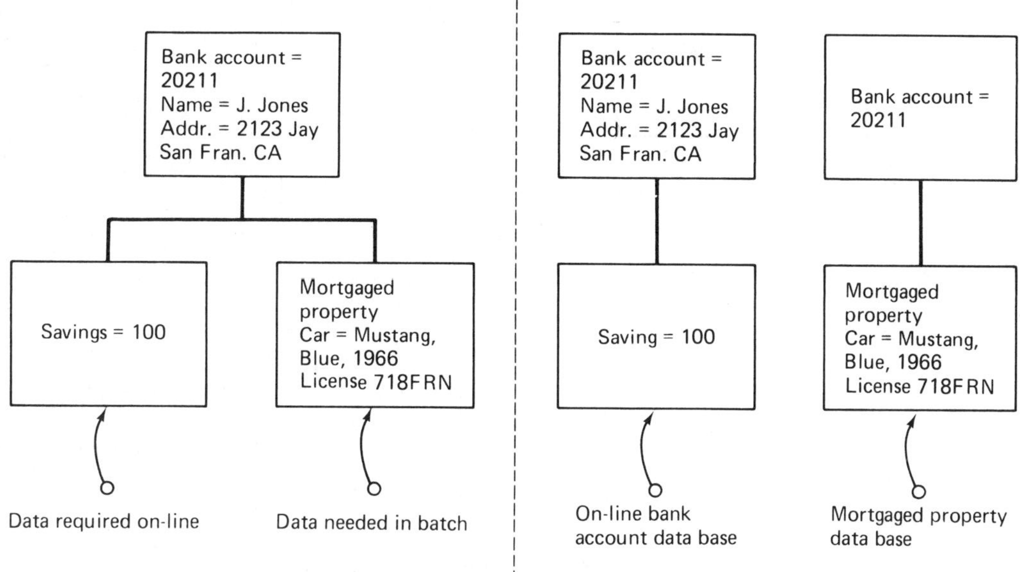

Figure 4.4 Separating data with widely varying functions reduces the overhead in the on-line environment at the expense of some redundancy.

minimum. The price of this simplicity is usually redundancy of data on a fairly large scale, and it may be necessary to have application programmer logic that imposes an artificial structuring on the data. The logic to accomplish this artificial structuring can be complex and in fact may cause some otherwise unnecessary I/O activity to occur. This is an example of shifting the complexity of the system from the DBMS to the application level.

The careful designer avoids creating long twin chains if response time is a factor. There are two varieties of twin chains—a chain that connects twins beneath the same physical parent and a chain that connects twins that point to another data base (Fig. 4.6). In the latter case each twin on the chain is likely to point to a separate segment. Processing any long twin chain is expensive, but processing a twin chain that points to another data base is most expensive because each access down the twin chain probably involves an I/O operation. Such is not the case when physical twin chains are processed.

If processing long twin chains is expensive, sequencing them in a particular order can be very expensive especially where the chain connects two data bases. If the twin chains are all loaded at one time off-line, and their ordering enhances on-line retrievals, there may be a good case for sequencing them. If the sequencing is done on-line, or done asynchronously, it may be very expensive. This point is

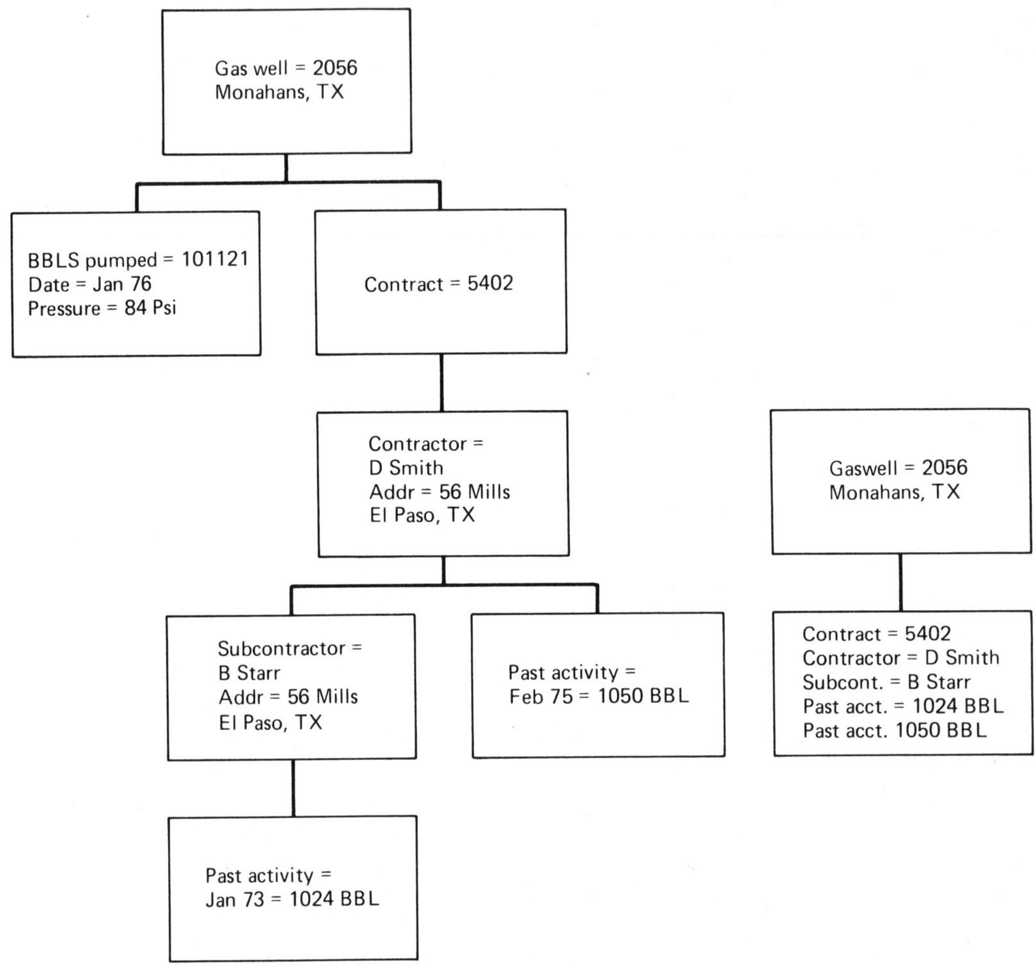

Figure 4.5 At the expense of redundancy and complicating the data, it is faster to retrieve data in a flatter structure than a deeper one.

shown by Fig. 4.7. Following the entire logical chain, it is seen that 1 I/O is done (on the average) for each dependent logical child as the pointer is followed to the personnel data base. Keeping the pointer segments in sequence may require much I/O.

Adding control fields to a segment may cut down on the number of calls necessary to the data base (Fig. 4.8). For example, suppose that n number of segments (twins) exist beneath a physical parent. As they are updated, the first $n - 1$ segments through contain a control field filled with a null value, whereas the nth segment has a nonnull value. As the segments are processed sequentially, it will not be necessary to

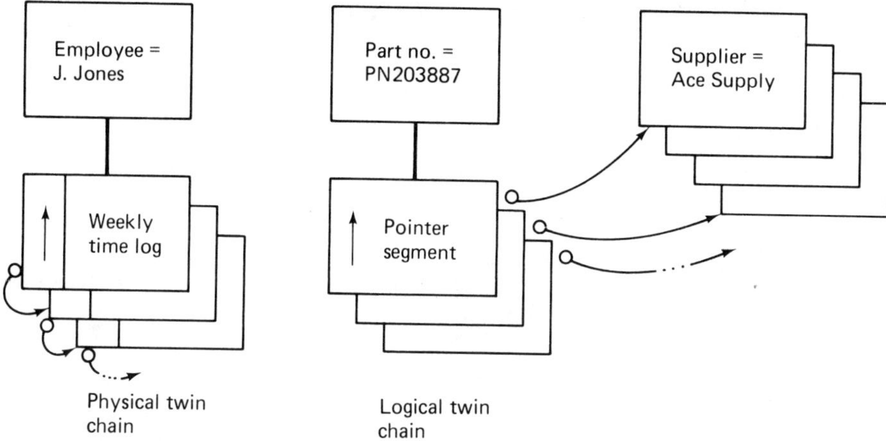

Figure 4.6 Processing long twin chains can be very expensive in terms of resources consumed. Logical twin chains can be more resource-consuming than physical twins, depending upon how the logical twin chain is implemented.

read beyond the *n*th segment to determine which is the last segment, thus saving one retrieval.

Control fields have limited use because, to be effective, they depend upon a specific sequence of events to occur. However, when those events do predictably occur, control fields can save processing time. In other cases the cost of their maintenance may be much more than their savings. Another type of control field that can be useful is a status field. Instead of

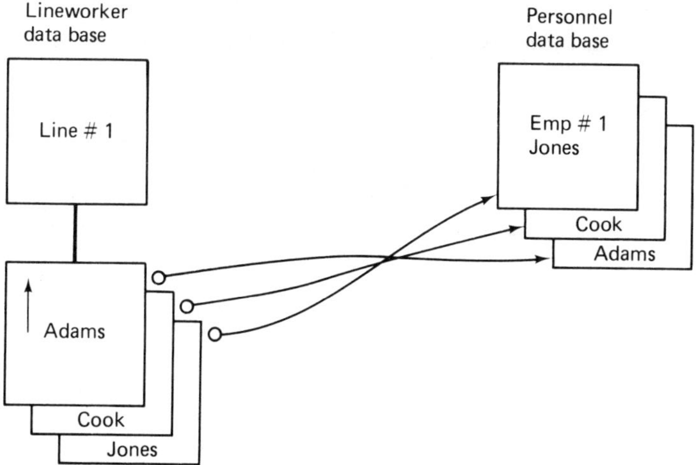

Figure 4.7 Maintaining logical twins in sequence can be very expensive if the twin chain is long and if the pointers are direct.

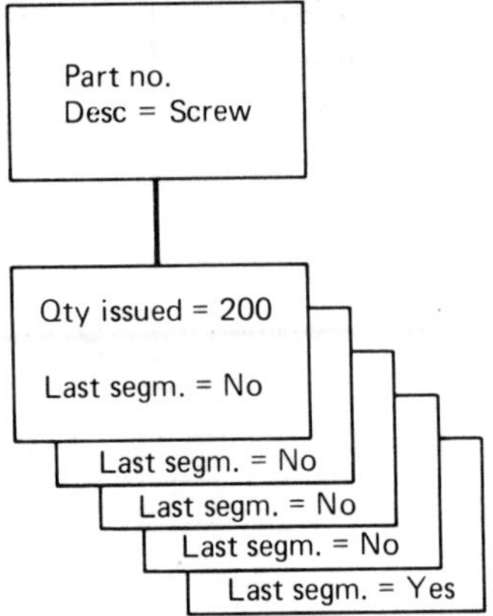

Figure 4.8 In some cases a control field can save a call to the DBMS. In this case, the field—Last Segm—indicates whether there is another Qty issued segment for a particular root. The programmer knows by the value contained in this field whether he should make another call to the DBMS to find all the segments under a given parent.

inserting a segment into a data base and then later removing the segment from the data base and reinserting the data (in one form or another) somewhere else when some status has changed, it is helpful to simply change the value of a status field in the segment and leave the data in place. This technique is shown by Fig. 4.9.

Ideally, a good design will capture data into the system, use the data in the place where it is initially stored, then delete it when it is to be purged. The data will exhibit very little movement across data segments and data bases.

Data does not have to be physically stored in order by key if that se-

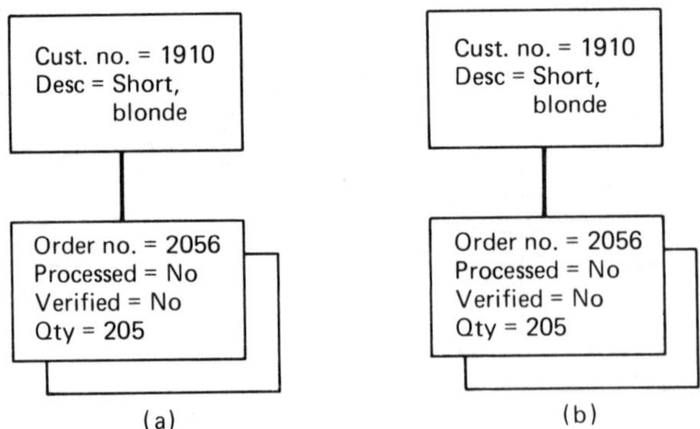

Figure 4.9 (a) Data upon initial entry into the system. (b) When status changes, only a control field changes.

quence is not the same one as its major processing order. Data can be stored in reverse order if it is useful to do so, or the keys may be encoded so that the natural order of the keys has no immediately apparent relationship to the order of the data.

Building redundancy into data structures in a judicious place can save much time during retrieval. The time saved should be balanced against the pitfalls of redundancy, such as increased update time, data synchronization problems, and the loss of flexibility. Where there is a limited amount of data (especially nonvolatile data), it may be cheaper to store pieces of data redundantly throughout the data structure than to force the programmer to make unnecessary calls to the DBMS. This is an example of optimizing only retrieval time at the expense of update time. Also, introducing redundancy adds a level of complexity to the programmer's task when he or she writes or maintains the update transaction.

Blocking data within a segment by the application program can save much time when done properly and under the right conditions (Fig. 4.10). Where many small twin segments exist beneath a parent, it may be useful to enlarge the segment so that a multiple of twin segments may be physically contained in a single segment. This saves some segment prefix space as well as time taken to insert each small segment. What occurs, instead of a series of inserts, is a single insert of a fully packed segment or one insert and several replacement calls as the segment is being packed, de-

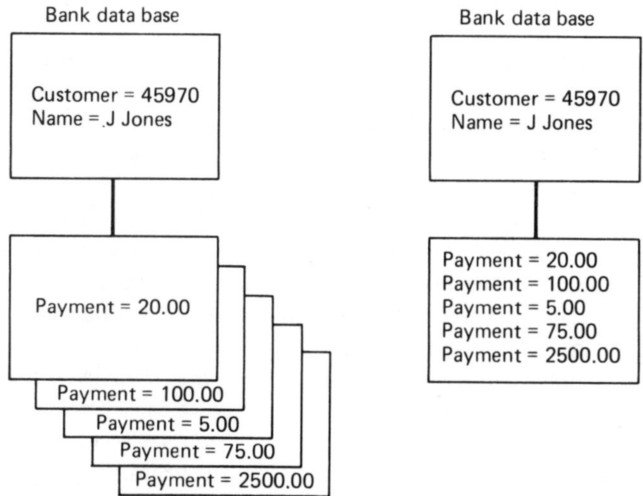

Figure 4.10 Blocking data elements into the same segment saves both segment overhead space and update and retrieval time when the data displays certain characteristics. Some of the characteristics are: repetition of a small amount of data, entry into the system and purging from it in a nonrandom (FIFO, en masse, etc.) sequence, usage by application in a sequential manner, and so on.

pending upon the load and update sequence. Both space and time are saved when data is entered into the system, as is retrieval time when the twin segments are accessed (e.g., one Get call retrieves *n* segments as opposed to *n* calls in the unblocked format). This technique is not applicable where the data is inserted or deleted randomly or when the distribution of the occurrences of the data is not reasonably uniform.

The price of blocking data is added program complexity (which may not be too severe, depending upon the characteristics of the data) and a limitation upon the structure of the data (e.g., it is questionable if a blocked segment can meaningfully have its own physical child).

USER EXPECTATION LEVEL AND PERFORMANCE OPTIMIZATION

It is never pleasant to have to explain to a user why he or she cannot have exactly what he or she wants out of a system. This is especially difficult to explain after the system is built. It is easier during the design phase of a system to be honest and frank, because at that point the user has a minimal investment compared to what he or she will have when the system is implemented. If there are serious credibility gaps that become apparent by the time the system is built, the user faces a loss of time and money already invested, and probably faces more work for which he or she has not budgeted. Correcting gross design errors and user misconceptions in the early stages of a project cause the least amount of pain.

One possible alternative to improving system response time and removing complexities is to reduce the scope of the system at the user level. This is especially true if the system has been oversold. The project may have to go through reorganization or redefinition of function—the specifications for the project will change—but the end result will be a system that has a chance of working and will provide a realistic level of performance and user satisfaction. This usually involves a separation of function into smaller and less interrelated units, and probably more user intelligence at the point of operation to make the system work, but the user ends up with more control and understanding of the system.

It is amazing how small extravagances at the user level can lead to unreasonable expectations and demands at the programming and data design level. Often, a small reduction in user expectations means a large reduction in system complexity and operation. The usual cause of unrealistic expectations is a shoddy feasibility or cost analysis study at the appropriate point in the life of the system design. The implications of the cost of certain features may not be understood. Experienced users tend to be more realistic in their expectations of the system, and consequently it functions better for them because the design does not have to be extraordinarily overoptimized in one direction or another.

OPTIMIZING SPACE IN DATA BASE SYSTEMS

Ordinarily, optimization of space is not a major issue. It is usually enough of an issue to ensure that data is not unnecessarily redundant and there are no gross errors in the usage of space. It is easier to buy space than to buy time, so savings in space usually takes a back seat. However, there is still the occasional case when space is an issue. That case often involves dealing with many data types of widely varying length—such as pieces of text or verbiage—that defy attempts at grouping the data into reasonably consistent structural arrangements. In such cases space optimization techniques may be justified.

The first place that space can be saved is in the removal of redundancies. Redundancy at the key level or in small isolated areas may be beneficial, but wholesale redundancy of many data elements that comprise a high percentage of the data base is not justified. It is worthwhile to take steps to reduce the size of the data elements or the number of occurrences of the elements in the data base.

A simple technique that can save space is that of encoding data (Fig. 4.11). Instead of explicitly spelling out a given value throughout a data base, the value may be shortened in its internal representation. When displayed outside the data base, it is translated back into its full representation.

Compaction can be used to save space. Compaction involves the repre-

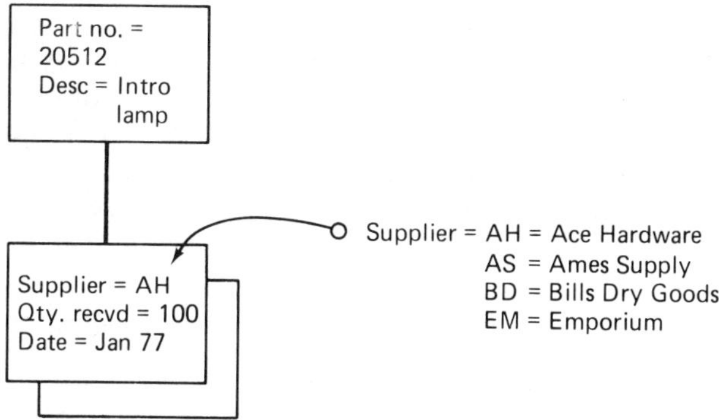

Figure 4.11 Encoding saves space but increases (slightly) the program logic.

Name = J. Jones
Name = Druscilla Woscieowski

	Bytes used
Compacted name = Jb̸Jones14b̸	10
Uncompacted name = Jb̸Jonesb̸b̸b̸b̸b̸b̸b̸b̸b̸b̸b̸b̸b̸b̸	21
Compacted name = Druscillab̸Woscieowski	21
Uncompacted name = Druscillab̸Woscieowski	21

Figure 4.12 **A simple form of compaction—repeating characters do not have to be iterated.**

sentation and control counts, so that more data can be packed into the same space than if compaction had not been used. A simple example of data compaction is shown by Fig. 4.12.

Compaction can be complex or simple. As a rule, the more elegant and complex the compacting algorithms are, the greater the savings in space. However, translation into and out of compaction requires CPU time and adds a level of complexity that otherwise would not exist.

Another technique to save space is to break a segment into finer and finer segments so that there is an absolute minimum of redundancy. This technique is self-defeating if carried too far (it wastes time as well as space), because the percentage of segment overhead grows as the size of the segment grows smaller. Any data base whose prefix space is more than 20% of the total space of the data base is suspect. Segmentation has probably been carried too far.

EXERCISES

1. Select an existing data base application for study. Select three or four major functions of the system and describe briefly how they are implemented. For each function, show how it could have been implemented in at least five other ways (by changing the data structure, the flow of processing, the relation of segments to each other, etc.). Evaluate the reasons for the current implementation in relation to the alternatives. Determine the advantages and disadvantages of each alternative over the others.
2. Consider some of the ways segments are put into a data base, such as:
   a) Initial load (off-line).
   b) Batch update.
   c) On-line update (randomly).
   d) On-line update (sequentially, with other related segments).

Break each of these operations into call flows, then into executable path lengths.

Based upon the path-length calculation, rank the operations by performance considerations.

3. a) Create a program that will load 100,000 segments onto a data base. Each segement will be 2000 bytes in length. Calculate the space used and the CPU and I/O necessary to load the data. Now introduce a simple compression subroutine so that the segments average 350 bytes in length. Run the same load program with compression, calculating space used and the CPU and I/O necessary.
   b) From the uncompressed data base, run a program that will randomly read 10,000 segments. Calculate CPU and I/O used. Perform the same program on the compressed data base, using decompression routines.
   c) Run a program that will insert and delete 20,000 segments into the uncompressed data base. Run it against the compressed data base. Run it against the compressed data base, using decompression routines.
   d) Compare the numbers generated from steps a), b), and c), and draw conclusions based on those numbers.
4. Optimize the compression algorithm, making it as elegant as possible. Repeat steps a) to d) using the complex algorithm. Create a data base with one root and 10,000 dependent segments (admittedly a strange request, but a good one to illustrate a point). Each dependent segment is unkeyed, with a single data element that reflects the order (sequentially) in which the segment was loaded.
   a) Retrieve the 9532th segment by reading each segment in the application program and continuing the retrieval until the desired segment is located. Keep track of I/O and CPU utilization.
   b) Retrieve the 9532th segment by using a single call with a designated search field. Keep track of I/O and CPU utilization. Redesign the data base so that the dependent segment is keyed on its only data element, order of insert.
   c) Now retrieve the 9532th segment by key, keeping track of I/O and CPU.
   d) Using data concerning I/O and CPU from steps a), b), and c), draw conclusions.
5. The *character occurrence data base* consists of two data bases that are explicitly connected. There are four segment types: (1) the alphanumeric segment, (2) a pointer from the alphanumeric data base to (3) the character data base, and (4) a dependent segment showing the number of occurrences of the character on the first 10 pages of the phone book (Fig. 4.13).

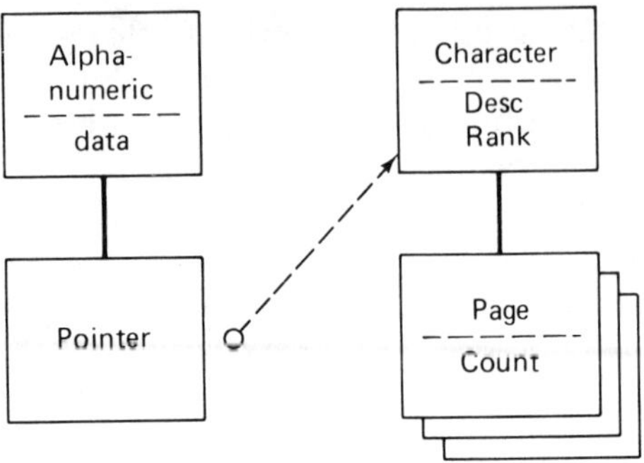

Figure 4.13

There are only two roots in the *alphanumeric data base*, ALPHA and NUM. All alphabetic character pointer segments are beneath the ALPHA root, and all numeric character pointers are beneath the NUM root (Fig. 4.14).

The *character data base* consists of a root whose key is the character represented (Fig. 4.15). The root contains two data elements, Description (a brief description of the character) and Rank (the order in the data base of the character). The dependent segment has a key Page, which corresponds to the page number of the phone book that Count refers to. Count contains the number of occurrences of the character on the given page of the phone book.

a) Construct the two data bases using the first 10 pages of the phone book of the largest city near you. Use symbolic pointers in the dependent segment of the alphanumeric data base. Use an index to locate the keys of the character occurrence data base. Organize

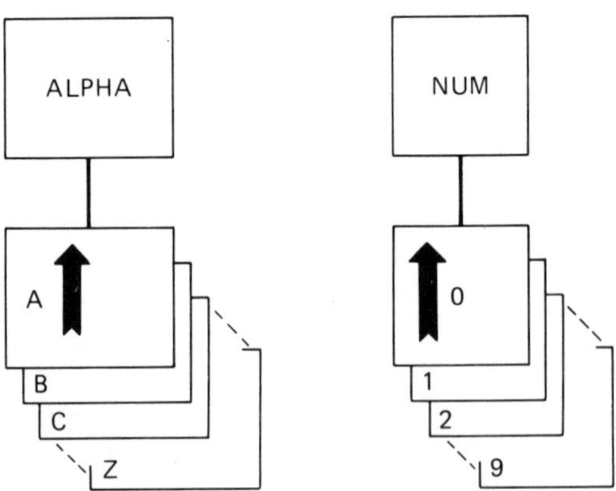

Figure 4.14 Alphanumeric pointer data base.

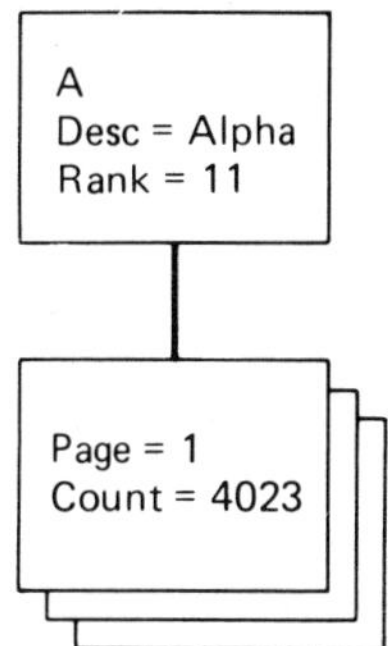

Figure 4.15 Character occurrence data base.

the blocksize and other necessary parameters so that no more than one root is inserted into a single block.

b) Locate the Page segments of "Q" by going through the alpha numeric data base pointer to the root of character occurrence. Calculate the total occurrences of "Q" from page 7 to page 10. Keep track of the I/O and CPU used.

c) Locate the last occurrence count whose value is greater than 1000 by accessing the character occurrence data base through the alpha numeric pointer data base. Keep track of CPU and I/O utilization.

d) Change the character occurrence data base from an indexed data base to a randomized data base. Repeat steps b) and c).

e) Change the alphanumeric pointer data so that the pointer is direct rather than symbolic. Repeat steps b) and c).

f) Based upon I/O and CPU utilization of the three cases, compare and draw conclusions.

6. Under what conditions is blocking data by application program a good practice? A bad practice?

FIVE

OPTIMIZING FLEXIBILITY IN DATA BASE DESIGN

Understanding flexibility in data base design begins with an understanding of the user environment and how it relates to the data bases associated with it. When change occurs in the user's world, it affects the data that is an abstraction of the user's environment. A data base is a portrayal of an entity or a relationship of some part of the user's environment. The data bears a resemblance (conceptually) to those things to which they are related. When the user's requirements change, it is necessary for the corresponding data structure to change.

It is a fact of life that change will occur over time. An effective and flexible data design will be able to be changed with a minimum of effort. Ideally, the programs and structures that deal directly with the changed data will be impacted, and no other programs or data will be affected. Figure 5.1 illustrates the relationship between the user's environment and the data bases that support his or her system and the impact upon data of a change in the user's environment.

Data structures have the property of either being elastic or inelastic to some degree. An *elastic* data structure is one that can withstand change

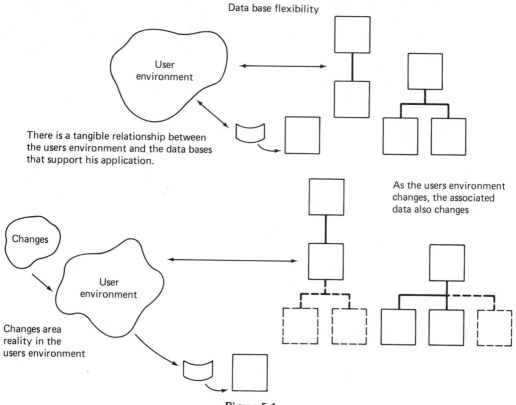

Data base flexibility

User environment

There is a tangible relationship between the users environment and the data bases that support his application.

As the users environment changes, the associated data also changes

Changes

User environment

Changes area reality in the users environment

Figure 5.1

with a minimum of impact; *inelastic* structures require large changes whenever any change occurs. It should be obvious that as high a degree of elasticity is desirable as is cost-effective.

How exactly does a structural change affect a data base? A simple example can be shown by the segment A in Fig. 5.2. Segment A contains five elements—a, b, c, d, and e. A new user requirement has just been generated due to a change in government requirements so that element d must have a new element—f—existing in the same segment with it (Fig. 5.3).

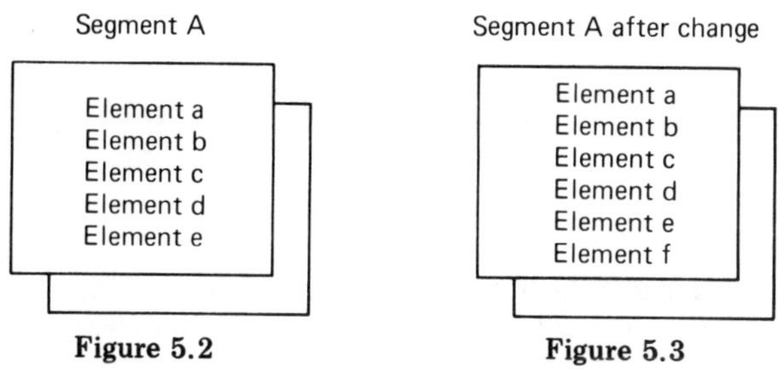

Figure 5.2 **Figure 5.3**

What changes must occur to reconstruct the new segment A? The first step is to change the semantic definition of segment A to the DBMS so that enough space exists for element f. All of the programs that access segment A must now be changed to account for the new segment size. The data currently in the data base in the old format of segment A must be stripped off and stored, then reloaded using the new format of segment A. Unnecessary work is done when programs that accessed segment A solely for elements a, b, c, and e must be recompiled. Work has to be done on them even though the change that occurred has no direct relation to anything they do. Change has unnecessarily impacted them.

In the simple case presented here change probably would involve nothing more than a recompilation and linkage of a few programs. But anywhere work is being done and changes are being made, there is a chance for complications to arise, no matter how trivial the task. Even in the case of simple recompilation, if there are many programs that are involved the chance for error grows. A library may run out of space. There may be a machine failure. One or more programs may not be recompiled because of oversight. There are a whole host of problems that can arise for even the simplest of conversions. Avoiding unnecessary work and reducing the chances for error is a very defensible objective. The full impact of change on the different parts of a system is described by Fig. 5.4.

The problems of change and the associated risks become even more acute when a data base must undergo a more complicated change than the one presented here. Good data base design takes into careful consideration the impact of change. The goal of the designer should be to ensure

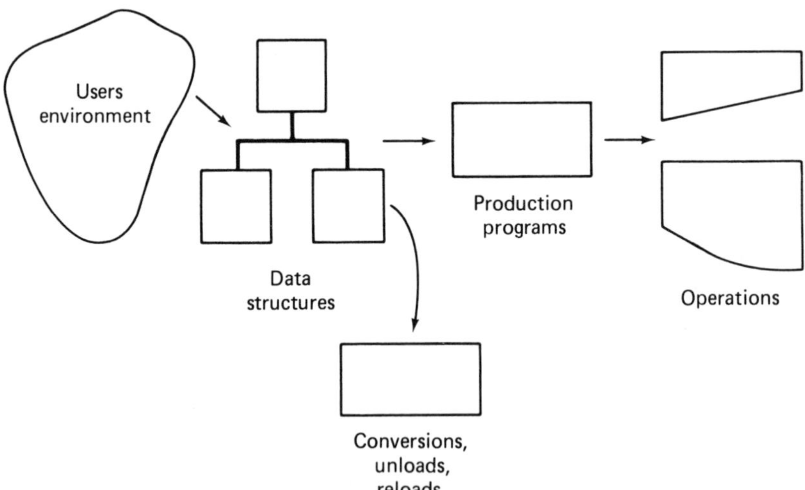

Figure 5.4 Data Base Flexibility: Impact of Change. Minimizing the impact of change at this point reduces total impact considerably.

that when changes occur in the user environment, the only structural changes in the data base will be in the area that directly relate to the changed part of the structure (i.e., no data element not directly related to the change in the user's environment will need work). "Innocent" data elements and segments should not be affected. The first step toward achieving this goal is to perceive data as it is physically bound together.

PHYSICAL BONDING OF DATA

In a hierarchical data base, data can be physically bonded together at four levels (Fig. 5.5). Data is physically bonded together when there exists an implied or explicit physical or logical relationship between two elements, two segments, or two data bases. The four basic levels of physical bonding are:

1. *Element bonding*—elements bound together within a segment. Elements are physically stored together, logically grouped together in a program, and are transported together. Elemental bonding represents the tightest level of physical bonding. When the designer

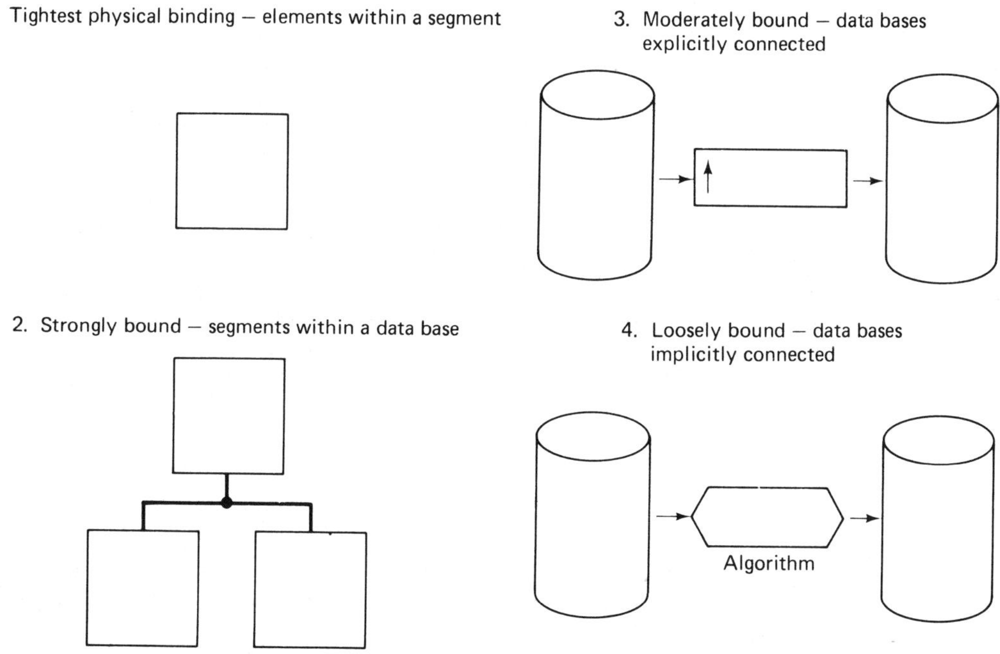

Figure 5.5 Data Base Flexibility: Levels of Bonding.

places elements into the same segment, he or she is binding them together in the strongest manner possible.

2. *Bonding by segment*—segments bound together in a data base. Segments are structured together or ordered uniquely within the format of the data base, and are mapped into this format by the DBMS and the programs that support the structure. This level of physical bonding is strong, but it is not as tight as elemental bonding.
3. *Closely bound data bases*—data bases that are closely bound together have one or more sets of pointer (symbolic or direct) segments that support the relationship between them. Closely bound data bases tend to be rather elastic (i.e., changes in pointer relationships probably will have little effect on the physical data structure).
4. *Loosely bound data bases*—the relationship between data bases is supported only by algorithms existing within an application program. This level of bonding is the loosest (and, strictly speaking, is not physical), since the two data bases can exist independently and are tied together only by an application program; they do not depend on the DBMS for existence and correctness of the relationship.

BONDING AT THE ELEMENTAL LEVEL

Data elements are subject to two kinds of change: their internal contents may change (i.e., the value of element a in segment A has a value of 6 and must be changed to 10), or their representation and meaning within a data base may change. The designer is not too concerned about change of internal contents when it comes to considerations of flexibility. The sort of change that concerns the designer is environmental change. Every data element has some propensity for environmental change, no matter how low. When the user's environment changes, one or more data elements will change. Over time, even the most stable data elements may be altered. Maps change, government regulations change, companies merge or go bankrupt, corporations are restructured, and so on. The data elements that support these organizations must, of necessity, change with them.

The greater the number of elements bound together by a segment, the greater is the chance that the segment will change over a period of time, regardless of the stability of the elements. Keeping the elements bound together by a segment to a reasonable number is a first step toward minimizing the impact of change. The impact of adding elements to a segment is shown by Fig. 5.6.

Understanding elemental bonding begins with a fundamental understanding of what components make a segment and how they are related.

		Probability of environmental change for an element –	Probability of environmental change for an element –
Segment A	Element a	Prob. (0.001)	
	Element b	Prob. (0.001)	Probability = 0.4%
	Element c	Prob. (0.001)	
	Element d	Prob. (0.001)	
Segment B	Element a	Prob. (0.001)	
	Element b	Prob. (0.001)	
	Element c	Prob. (0.001)	
	Element d	Prob. (0.001)	
	Element e	Prob. (0.001)	Probability = 0.79%
	Element f	Prob. (0.001)	
	Element g	Prob. (0.001)	
	Element h	Prob. (0.001)	

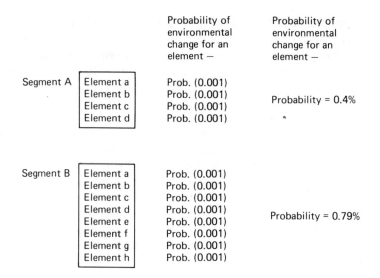

Figure 5.6 Data Base Flexibility: Propensity for Change. Each element has some propensity for change, however small. The propensity for change for elements within a boundary correlates to the propensity for change of each of the elements within the boundary.

A *segment* is an organization of one or more data elements into a recognizably unique unit of data. When the DBMS stores (and later accesses) the segment and when the programmer uses data values contained in the segment, there is general agreement as to the meaning of the contents of the segment. All other segments of the same semantic type will be similarly interpreted, even though they probably will contain different data values. All occurrences of the same segment type are distinguished by a *boundary* that logically and physically ties the segment together. When the DBMS is called upon to retrieve a specific segment, it determines the location of the first byte of the segment, then references the predefined boundary of the segment to calculate how much space the segment occupies. When the programmer receives the segment, he or she determines what the data values within the segment are by fitting the appropriate mask over the boundary of the segment. The most fundamental relationship between data elements exists when they are surrounded by the same boundary.

Data elements within the same boundary necessarily have a relationship to that boundary.* The boundary represents some logical grouping

*This discussion of data elements and boundaries assumes that the segment and its elements have been mapped into a static format prior to programming and loading of the data base. When this is not the case and an unrestricted formatting of data elements occur, other concepts of boundaries and segmentation apply. See the Appendix.

of data elements that has meaning in the user's environment, and just as the data elements have a relationship to the boundary of the segment within the computer, the entities in the user environment that are represented by data elements have a correspondence to the boundary as it exists external to the computer. The boundary may represent a bank account, an oil well, an employee's work history—in short, some division of information meaningful to the user.

If the segment has one or more data elements that serve as a key, each *element* in the segment has a relationship to the key as well as to the boundary of the segment. The impact of change can be minimized by grouping data elements by a common relationship to the boundaries of the segment or, if it exists, the key of the segment. On the other hand, data inelasticity is introduced at the most fundamental level—the elemental level—by allowing data elements to exist in the same segment type that have no common relationship to their boundary. These relationships are illustrated by Fig. 5.7.

Grouping data elements together because of their similarity of relationship to a common boundary or key greatly enhances elasticity. This is true because changes that occur in the user's environment happen to the logical division of data (represented by the segment) as a rule, and not to individual, random entities. Separating data elements that have dissimilar relationships to a boundary or a key into different segment types accounts for the fact that when change occurs and the user's environment is altered,

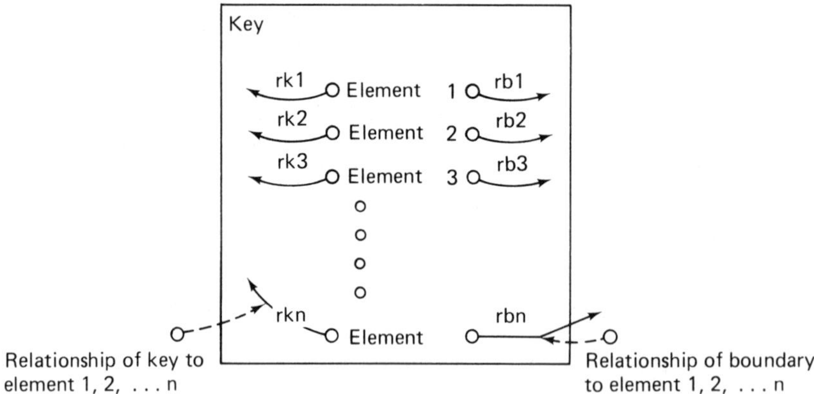

Figure 5.7 Data Base Flexibility: Data Elasticity. Minimizing the impact of change produces structures that are elastic. Elasticity can be expressed in terms of elements, boundaries, and relationships. The most elastic data structuring occurs when rk1, rk2, . . . , rkn and rb1, rb2, . . . , rbn are closely similar to each other. The most inelastic data structuring occurs when rk1, rk2, . . . , rkn and rb1, rb2, . . . , rbn are widely dissimilar from each other.

all of the appropriate elements will be grouped together and all of the nonaffected (innocent) elements will already be segregated elsewhere.

When the same data element exists in more than one place, the data structure becomes inelastic because the impact of change is multiplied when a data element must be altered. Instead of needlessly impacting "innocent" elements in a single place, innocent elements are impacted in several places. Maximizing flexibility dictates that an element exists in only one place. When a data element exists in more than one place, it is an indication that there may be some duplication of meaning as to the boundary of the segments of the data elements. If the data elements fit comfortably in more than one segment, the question may be asked: Why are the boundaries of the segments similar, and should they be combined? If they are very similar, they will inevitably create inelasticity in the data structure. The result of applying the strategy of segregation by similar relationship to a common boundary leads to the following rules:

1. A data element should appear only once in a data base.
2. Data elements that participate in different relationships in the user's environment should be separated into different segment types.

BONDING AT THE SEGMENT LEVEL

Hierarchical data structures are made up of segments that are ordered into a predefined format. The simplest relationship (or ordering) between segments is that of parent/child. In this relationship the parent segment is associated with zero or more child segments. The parent/child relationship can be either descriptive or structural (or a combination of the two). It is a descriptive relationship if the child segment describes something about the parent segment or denotes something that belongs to the parent. It is a structural relationship if the child segment contains pointer data. A structural relationship differs from a descriptive relationship in that in a structural relationship no direct information is given about the parent, only information concerning the location of another segment that has some relationship to the parent segment.

In a descriptive child segment, the key or boundary of the segment represents a description of some aspect of the parent segment. To achieve elasticity, the key of the parent and the key of the child should be an abstraction of different entities in the user environment.* Allowing both keys to be an abstraction of the same entity in the real world automati-

*Ironically the widely used terminology of "parent/child" depicts a highly inelastic relationship, since both "parent" and "child" portray the same type of entity as it exists in the real world.

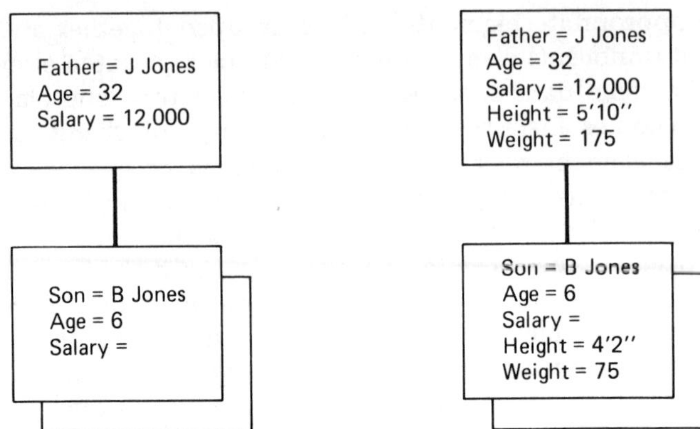

Figure 5.8 A change in the user's requirements, the addition of height and weight, affects two segments, not one.

cally produces redundancy and a normally unacceptable form of a recursive relationship. Where both keys are an abstraction of the same entity, a change in the user's environment that affects that entity affects both segment types (Fig. 5.8).

Furthermore, if a key is described in terms of itself once (i.e., a parent is described in terms of a child), it is likely that it will be desirable to describe the key in terms of itself at a new level, in this case producing a grandparent, parent, and child (Fig. 5.9).

Structurally, this means adding a new level of segmentation, and compounds the problem of data elasticity. Furthermore, there may be no end in sight to this process of describing a parent in terms of a child. The structure may be required to grow to *n* levels, creating a highly inelastic structure. A convenient generalized way to solve this problem of proliferation of child segments to many levels is to use a parent/child relationship in which the child segment is a pointer and points up to the root (or parent) segment (Fig. 5.10).

In this fashion, knowing a father—B. Jones—an access is made to the root segment. To determine the children of B. Jones, the pointer segments beneath him are read, and each one points back to the root segment, but to a different occurrence (B. Jones cannot be his own father!). The process is reiterated until the desired level of the family structure is reached. In this case, when a user wants to add a new data element to the segment type of a parent, he or she has only one segment type to deal with, which would not be the case if the family tree were represented with a physical segment type for each generation of the family (see Fig. 5.11).

Redundancy in a data base occurs not only in the form of multiple

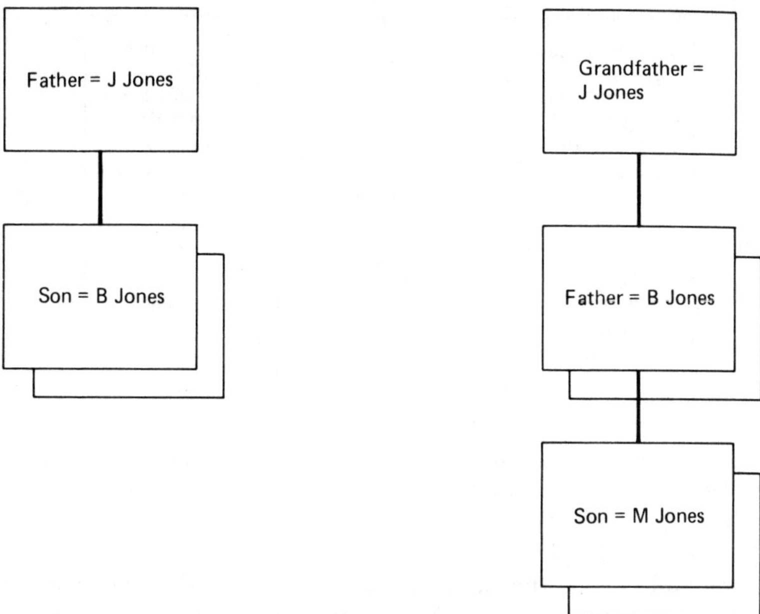

Figure 5.9 Once having described the father in terms of the son, describing the son in the same way requires the addition of a new level of segmentation.

data elements but also in the form of internal data structures. An example is shown by Fig. 5.12.

The activity segments have the same internal structuring even though they apply to separate subaccounts. Suppose that the user requires an

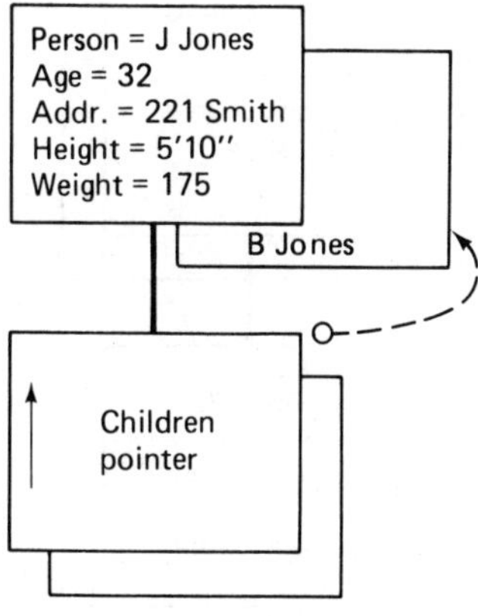

Figure 5.10

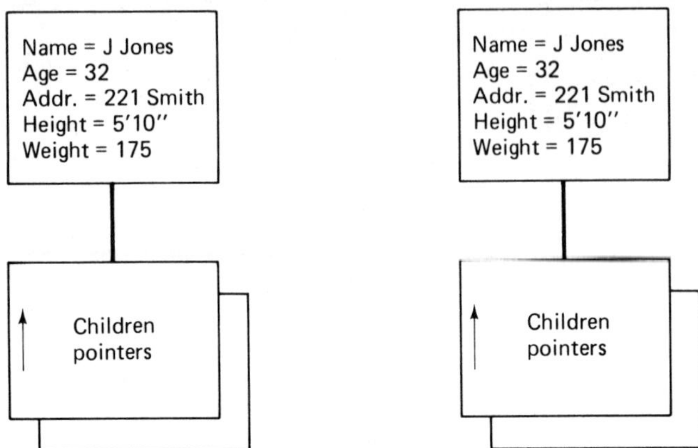

Figure 5.11 Because of a change in user requirements, a new data element—sex—is to be added to the data base. The impact is felt by only one segment type.

environmental change that affects activity. The result is a change to more than one segment type. Had the activity segments been designed differently so that similar internal data structures were consolidated into a single segment type, the impact of environmental change would be mini-

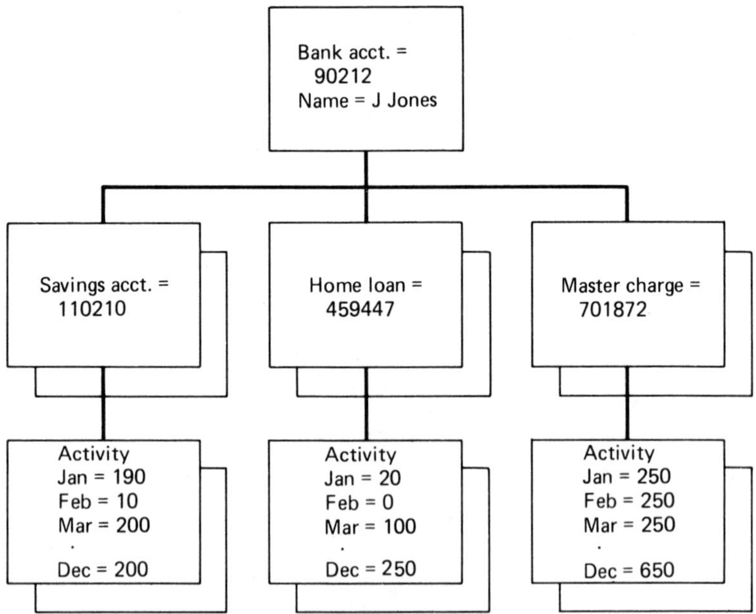

Figure 5.12 When the bank decided it wanted quarterly subtotals on all activity, more than one segment was impacted.

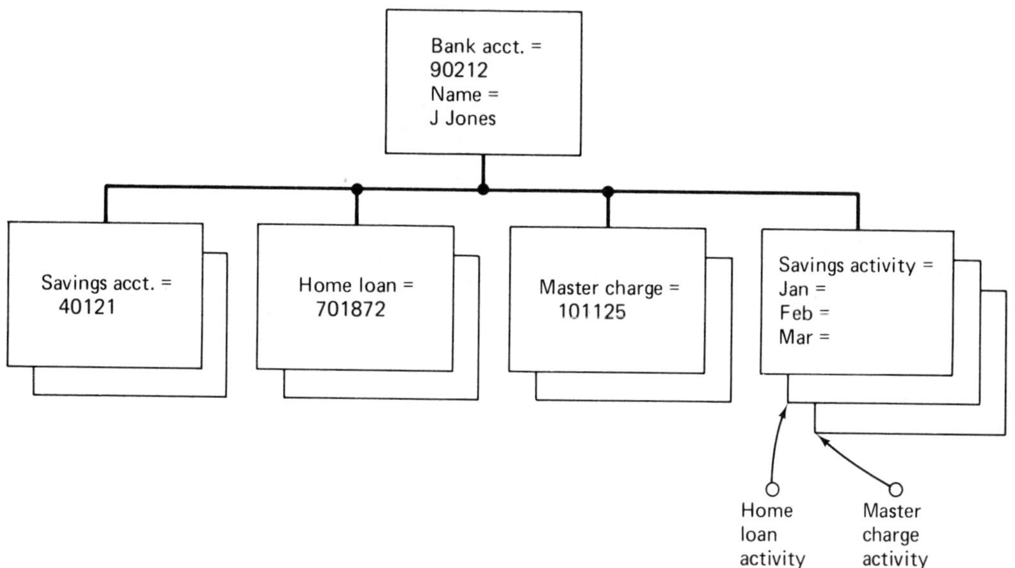

Figure 5.13 When the bank asked for quarterly subtotals for all activity, only one segment type was affected.

mized and the data base would be much more elastic. An example of this design strategy is shown by Fig. 5.13.

When data elements exist within a child segment that have a widely differing relationship to the boundary, the designer may opt to create sibling segments beneath the parent. When change occurs in this case, it is likely that only one of the sibling segments will be affected, not both (Fig. 5.14).

The net result of organizing data into elastic structures is to create a hierarchy with many levels and many siblings with no redundant data elements. The resultant data base will have many segment types. A given data element will occur at only one place in the data base, as do internal structures of data. Every relationship between a parent and a child is structural or descriptive, and every key within the data base describes a unique entity in the user's environment that is not described by another key.

When analyzing the degree of elasticity of a data base, two levels of analysis must be carried out—at the elemental level, and at the segment level. At the segment level, if a given boundary (or segment) represents the same thing (in the user's environment) as any other boundary in the data base, the data structure is not elastic. This can be stated as shown in Fig. 5.15.

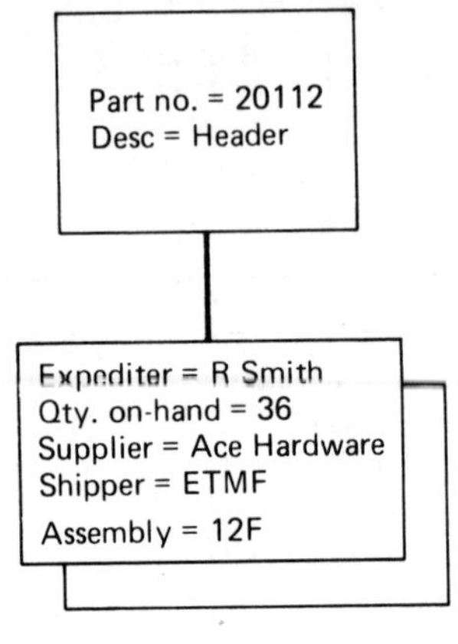

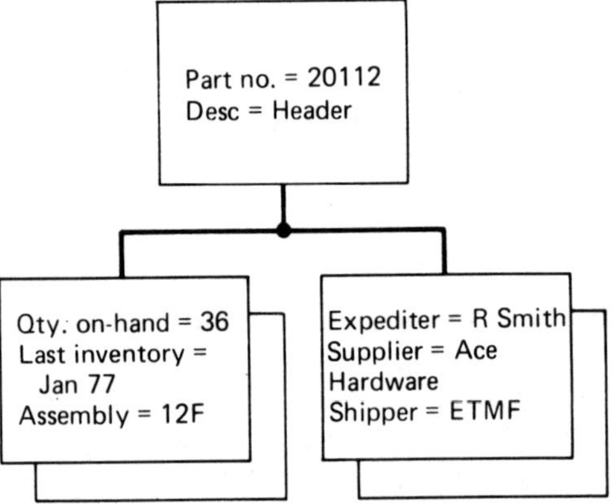

Figure 5.14 (a) When widely dissimilar elements exist within a segment beneath a parent, the impact of change is increased. (b) Breaking the data into sibling segments meant that adding the last inventory date to its associated element—Qty on hand—did not affect expediter, supplier, or shipper.

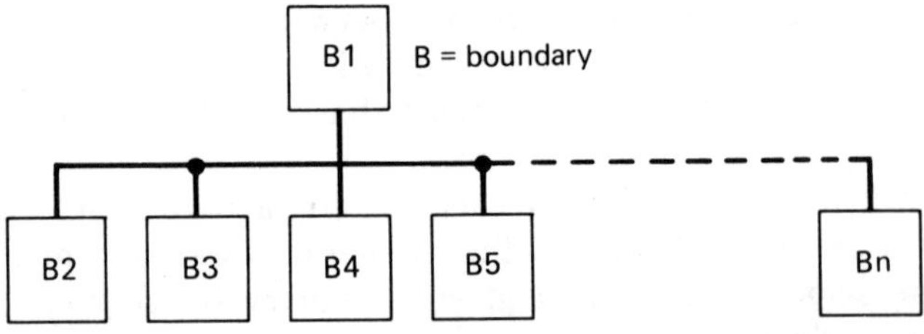

Figure 5.15 Data Base Flexibility: Data Elasticity over Multiple Segments. In examining the segments of a data base, the most elastic structuring occurs where all B1, B2, . . . , Bn are dissimilar.

BONDING AT THE DATA BASE LEVEL

Two data bases are physically bonded together most closely when they are connected by pointers that directly point from one data base to the physical address in some other data base (Fig. 5.16). This type of arrangement is the most inelastic because as the data base being pointed to changes, the pointer in the other data base must also change. If the data base being pointed to is affected by an error (such as an invalid pointer due to hardware failure), it is likely that at least a few of the pointer segments that direct themselves to the impaired data base are invalid. Furthermore, if the data base being pointed to is physically moved from one device to another, the pointer chain must be reconstructed. Such a relationship is very delicate. The advantage of direct pointers between data bases is that when the pointer is being followed, no randomizer or index has to be used; hence it is very efficient operationally.

Symbolic pointers can be used to connect two data bases (Fig. 5.17). In this case the pointer contains the key information necessary to locate the segment being pointed to. This means slightly less efficiency because of mandatory use of the randomizer or index, but it also enhances flexibility by allowing the data base being pointed to to be transported from one location to another without having to reconstruct the whole pointer chain. This increases the elasticity of the relationship.

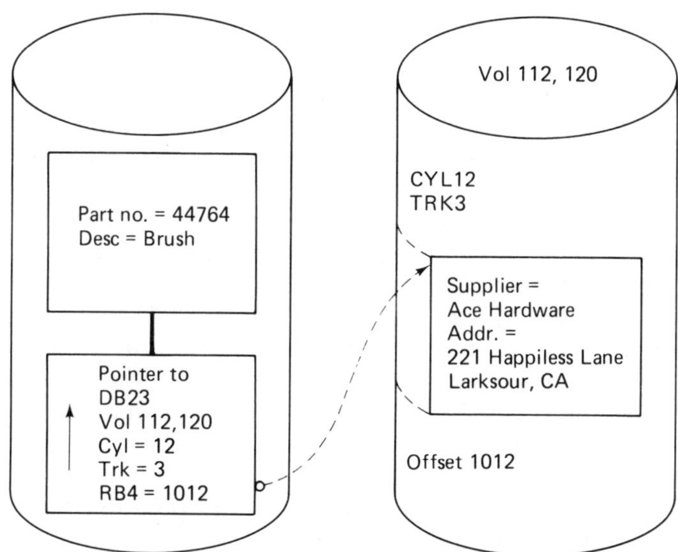

Figure 5.16 Direct pointers contain specific information as to the address of a given record. A randomizer or index does not need to be used. When the physical location of the segment being pointed to changes, the pointer needs to be reset.

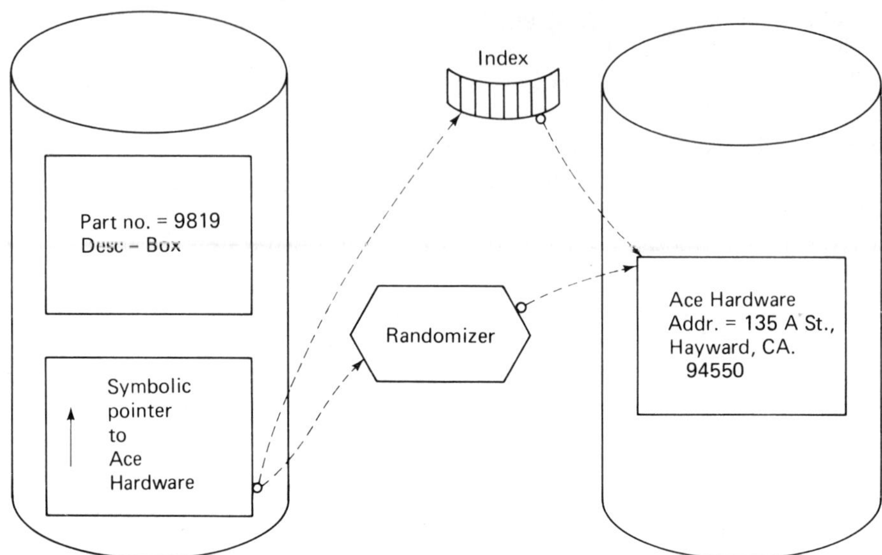

Figure 5.17 To use a symbolic pointer, the key value stored in the pointer segment is sent to the randomizer or the index structure and then the segment pointed to can be located. This allows the supplier data base to be physically moved without altering the part number pointers.

Symbolic pointer segments may be constructed by using features of the DBMS or by an application program external to the DBMS. The highest degree of freedom in bonding between data bases can be achieved by creating pointer segments with application programs because the structures that are produced are not limited by the constraints of the DBMS. Some examples are shown by Fig. 5.18.

There are some distinct advantages to creating symbolic pointers external to the DBMS. When a pointer chain is broken or invalid, the recovery routines of the DBMS must be relied upon to recover the pointer chains if the pointers are defined within the DBMS. However, if the pointers exist strictly as part of the application, the programmer has direct control over the recovery of the data base. A disadvantage here is that application constructed pointers must have hand-built software written to handle activity such as recovery. Each set of external pointers requires its own software, which typically includes routines that verify the existence of all segments being pointed to, rebuilds pointer chains, searches for the existence of a single pointer, and so on.

Flexibility at the data base level may involve the creation of multiple data bases (redundant at the root level) when the segments that make up the data base have a widely varied meaning or where the volatility of the segments in a data base varies widely. For example, suppose that a data

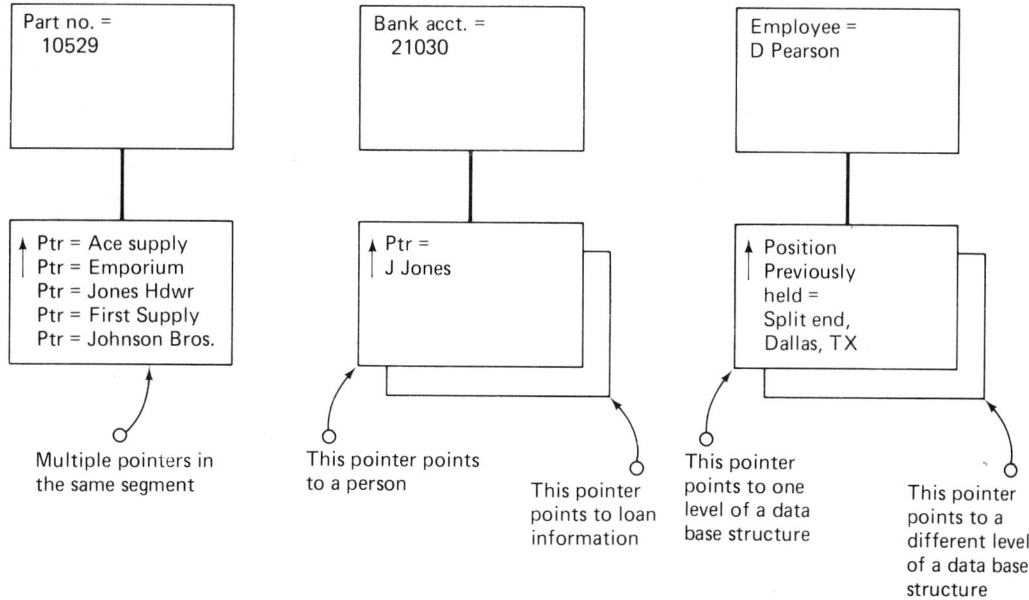

Figure 5.18 Some of the ways pointers can be used when programmed within the application, external to the DBMS.

base whose root is an oil well has a child segment containing information about parties to contact for leasing the well, and suppose that another segment type exists concerning the monthly production of the well. It may be a good design decision to split these two segments into separate data bases, because they are only incidentally related to each other and because their volatility is quite dissimilar. Suppose that a change is to be made to the activity segment. While the change is being made, the segment concerning the leasing of the well is affected even though it has no relationship to the change being made. It is an "innocent" segment.

LOOSELY BOUND DATA BASES

The loosest degree of physical bonding between data bases occurs when implied data relationships are created. The relationship is supported entirely by an application algorithm. If one data base gets out of synch with another, there is no way of detecting the error except through the algorithm that connects the two. An implicit relationship differs from an explicit relationship with a symbolic pointer in that symbolic pointers explicitly tie two data bases together by the existence of the keys of one data base residing in another whereas an implied relationship has no such direct tie.

DATA ELASTICITY

Elasticity of data is understood in terms of the physical bonding of data. Bonding of data occurs at the elemental, segment, and data base level. The net effect of introducing elasticity into a data structure is to separate data into units that are the least susceptible to future unnecessary work caused by change.

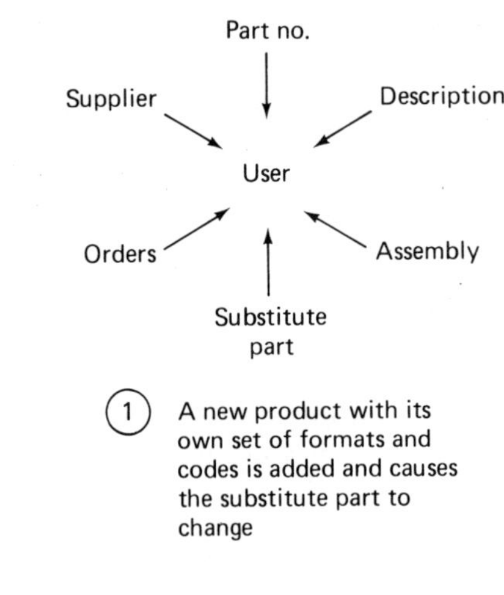

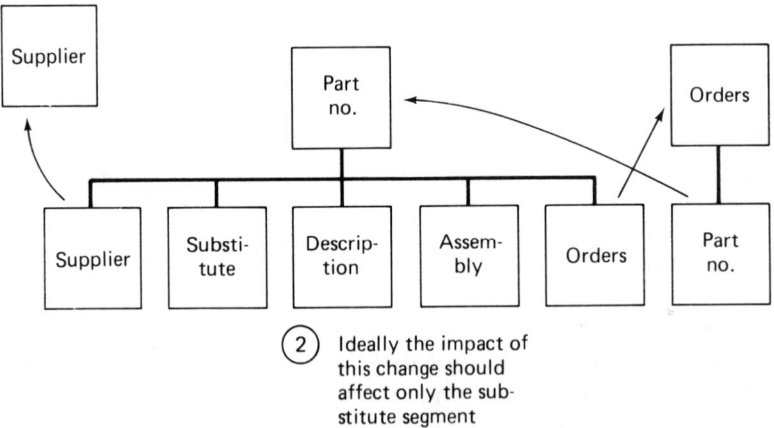

Figure 5.19 Data Base Flexibility: Strategy for Minimizing Impact of Change. When change occurs, only those elements impacted in the user's environment should be impacted in the data base. A change to a single logical unit of information in the user's environment produces a change to no more than a single data element. Simple strategy, not so easy to implement.

A good design will allow for the fact that there is a relationship between physical data bonding and data complexity. If a data structure is highly complex or if there is a high propensity for change, the designer should separate the data elements as much as possible using the loosest level of binding possible. Complex data structures that are tightly bound are almost sure to change, and the more tightly they are bound, the greater the amount of work needed to reshape them.

The cost of elasticity is not cheap. A high degree of elasticity is operationally expensive. The cost/benefit ratio of data elasticity is derived when change occurs and the elastic structure is easily manipulated, thereby saving money by minimizing program changes and data manipulation. Figure 5.19 discusses the strategy for achieving data elasticity and shows how the impact of change might be minimized.

Another perspective of data elasticity is to view the structures of data and their source. Data structures closely resembling the data as it has been abstracted from the user's environment (*natural data*) tend to be elastic, whereas data designed purely and simply from a given set of system requirements tends to be inelastic. This is so because a given set of requirements necessarily causes the designer to perceive data to be in a finite state, whereas data patterned naturally tends to view the data more generally, fulfilling many views of the data. Data patterned after a set of requirements is optimized for those requirements, which leads to good system performance. Data patterned naturally is oblivious to any given requirement.

EXERCISES

1. Review the oldest data base application in your environment (preferably 3 or more years old). If available, read the initial set of user requirements and determine how well the initial design of the application fits the requirements.

   Identify all major changes in the user's environment to the present and correlate changes in the data structures that were made because of the changes in the user's environment.

   If records have been kept of coding changes in the application, relate those changes back to changes in the user's environment.

   Critique the system on the status of its design as it currently exists (e.g., how clean is the code today?) Identify any peculiar structures or practices that exist that accommodate changes in user requirements.
2. Select an existing application with a large amount and wide variety of types of data. Analyze the elasticity (or inelasticity) of the data based on the following criteria:

a) Number of data elements in a segment.
b) Similarity of all data elements in relation to the segment.
c) Similarity or dissimilarity of segment types to each other in a data base.

3. Choose an existing application. Analyze the impact of change on existing code in light of the following:
   a) Data element A must be enlarged and a new element, B, is to be added to the segment where A exists and is to be accessed in conjunction with A.
   b) Data element A is to be moved from its existing segment to a new segment.
   c) Segment A is to be removed from the data base and used to create a new data base.
   d) Segment A and its dependent, B, are to be combined.
   e) Segment A is to be split into sibling segments A and B.
   f) The key sequence of A is to be rearranged.
   g) Data bases A and B are related by a direct pointer. The pointer is to become symbolic.
   h) The explicit relation between data bases A and B is to be changed so that the key structure of B can include a new element.
   i) When element A in data base A is updated, a segment in data base B is created. Now data base B is to be divided into two physically separate data bases.
4. Some DBMSs are able to allow for change of data structures quite easily. In some cases this is because they operate at a level of field sensitivity, not segment sensitivity. In doing so, changes are fairly easy to accomplish. However, there usually is a price to pay in terms of performance. Analyze several fundamentally different DBMSs and examine the trade-offs associated with flexibility and performance.

SIX

COMBINING CONSIDERATIONS OF FLEXIBILITY AND PERFORMANCE

The goals of efficient operation of a data base system and a flexible design of data structures are nearly diametrically opposed. Data structures built for efficiency tend to have few segment types, shallow and narrow structures, short twin chains, and segments that contain data elements that are only vaguely related. Data structures that optimize flexibility have many segment types, intricate structuring of segments, and all elements within a given segment have a common relation to the boundary of the segment. It is the usual case that somewhere in between these two polarities lies an acceptable set of design criteria.

FLEXIBILITY OR PERFORMANCE

When considering trade-offs of performance versus flexibility at the start of the design process, it is always easier to opt for performance because the utility of performance is apparent and immediate, while the

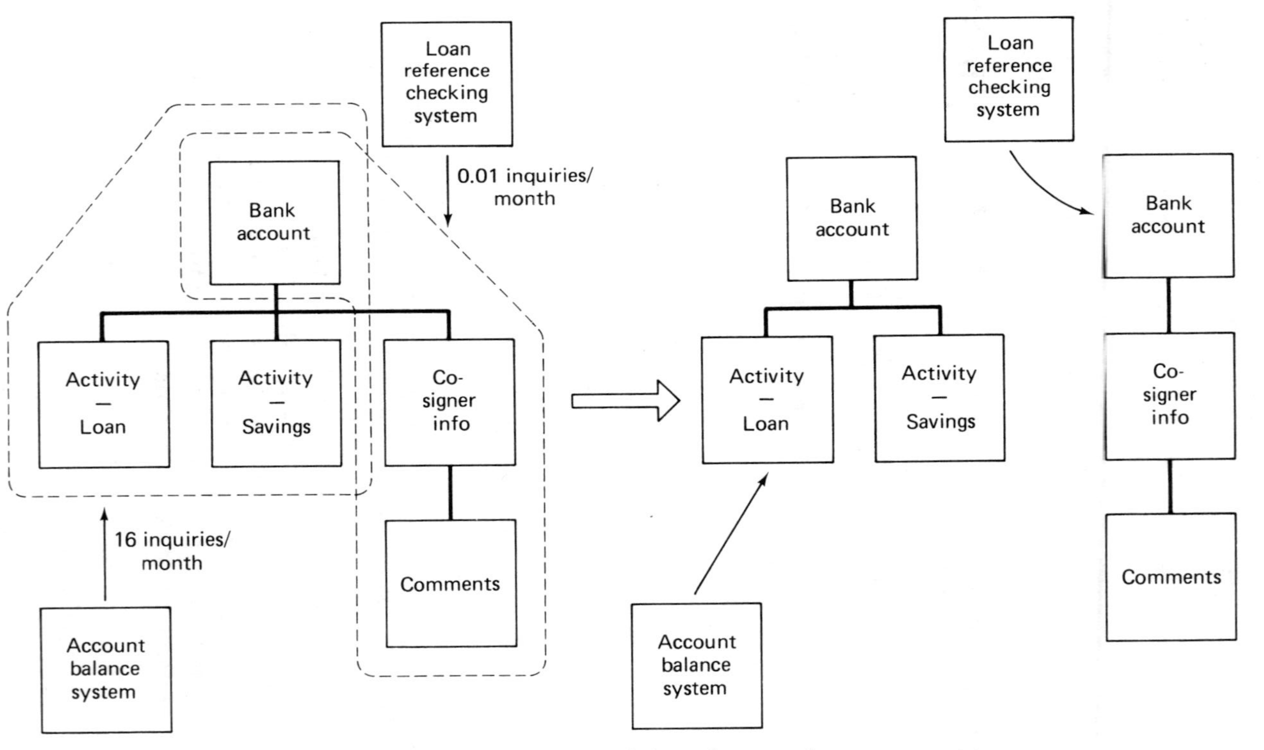

Figure 6.1 Combining Flexibility and Performance: General Agreement of Design Criteria. Data that is physically stored together but differs widely in function should be physically separated.

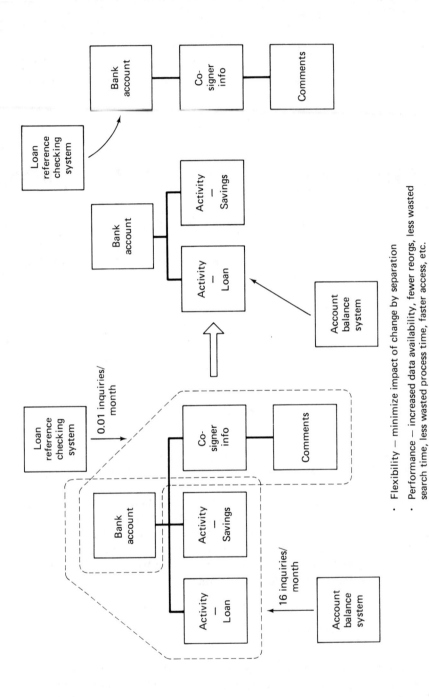

utility gained by building elasticity into a data structure is latent. Data that is elastic survives best in the face of environmental change. It is only when data that is inelastic undergoes environmental change that the wisdom of building flexible data structures becomes apparent.

The actual design of a data structure is a compromise among several differing considerations. One of the earliest design philosophies that must be decided is a *prioritization* of the goals of the system—that is, what features are the most important, what features are merely useful, and what features are nice to have only if they do not cost too much. Allowing this prioritization to be done informally or by default can lead to confusion and wasted effort at a later time. Prioritization should be done based upon an awareness of what the issues are, their costs, and how the needs of the user can best be met realistically and at the least expense.

There is one curious item agreed upon by both considerations of flexibility and performance. Sibling segments should be separated into different data bases when they contain data that is not similar in content, when their volatility or frequency of access and update varies a great deal, and when they are used exclusively in different environments (on-line, batch, etc.).

From the standpoint of flexibility, this split is desirable because it means that if environmental change occurs and affects one segment type, other unrelated segments will not be affected, because they are in a separate data base. From the standpoint of performance, when a segment that is never used for certain processes resides in the same data base with a segment that is used exclusively for other processes, then splitting them into two data bases reduces the overhead that must be done (see Fig. 6.1).

ANALYSIS OF RISK FLEXIBILITY

To best determine where risks can be taken with the least likelihood of a bad outcome, it is a good policy to examine what factors can cause data elements to have a high propensity for change. A few typical considerations are:

1. Is the system new or are new features of magnitude being added to an existing system? Nearly every new systems analyst suffers from the syndrome of "give me what I say I want, then I can tell you what I really want." Even competent and experienced personnel can miscalculate the requirements of a new system. The data structures that will support the initial cut at a system are best designed with a high degree of flexibility.
2. Is the nature of the data unstable? Typically, government regula-

tions and organizational charts change on a predictable basis. Not preparing for change when handling this type of data is dangerous. Other types of data, such as general ledgers, are static and do not undergo structural change with great frequency. If the nature of the data is inherently unstable, prepare for that fact.

3. Is it a known fact that the structure of the data will change? If so, prepare for it. Sometimes a system designer knows data will change in the foreseeable future but will not know the specifics of the change. An elastic structuring of data allows ongoing system development to occur without a fear of having to rebuild the system from scratch when changes occur.
4. Are there many interrelationships among data elements? Is the structure complex? Are there many data elements logically connected by one or more fragile algorithms? The more complex and interrelated the data, the greater the impact of change. Also, the probability of change seems to be higher in the presence of fragile and complex data.
5. Is the user either unreliable or inexperienced? If so, it is inevitable that changes will occur, usually large ones. This factor should be tempered with other factors, but in its own way it is the most important factor.
6. Are there many internal structures of data within a segment? If a segment is packed with several iterations of the same data element (blocked), is the segment and its supporting program able to withstand the change of adding a few more iterations of the data element into the segment? Segments that contain data that has its own structure within the segment are more susceptible to change because the probability for change is greater than if there were no internal structure. This is so because the propensity for change must account for the normal probability for change of each data element as well as the probability of change for the internal structuring of data.
7. Is the political environment of the user unsettled? Even when an experienced and competent user contributes to the system specifications, if his or her own environment is unstable, the system being constructed is likely to change.

Just as there are poor risks that should not be taken when determining how elastic the data structures should be, there are good risks as well. They are:

1. Is the system stable and well defined (possibly a conversion)? If the user is aware of what to expect and how to manage the system, it is reasonable to structure data in somewhat less than a flexible manner.

2. Is the user experienced and reliable? Has the user experienced the rigors of creating a system in the past? Has the user demonstrated foresight and good judgment in making past decisions? If the user has gone through more than one iteration of system design and development, knows what to expect, and has had a record of success, it may be safe to build somewhat inelastic structures for him or her.
3. Is the very nature of the application stable?
4. Is the structuring of the data simple? Is there a minimum of complex relations, internal structures, and redundancy? If so, the designer may take some liberties with the elasticity of the design.

COMBINING UNLIKE DATA ELEMENTS

The data designer normally trades flexibility for performance by combining unlike data elements into the same segment. This means that the various elements will have dissimilar relationships to the boundary of the segment, and thus are susceptible to unnecessary change. But, by having more data available for any given access, the total number of calls to the DBMS is reduced. This means less program logic, less I/O, and less time spent in execution of the code in the DBMS.

Unlike data elements may be combined into the same segment type to reduce space requirements. When a segment contains one or two short data elements and the prefix of the segment is close to the size of the data portion of the segment, the existence of such a segment should be questioned.

Another motivation for combining unlike data elements into the same segment is to simplify the structure of the data base and the processing that must occur. This is a rather weak motivation, however.

The boundary of a segment becomes broadened or reinterpreted when unlike data elements are placed in it. In some cases this may amount to an enlargement or annexation of the original interpretation of the boundary of the segment, or it may merely represent the intersection of two entirely different boundaries wed out of necessity.

SAFELY COMBINING UNLIKE ELEMENTS

Combining unlike data elements into the same segment takes the least amount of risk when:

1. The risk of environmental change is minimal. The user is experienced and predictable, the application is well defined and the risk

of wide new interpretations is minimal, and the nature of the data is simple.

2. No data element appears more than once throughout the structure.
3. No structuring of data elements internal to a segment is repeated.
4. Data has been thoroughly analyzed by asking more-than-enough "what if" questions.

PLANNED AND CONTROLLED REDUNDANCY

Redundancy can be wasteful and produce inelastic structures, but in certain cases it can be used as an effective tool by the designer. When redundancy creeps into the system and is unplanned, it is almost always harmful. However, there are situations where planned redundancy can enhance system performance and can be used to create alternatives for processing that would otherwise be awkward or unfeasible. To understand how to apply redundancy as a tool, it is first necessary to understand what the pitfalls of redundancy are:

1. Redundant data requires more work (programmer time, execution time, etc.) to maintain.
2. Redundant data uses unnecessary space.
3. Redundant data, through hardware or software error, may get out of synch. A data element in one place may have a different value than a data element in another place at the same time. Which value is correct and which is incorrect may be a difficult thing to determine.
4. The impact of change in the environment is unnecessarily proliferated. A change in the environment of a redundant element has an impact whenever the element exists.
5. Program maintenance, even routine maintenance, becomes complicated. Whatever program changes occur in one place must be applied wherever else the data element is manipulated to keep the system functioning in a consistent fashion. A programmer may correctly change one program but may not be aware that other programs need the same change.

TYPES OF REDUNDANCIES

Redundancy occurs in many forms. Sometimes, it is explicit and obvious. Other times, it takes the form of data elements that are very similar but not quite the same. Often when data elements are very similar,

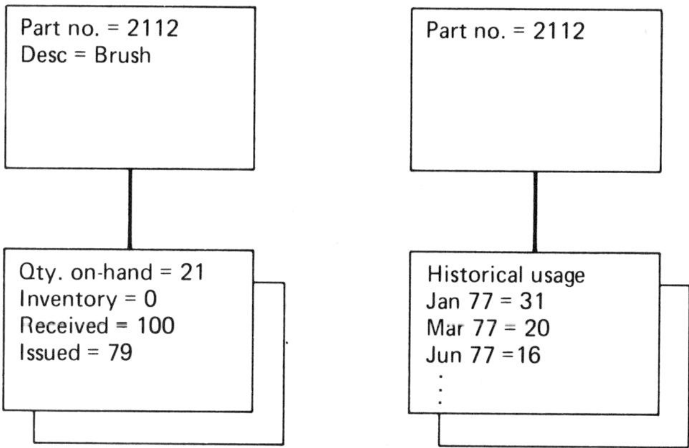

Figure 6.2 Redundancy at the key level is used to separate data keyed the same way but used for entirely different purposes.

perceiving them abstractly reveals that they represent the same entity in the user's environment.

There are two basic categories of redundancy: physical or semantic. *Physical* redundancy occurs when the same data values exist over and over again in the data base. Except for the storage occupied, physical redundancy is seldom a problem. The real problems of redundancy are *semantic*—where the same data element, segment, or structure appears multiple times in a data base(s).

Some of the different types of semantic redundancy are:

1. *Key-only redundancy*—when used correctly, it can be a powerful tool (Fig. 6.2).
2. *Elemental redundancy*—this may or may not be a useful tool, depending upon its usage and the amount of inelasticity it produces (Fig. 6.3).
3. *Structural redundancy*—this is seldom if ever useful (Fig. 6.4).
4. *Wholesale-data-base redundancy*—this type of redundancy should be scrutinized closely (Fig. 6.5). The worst cases of waste and inelasticity occur when this type of redundancy is encountered.

REDUNDANCY AS A TOOL

When can redundancy effectively be used as a tool? Redundancy can be used to split data into separate data bases that have the same root key. Making the root redundant is cheap (in terms of space) and allows the dependent data to functionally exist independently in different places. It is expensive when the dependent data that is split must be accessed by

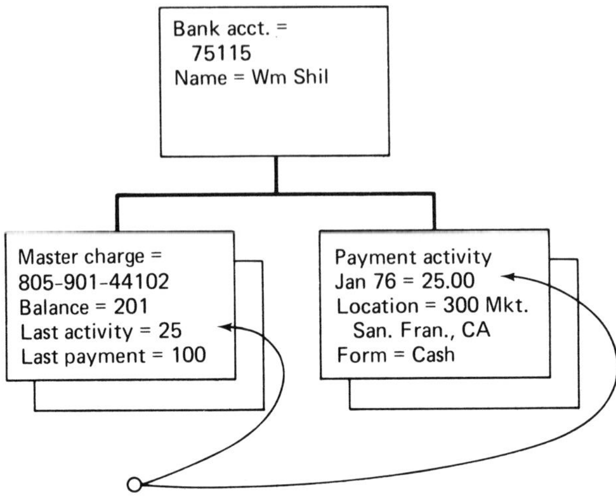

Figure 6.3 Keying the last activity in to places means that an inquiry to the Master Charge segment does not require an access to the payment activity segment to determine appropriate information. This type of redundancy (on a limited basis) can be beneficial.

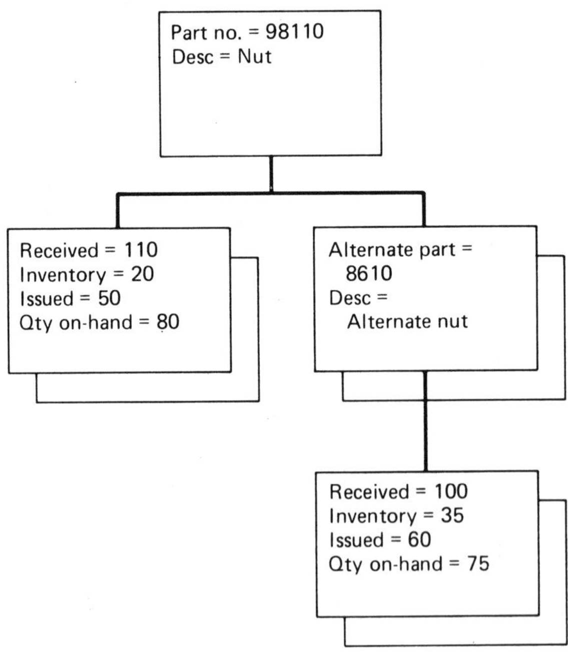

Figure 6.4 The appearance of similar internal data structures should be a warning that the design may need review.

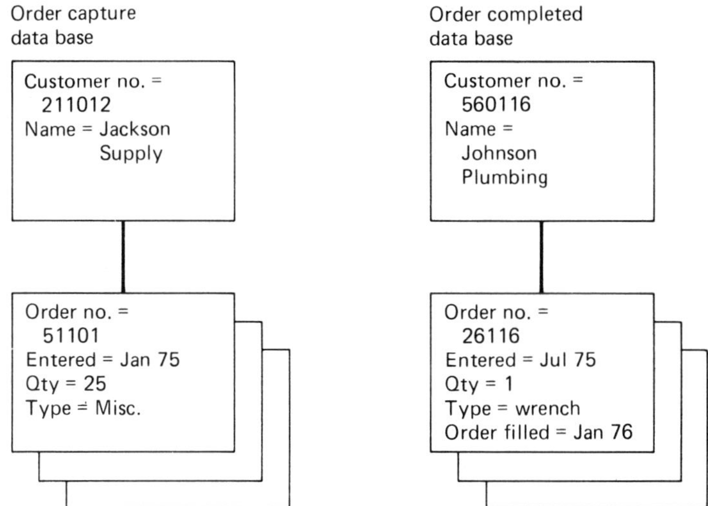

Figure 6.5 Data redundancy at the data base level is usually extremely wasteful but is surprisingly common. It often occurs because of separation rather than combination of development effort.

the same program because the amount of I/O is considerably more than if the dependent segments were still physically joined at the root level.

Before redundant data elements can be used successfully, a "ground rule" must be established. There must be one and only one place into which the data is updated, and this location by definition contains the "correct" value of the data element in case there are discrepancies elsewhere. Having updated the data element in its prime location, other occurrences copy the value from that location. This may amount to no more than an exercise in semantics, but it is important to have a single reference point which can be used to settle any disputes as to the correct contents of the data element. Figure 6.6 discusses the concept of "source and copy" philosophy.

Having established a common point of reference, it is safe to create redundant elements. The redundant elements can be placed into segments that are likely candidates for on-line retrieval, so that a minimum number of calls to the DBMS is achieved. Redundant elements may also be used to interface between two systems. The simplest sort of elemental redundancy as a system interface occurs as a symbolic pointer in an explicit relation between two segments. Its use as an interface is not limited to a symbolic pointer, however. Redundant data elements can be used in cross-reference data structures, in indexed data structures, and in a wide variety of interfaces.

Wholesale data redundancy is useful when data is to be aged or ar-

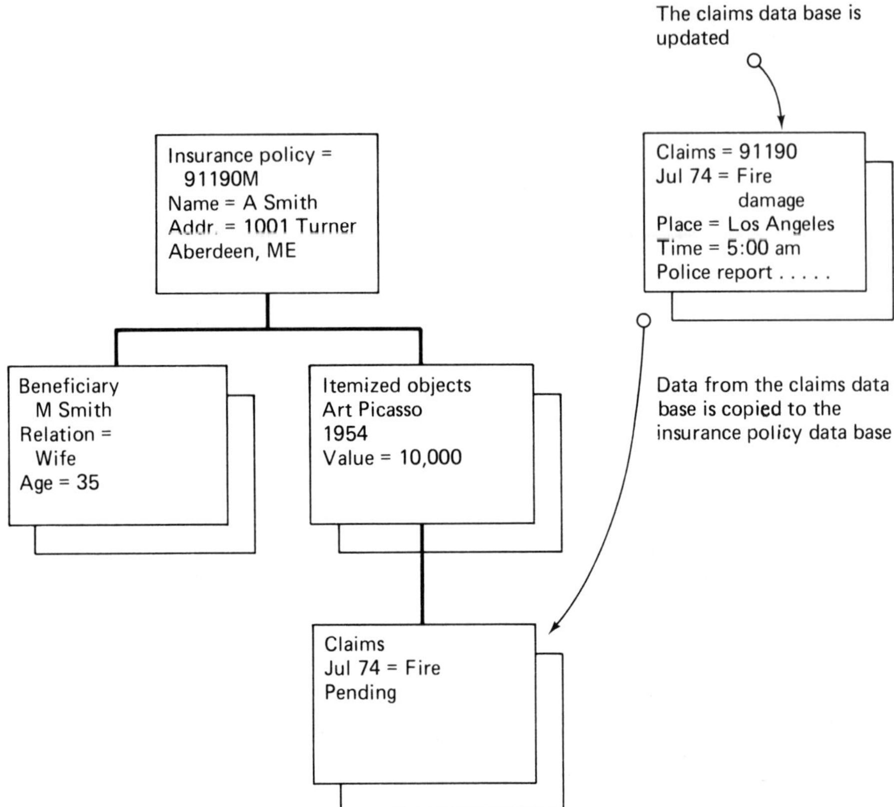

Figure 6.6 One data base is updated and is considered to be the authoritative source for the redundant data element. Information from it may be copied to other data bases. If a conflict arises, the data base that is updated is considered to be correct.

chived. In this case, some portion of the data in a data base is to be deleted because its usefulness is past and space is needed for new data. Rather than throw away the data, it may be desirable to keep the data for historical purposes. This usually amounts to removing data from a direct-access device to tape. It is useful to transport the data in the structure as it resides.

REDUNDANCY AS A DESIGN TOOL

Redundancy can be used as a design tool (Fig. 6.7). As an example of how redundancy (which reduces the elasticity of the data) can be used to enhance performance, consider the following design problem.

- Guideline – No data element should be semantically redundant.
- Semantic redundancy can be useful in the following exceptions where circumstances warrant –
  - Key-only redundancy – Useful for splitting large data bases
    – Useful for enhancing performance
    – Useful for enhancing flexibility
  - Elemental redundancy – Useful for enhancing performance by reducing the I/O at retrieval time
  - Data base redundancy – Useful for separating data into groups whose functional usage widely varies
    – Useful for archiving data

Figure 6.7 **Redundancy: Redundancy as a tool.**

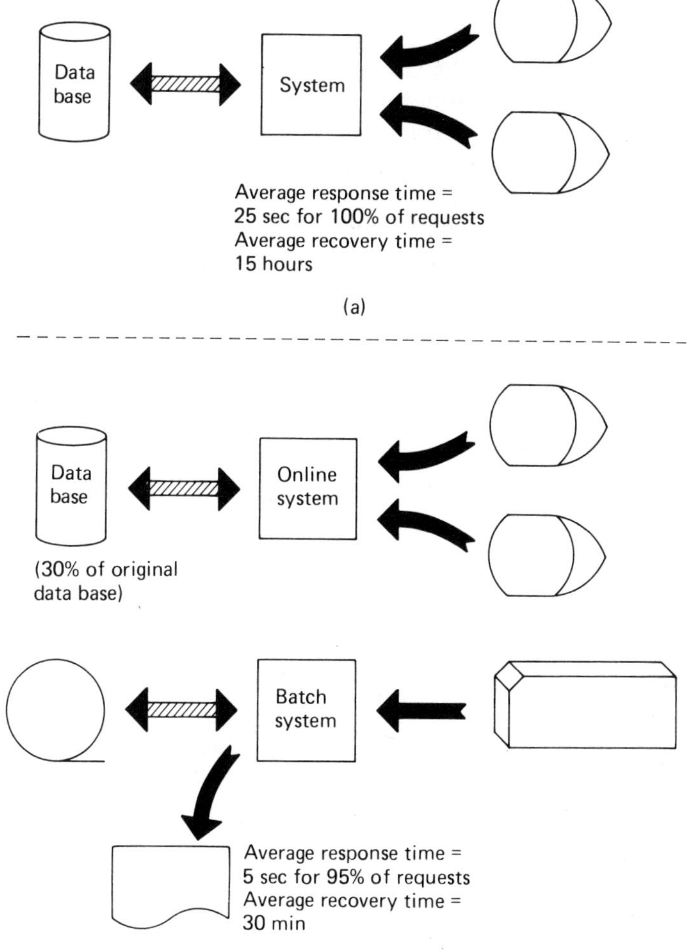

Figure 6.8 (a) Original system specifications. (b) Revised system specifications with data redundancy and a smaller on-line data base.

A data base that is very large exists to which many inquiries (no updates) on-line are made. Because of its size, data reorganization is done only once a year, and consequently each inquiry results in more I/O than would be necessary if the data were organized more frequently. A decision has been made to reduce the on-line data by 70% and to store all the data on tape (redundantly). Because the 30% of the data remaining on-line has been carefully selected, 95% of the on-line inquiries will still be satisfied. The remaining 5% that are not satisfied will be run against the tape. Figure 6.8 illustrates some of the trade-offs involved.

EXERCISES

1. The Four-Step Assembly Company has decided to construct a data base to reflect the manufacturing of its product. The system designer has decided that each segment needs an ID, a Description, and a Qty. Those elements will satisfy all existing reports and queries. The data base is shown in Fig. 6.9.
   a) Build the Four-Step data base and load with random values.
   b) Write a batch report program that will report:
      i. The level of an ID.
      ii. The ID.
      iii. The Qty of the ID.

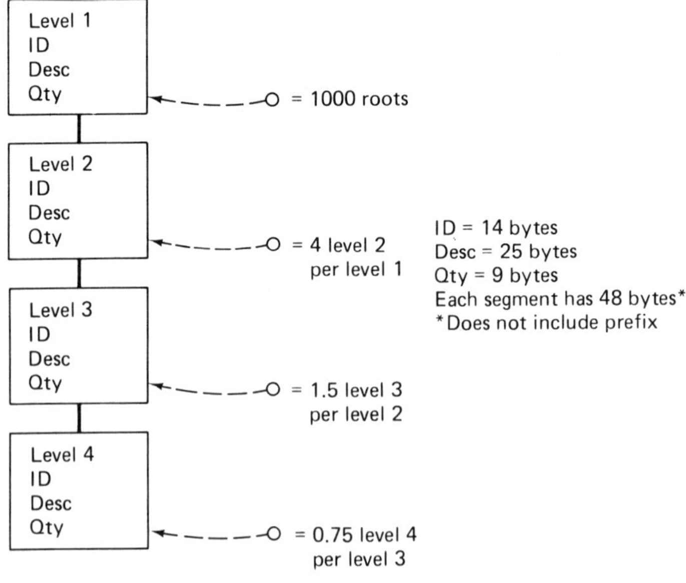

Figure 6.9

c) Write an on-line transaction that will:
   i. Locate any given ID.
   ii. Report its level and Qty.
   iii. List all IDs beneath it by ID and Desc.

d) Keep track of the time necessary to program and generate a), b), and c).

Five-Step Associates has just acquired Four-Step Assembly. Part of the assets they bought were the programs and data bases of Four-Step.

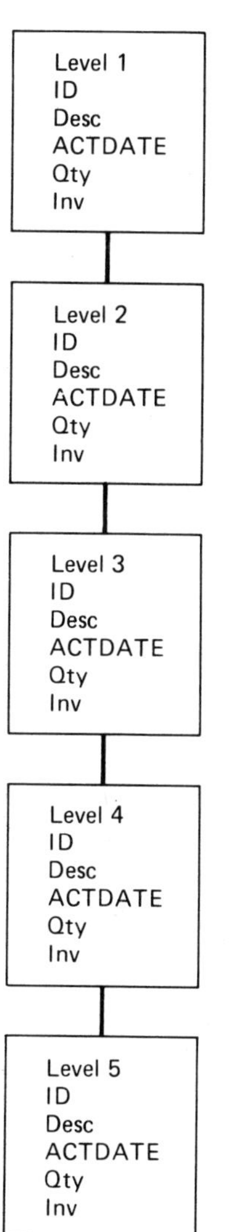

ID = 15 bytes
Desc = 25 bytes
ACTDATE = 5 bytes
Inv = 10 bytes
Each segment is 64 bytes*

*Does not include prefix

Figure 6.10

Because Five-Step is a modern, progressive company, their reports are more extensive than Four-Step's. One of the first decisions is to convert Four-Step's system to Five-Step's operation. To do this, a new level must be added to the data base, and activity date and inventory amount must be added. ACTDATE is required to be placed between Desc and Qty. The new data base is given in Fig. 6.10.

e) Convert the Four-Step DATA BASE according to the Five-Step requirements. Convert the report and transaction to reflect the new data base and display the ACTDATE and Inv in the report and transaction. Keep track of programming and data regeneration and conversion time spent.

When the Six-Step Automation Company tenders an offer to buy the stock of the Five-Step Associates, a data analyst proposes the new data base design shown in Fig. 6.11.

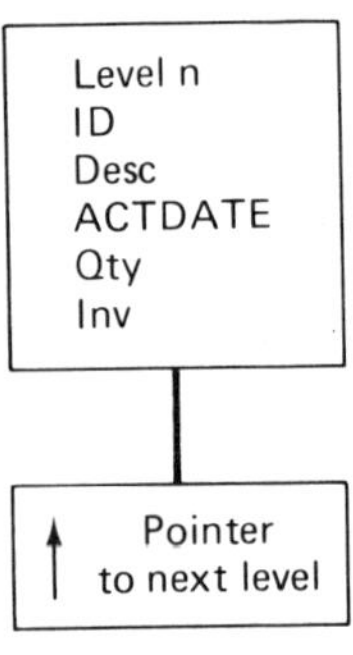

Figure 6.11

f) Comment on this program based upon previous program changes and amount of conversion (both data and program).
g) Comment on this program based upon performance considerations.

2. Given the following environments, comment on the propensity for environmental change:
   a) King James version of the Bible (each verse is a segment).
   b) The National Football League (structured by standings).
   c) Kentucky Derby entries.
   d) Litton Industries corporate structure.
   e) Robert's rules of order.
   f) *The Guiness Book of Records.*
   g) Chemical table of elements.
   h) World money market.

   i). Which environments might be safe for optimizing performance?
   ii). Which environments require optimizing flexibility?

SEVEN

LARGE DATA BASE DESIGN

There are two ways in which a data base can be large: It may contain a voluminous amount of a few types of data or it may contain a large and varied collection of data types which when put together form a massive amount of data. In each case the implications of the volume of data are different depending upon the nature of the data base. When a few massive types of data are strung together, the impact is usually in the area of performance for the one or two environments in which the data base participates. When many data types are connected and form a large data base, the impact tends to be spread over many environments. Figure 7.1 shows the ways in which data bases can be large.

PROBLEMS WITH LARGE DATA BASES

A large data base can become its own limited resource when it is used in conjunction with many other data bases in widely varying conditions.

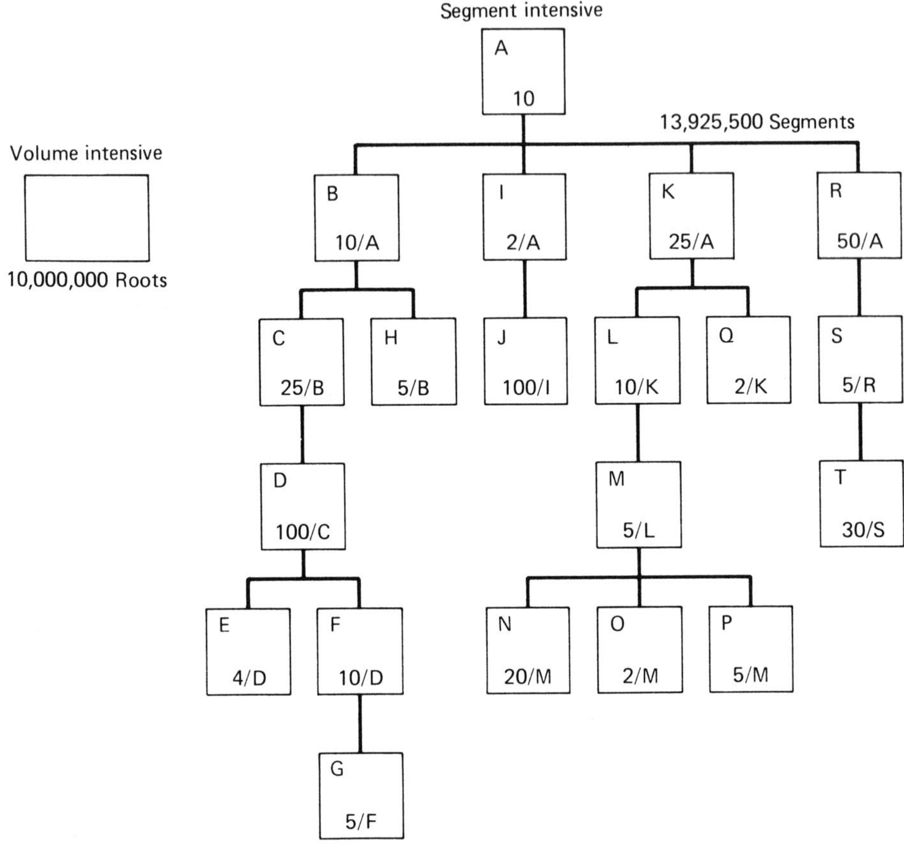

Figure 7.1 Large Data Bases: Types. In the case of a single segment type being voluminous, the problems of size impact only those parts of the environment that touch the segment. Where many segment types are connected and the size of the data base is a problem, various other environments are affected as they compete for the data base as a resource.

The problem is intensified when the data base must be used restrictively (i.e., while interfacing in one environment, no other uses may be made of the data). The inaccessibility of the data then impacts other systems, and the goal of a single centralized, unified data base becomes less than desirable.

A large data base that is highly volatile presents problems when it needs to be reorganized. As segments are inserted and deleted, data tends to become poorly organized. Long and complex pointer chains from primary to overflow areas are created and normal access of data requires much more effort than if the data were freshly organized. This is a result of the way updating is handled by the DBMS within the given native data organization (direct, indexed, etc.).

For instance, the space occupied by a segment after it is deleted may or may not be reusable. Or an insert may be made to an area that is already occupied and pointers will be constructed to show the location of the new segment. As more activity occurs, the DBMS requires more and more pointers to build the data base.

The general solution to keeping the data well organized is to read it sequentially onto a tape and reload the data base in an order that will create the best structuring of the data. The larger the volume of data, the more resources this unloading/reloading process consumes.

In some data base management systems, such as IMS, another need for reorganizing a large data base occurs when a structural change needs to be made to the data. A segment type may need to be added, or changed, or deleted, or a segment type may need to be reordered or even have its parent changed. In any case, from time to time, data bases require a change of their definition to the DBMS. Other changes may involve enlarging the total space allocated for the data base, a change in the physical blocking of the records, or a change in indexing. Such changes require the data to be unloaded in its current format, the new definition of the data described to the DBMS, and the data then reloaded into the new format. A large data base is necessarily awkward to handle at reorganization time for no other reason than the amount of time it takes to process the volume of data.

Another major problem with large data bases is recovery. When a small data base must be restored (and over time, it is likely that any data base is going to need to be restored), recreating the data base or running utilities to correct the problem takes a short amount of time. For a large data base, this is not so. Because of the size of runs that must be executed, recovery will take a relatively long time. Large data bases further complicate recovery insofar as their size alone makes problem analysis and correction a risky business. If a designer insists on building large data bases, he or she should plan on some downtime, estimate that time, and alert management and the user to the risks. Not doing so leads to ultimate dissatisfaction.

SPLITTING A DATA BASE BY KEY

One possible solution to some of the problems caused by large data bases is to logically create a data base by defining more than one physical data base, all with the identical semantic structuring, except that data is spread over them based upon the value of the key of the root segment. In the example shown in Fig. 7.2, if the key of the root lies between 000 and 333, it will exist in data base 1. If the key is between 334 and 666, it will be in data base 2, and if the key is between 667 and 999, it will be in data base 3.

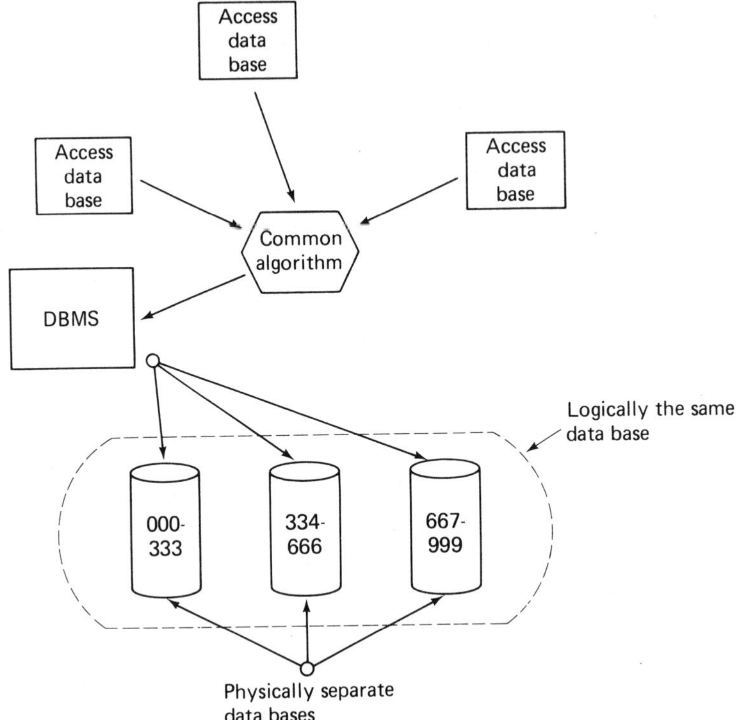

Figure 7.2 Large Data Base: Alternatives. Splitting DB algorithmically by key. Note: Best key split is not done along lines meaningful to the functional organization of the data.

The implications of splitting data bases by the value of the key of the root segment should not be taken lightly. The data should be spread evenly over the data bases if growth is to occur in a random order, or in a skewed fashion if growth will not be random, allowing the most free space where growth is expected to occur. The frequency of access and update should determine what values are appropriate for the splitting of the keys. If at all possible, empirical information should be used to determine the best values for key splits.

There are several advantages to splitting a data base by key into more than one physical data base. They are:

1. Partial recovery and reorganization—when one of the data bases that has been physically split is unavailable due to software or hardware failure, it will not be necessary to recover all the data—only the data in the affected physical data base.
2. System reliability—when part of the system is unavailable, the rest of the system will not be unusable.

3. Breaking of recovery, reorganization, and so on, into smaller, more manageable jobs.

Although data base splitting by key has desirable features, there are some surprisingly severe drawbacks. Some of them are:

1. Operationally, split data bases are difficult to handle. Specifically, synchronization becomes a problem. Coordinating and keeping track of what work needs to be done and has been done to a data base becomes complex and prone to error. The normal maintenance problems are multiplied.
2. A new level of complexity has been added to the system. The job of coding is more difficult (but can be eased by using a common program interface that does all accesses and inserts to the data base), and debugging and testing have more variables to go wrong.
3. The design options are limited. Specifically, when pointer segments are to be used (especially when the pointers are handled within the DBMS) the design quickly becomes very complex. Such questions arise as: Should each data base have its own separate logically related data base, or should each data base point to the same logically related data base? Indexing, implicit relationships, and many other design features are adversely impacted by the use of split keys.
4. Overhead of many data bases. Each data base and its definition to the DBMS involve some overhead. When there are not too many data bases involved, this overhead is not significant. However, when data bases are split by key, the overhead the DBMS has to handle can become a factor.
5. Evolution of one data base away from others. If the split by key is involved in a logical division of root keys by some category, such as location, division, territory, and so on, it is natural for the data bases to evolve in separate directions over time. The requirements and wants for one territory will differ from other territories, given enough time. As this occurs, there will be a temptation to alter the definition of one data base without altering the other data bases. This will have a big impact on existing programs and on future capability to reconsolidate the data base.

SPLITTING DATA BASE BY DATA TYPE

Another way to break a data base into smaller, more manageable pieces is to separate it into several smaller data bases by splitting off entire segment types. This necessarily implies redundancy of the key of one or more roots, but provides many of the advantages of smaller data bases without having as many disadvantages as splitting data by key. Figure 7.3 shows data bases split by data type.

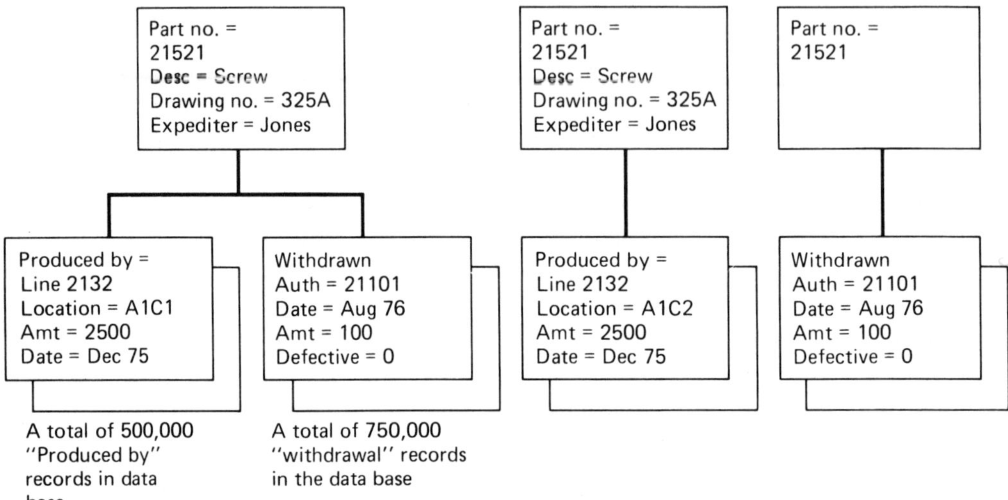

Figure 7.3 Total data base segments—500,000 + 750,000 + r (number of roots) = 1,250,000 + r. Splitting the data base by data type creates redundancy and more records at the root level. Total data base segments—500,000 + 750,000 + 2r = 1,250,000 + 2r.

Some of the advantages of splitting data bases by data types are:

1. Reduction in the number of segments and space of any given physical data base. Recoveries, backups, and sequential scans of the data base have a smaller impact on the system.
2. Data is not concentrated as heavily in one resource. This means that when one physical data base that participates with other physical data bases to form a logical data base is being used exclusively, the other data bases with which it is associated may be free for other processing (see Fig. 7.4).
3. The problems of evolution of data into a different form (as in the case of splitting data bases by key) are not applicable. It is quite natural to let data bases evolve when all segments of a given type are in the same physical data base.

There are some disadvantages, however, to breaking up large data bases by data type. They are:

1. System overhead—each data base requires overhead in its handling. The more data bases, the more overhead the DBMS must handle.
2. Increase in number of root segments in the system and redundancy at the root level.

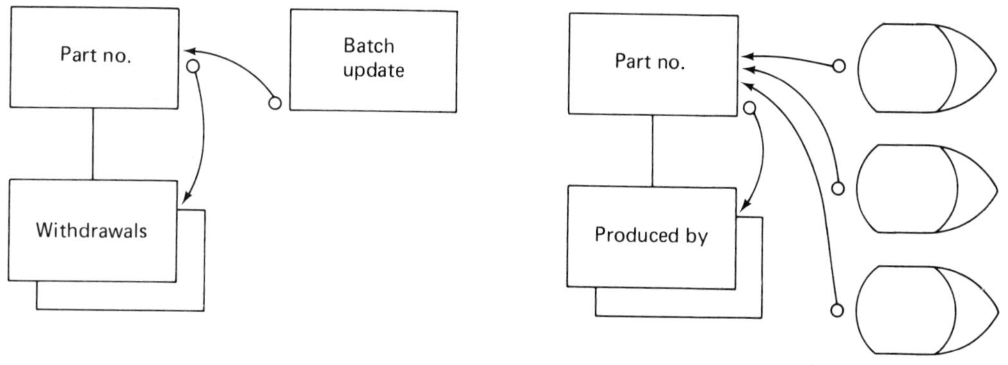

Figure 7.4 Batch update will not let any other resources use the part no.-withdrawals data base while it is executing. Breaking a data base by type allows processing to occur that otherwise would be awkward or impossible if the data bases were joined. On-line retrievals are being made against the part no.-produced by data base.

3. Synchronization problems—whenever redundancy occurs, synchronization problems occur.
4. An added level of complexity—the greater the extent to which data is broken up and the less streamlined it is, the more complex the management of it becomes.

DECENTRALIZATION OF DATA AT THE USER LEVEL

Correction of a design mistake is most expensive when the error is discovered during or shortly after implementation. Unfortunately, the major disadvantages of building massive data bases first become obvious at the time the system begins to perform under real stress. Having to redesign a system or major parts of it soon after implementation is discouraging to the user, expensive, and embarrassing to the designer.

Another alternative to breaking up large data bases into smaller ones by key splits or separation of segment types is to fulfill user requirements by gathering data from several sources, not one conglomerate. In essence, the data the user needs to run a system is supplied by a diverse set of data bases. This may cause a reduction of function as the user sees the system, or may cause the user to separate the operation into smaller and separate pieces. In a system that has been oversold, a slight reduction in user expectation may amount to a dramatic easing of constraints. From the designer's standpoint, a reduction of user requirements may mean that the system is feasible to build when otherwise it might not be possible.

A system that is simplified and streamlined can be extended to meet future needs, can be fine-tuned by operations, and is easy to modify—in short, it is pliable—whereas a system that is complicated, elegant, and oversold may have a short life span. It may be beneficial to the designer to convince users that a few more personnel doing more and simpler tasks are worth the benefit of being able to manage the system in the future.

REORGANIZING LARGE DATA BASES

One of the major bottlenecks of large data bases is data reorganization—either to clean up the pointer chains left by volatile activities or to change the configuration or definition of the data base. This conceptually simple process is shown by Fig. 7.5.

Although technology will undoubtedly improve in years to come in this area, currently the designer is left with what tools there are at hand. There are some things that can be done to minimize the impact of reorganization.

1. Develop in-house, tailored unload/reload programs. A tailored program should always be faster than a generalized program. There are some drawbacks to building in-house software. The software vendor may well make software changes that affect the unload/reload program and the vendor does not have (and should not have) an obligation for privately built software of this nature. Also, a separate program will have to be written for each data base that needs to be reorganized.
2. Keep relations between data bases symbolic. By doing so, it will not be mandatory for more than one data base to be reorganized at a time. When direct pointers are used between data bases, reorganizing one data base makes it mandatory that another data base be reorganized before the system is operable.
3. At the outset of the loading of the data base, allocate plenty of

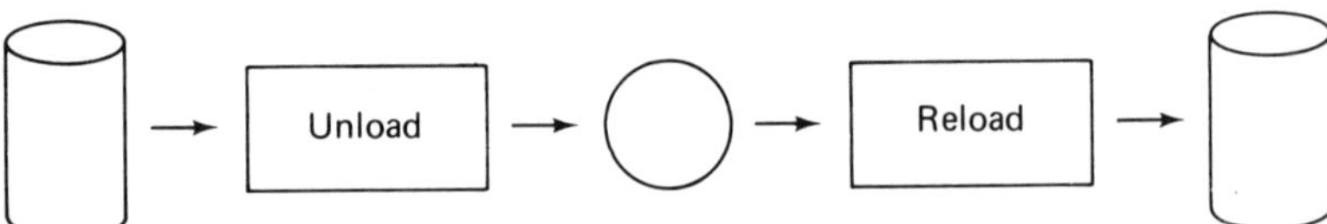

Figure 7.5 Large Data Bases: Problems. Because of the amount of data involved in reorganizing a large data base, reorganization becomes an awkward problem. The length of the run makes the data unavailable for X hours; X may be a painfully large number. The susceptibility to machine failure is high. The susceptibility to mechanical errors is high. The cost is expensive. The chance for encountering previously undetected errors is high.

space and use the features of the randomizer or index to the best advantage. This means identifying where the activity is going to occur in the data base and preparing space and the native data organization for it.

4. Avoid oversegmentation. The more segment types a data base has, the more overhead the unload/reload process will have to handle. Oversegmentation also has an adverse effect on programs and, in some cases, on program logic.
5. Organize updated programs so that they will create as few overflow chains as possible. Analyze the way the data will be updated and then stored internally, and design the order of the data so that segments will go to overflow only when necessary. This may mean using such techniques as a 9's-complement representation of the key. This strategy has only a limited usefulness. When the data base begins to fill up, one update strategy is as ineffective as any other.

EXERCISES

1. Write specifications for a "tailor-made" data reorganization in IMS. Write unload/reload specs, including all necessary information for:
   a) Pointers.
   b) Delete bytes.
   c) Segment codes.
   d) Programmer data layout.
   e) Overflow pointers.
   f) DBMS overhead (FSAP, RAP, VSAM, etc.).

   Include details of updating control fields necessary to operation of data base.

   Allow for a new allocation of space from the old data base to the new one (with or without changes in block size).

   Allow for synonym resolution and chaining.

   Allow for logical data bases.
2. (*Note:* SUPERZAP is standard terminology and utility for the direct alteration of data values on a disk external to any DBMS software.)

   Write clear, easily understood, step-by-step instructions for doing a SUPERZAP to a data base. Include requirements for documentation (such as DBDGens, available SMU reports, last reorganization output, etc.), backup procedures, and testing procedures for structural and data integrity. Identify the case where SUPERZAP should simply be used for deletion of a segment and cases where SUPERZAP can be used to alter the contents of a data element. Estimate the time necessary to do a SUPERZAP. Suggest preparations that can be made prior to an emergency that necessitates one or more SUPERZAPS.

3. a) Analyze how each item in the following list affects synonym collision:
      i. Blocksize.
      ii. LRECL.
      iii. Randomizer.
      iv. Initial space allocation.
      v. Average record length.
      vi. Distribution of segments by key.
      vii. Median record length.
   b) What controls does the data administrator have to minimize synonym collision?
   c) What existing tools are useful in determining whether or not a data base is poorly organized? What constraints are there on the use of those tools? What are the problems with writing tailor-made utilities for data organization analysis?

EIGHT

RESTRUCTURING DATA BASES

When it comes time to change the structure of a data base, the impact is felt throughout the system. Programs that support and use the data base are subject to the greatest impact. Programs involved with the old data structure must be modified or discarded. New programs may have to be written to support features of the new structure. When the data base is transformed, activity must be coordinated so that at one moment the system exists in its old form and at a later moment in its new form.

The data base is especially vulnerable during and immediately after its transformation because the risk of malfunction is greatest at the very time that it is most difficult to handle errors. Typical problems that arise at this time are data integrity problems, data conversion problems, and unforeseen and previously unexperienced program problems. The conversion itself may be a simple one-step task or a complicated series of tasks. While the conversion is occurring, no system really exists at all. This fact alone should justify the work necessary to achieve a high degree of confidence in the conversion prior to its initiation.

Changing a data structure may produce a ripple effect on other data bases when the structure to be changed is implicitly or explicitly related to other structures. Prior to the writing of any programming specifications, the interface between the data bases should be closely investigated. Even if there is a clean conversion of data and the new set of programs are adequately tested, the restructuring of the data may be a failure if relationships related to the newly structured data are not supported.

PREPARING DATA FOR RESTRUCTURING

There are two basic practices that a designer should follow to minimize the problems of restructuring. The first practice involves implicit relationships. When the data in one structure is related to data in another structure (or another part of the same structure) solely by application programs, the data elements are implicitly related. If the algorithm that defines the relationship is simple and if a manageable number of elements are involved, the data may not be difficult to handle when the restructuring occurs. On the other hand, when the algorithm is complex and there are many data elements that participate in the relationship, restructuring may be a big task. The complexity of the algorithm is often made more difficult when the algorithm in fact exists only in pieces spread over several programs, which is not an uncommon practice. The careful designer will attempt to keep implicit relationships simple for no other reason than to prepare for a successful restructuring of data, even though at the time of initial design there is no plan for future restructuring. Imagine the work involved in restructuring the complex relationship shown by Fig. 8.1.

The second practice that the designer should follow to minimize the effort of restructuring is to specify coding standards so that every program is written as independently as possible of the current form of the data base (i.e., the code should be as generalized as possible, not tailored to a specific data structure). Coding practices are highly dependent upon a given DBMS, so it is not possible to list a comprehensive set of techniques that will ensure generalized calls to the DBMS. Instead, a few broad suggestions will be mentioned. The designer should greatly expand upon these guidelines given a choice of a DBMS.

Some general rules are:

1. When searching for a specific unit of data, specify the search criteria as fully as possible. Specify the type of data to be retrieved and, if possible, selection criteria (key or data values) or other criteria, such as first or last segment encountered, and so on.
2. Never blindly retrieve data without knowing what type it is prior to the call (a valid exception to this rule might be in certain data

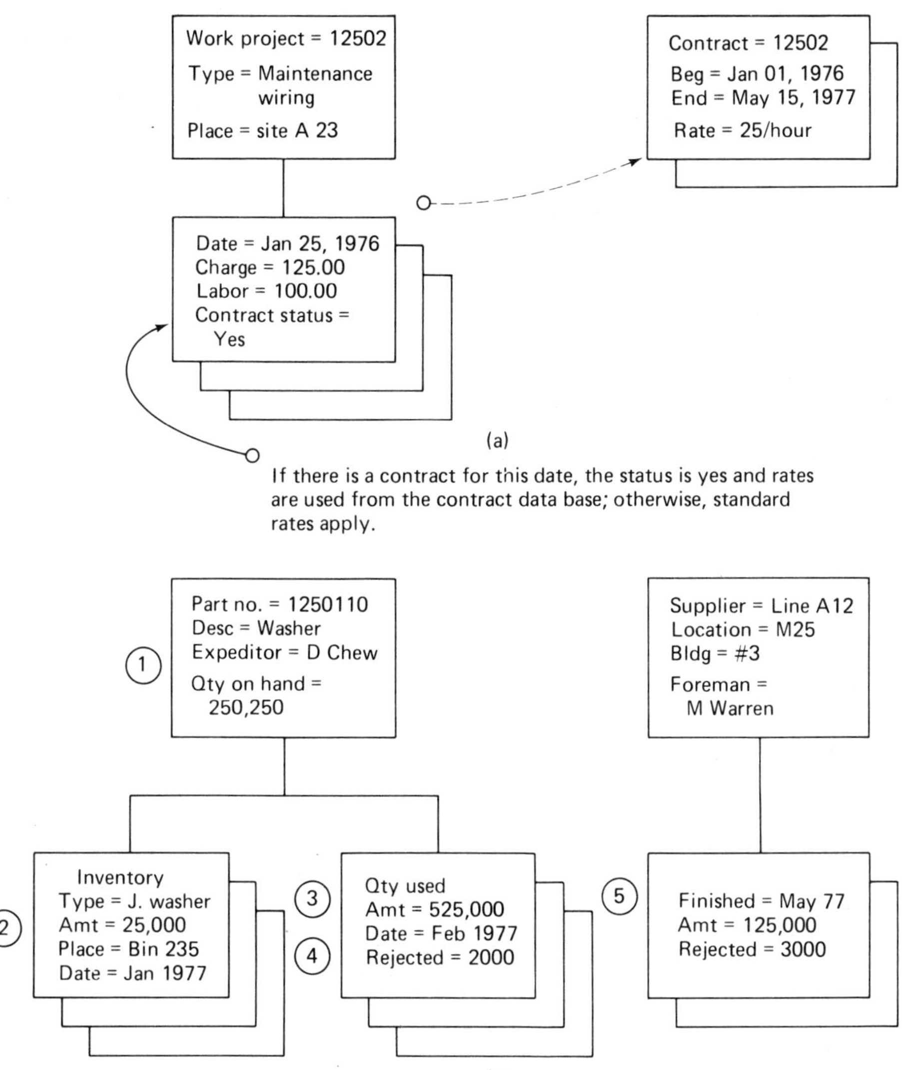

Figure 8.1 (a) Example of a simple implicit relationship—easy to change if data is restructured. (b) The more complex an algorithm gets and the more variables involved, the more difficult it is to restructure data. Qty. on hand. ① = Most current inventory ② + [Σ (since last inventory) amount finished ⑤] − [Σ (since last inventory) quantity used amount ③] + [Σ (since last inventory) rejected amount ④].

management software doing entire data base extracts or scans). This means controlling calls to the DBMS to the point of not allowing an arbitrary retrieval.

3. When more than one unit of data is being retrieved in a single call (i.e., retrieving a single path of segments, from highest to lowest), fully specify each data type and, if possible, selection criteria.
4. Make no assumptions about the existence (or nonexistence) of any given data. The programmer should ignore any application specification "guaranteeing" the existence of data under a set of conditions. (In certain instances, this may adversely affect performance, in which case the risk of data base malfunction should be weighed against the cost of not trusting system specifications.)
5. Make no assumptions about the order of occurrence of data. If it is necessary to switch the order of occurrence of data and the programmer has not originally written code that will prepare for this turn of events, there may be an adverse impact. (*Note:* There may be some real performance considerations in not making assumptions about the order of occurrence of data.)

SIMPLE RESTRUCTURING

A simple restructuring typically includes the semantic removal of data, addition of data, or modifying the physical characteristics of data due to the addition, deletion, or modification of one or more data elements. The impact on coding should be small. One of the questions that should be asked as program specifications are being written is: What would be the effect if this data (or this element) changes? Again, the impact on coding should be small. If it is not, it is probably the sign of a poor data design, poor program design, or both. The conversion effort for a simple change should be small. A difficult conversion is another sign of poor design.

MODERATELY COMPLEX RESTRUCTURING

Other types of changes to data structures may have a larger impact. The same type of change in one instance may have a small impact, whereas in another case, the same change will have a very large impact. This is due to the varying interrelationship of data to its environment. As a general rule, a well-designed system will not be susceptible to a change that causes a major part of the system to be rewritten. In a hierarchical environment, some types of changes that typically may cause a large effort are:

1. Changing the key sequence of one or more segments—This may entail an enlargement or a shortening of the key or a rearrangement of some elements internal to the key. Since each element in the segment relates to the key, nonkey elements may also be affected. The change may be small but can have a large impact where the segment interfaces with other systems.

   Processes (especially sequential) may depend upon the order in which the segment occurs, and a changing of the sequence may cause problems. When this type of error occurs, it may not be at all obvious. Furthermore, when the change occurs at the root level, performance may be affected. Any change at the root level should take into account the data organization (indexed, direct, etc.) of the structure and the current and future processes that will use the data base.
2. A change of an explicit relationship—This type of change is usually simple. It becomes complicated, however, when the two segments involved in the relationship are connected in a complex manner. The impact of the change for one segment may be obvious, but for the other segment may be difficult to ascertain.

   Also, a change in an explicit relationship may involve performance problems. For example, changing the pointer type from direct to symbolic may cause I/Os that were never made before. Another danger in altering an explicit relationship is the risk of misrepresenting the relationship in a fashion unacceptable to the end user. What may appear acceptable to the programmer may be entirely unacceptable to the user. Figure 8.2 is an example of this.
3. A change of an implicit relationship—This type of change is simple when the relationship is simple. Complications can arise for several reasons: more than two segments may be involved, the segments are tied together by an algorithm that may be spread throughout several programs, or the algorithm itself may be complex. From an implementation standpoint, a change to an implicit relationship is easier to achieve than a change to an explicit relationship, because no data needs to be redefined to the DBMS (i.e., only changes to application programs are needed).
4. The redefinition of a segment—This practice (commonly used in sequential processing) involves redefining the nonkey portion of a segment to contain an additional masking of data elements. Figure 8.3 is an example.

If the designer did not originally intend for the segment to have multiple definitions, there may be a surprisingly large impact on existing programs that access the segment.

There is another inherent danger in redefining a segment. When the

Insurance agency =
Ray Zapper
Addr = 147 Daly

Insurance policy =
125011201M
Type = Commercial
property
Date = May 1978

Policy pointer
125011201M

Building no. = 1
Addr = 25 Market
San Fran. CA
Value = 5,750,000
Date appr = Mar 1977

Owners =
Bill Johnson
Addr = P.O Box 210,
Atherton, CA
Phone = 415/420-6457

Special riders =
Fountain, Veranda
Location = Lobby
Value = 105,520

Claims
June 1977
Vandalism
Claim = 2,500
Paid = 2,500
Auth = R. F.

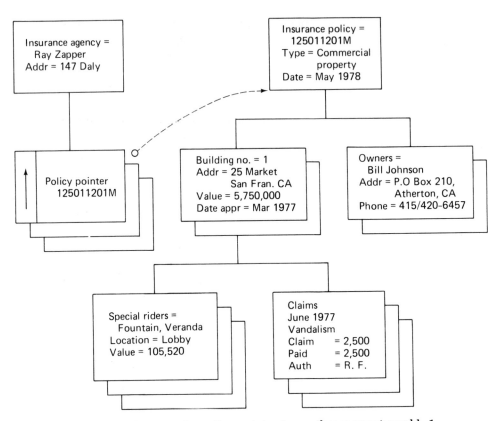

Figure 8.2 Changing the policy pointer to another segment would—1. Cause the meaning of the policy pointer to change. 2. Cause a search through the whole data base to be impaired.

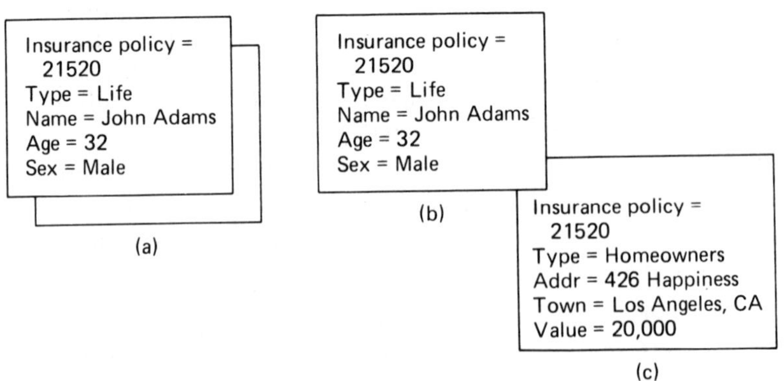

Figure 8.3 This data base (a) is redefined to handle more than one type of data (b) and (c), based upon the field type.

data structure was originally designed, part of the design included an estimate of the expected occurrence of each segment. When space for the data base was allocated, it was probably allocated for the projected number of segments. Redefining a new masking of data over an existing segment usually means a new projected occurrence of the segment type, and the data base allocation may need to be enlarged.

5. Separating a segment into more than one segment type or consolidating more than one segment type into a single segment—This type of change may involve the creation of sibling segments from a single segment or creating parent/child segments from a segment or combining segments currently existing in another form. For example, see Fig. 8.4.

Splitting or combining segments necessarily affects existing programs that handle these segments, as well as adding new codes to support the new structure of the data base. Surprisingly, the impact is not severe as long as all of the original elements exist in one place or another in the new definition of the data base. When elements are removed entirely by splitting or combining segments, there is a risk of large unplanned code maintenance if the designer has not been very careful. When all original elements are in the new data base, change comes in the form of retrieval of segments in the proper fashion, and once retrieved, the normal flow of the program may continue as if no change to the structure had occurred.

Obviously, splitting or combining segments calls for a retuning of the data base, so that performance will not be adversely affected.

6. Combination of structural changes—Occasionally, a change in the user environment happens so that more than one structural change has to be made. Typically, a segment needs to be enlarged, another segment is to be added, and the key field of another is to be modified. When such changes occur in combination, the impact seems to have an exponential effect. Often, it is difficult to fully comprehend the impact of a single change, and when other related changes occur, the problem becomes very complex. Creating simple structures that are utilized in a straightforward manner at the outset helps to minimize the complexity of multiple structural changes.
7. Splitting a data base into more than one data base—This type of change is not uncommon and can be quite a useful tool to the designer. Splitting a data base can be very costly unless the designer has initially specified the following rules:
   a) A given program (or transaction) updates only one segment.
   b) A given element is updated from only one source.
   c) Data redundancy is kept to a minimum and is controlled.
   d) A segment is accessed a minimum number of times by retrieval and report programs.

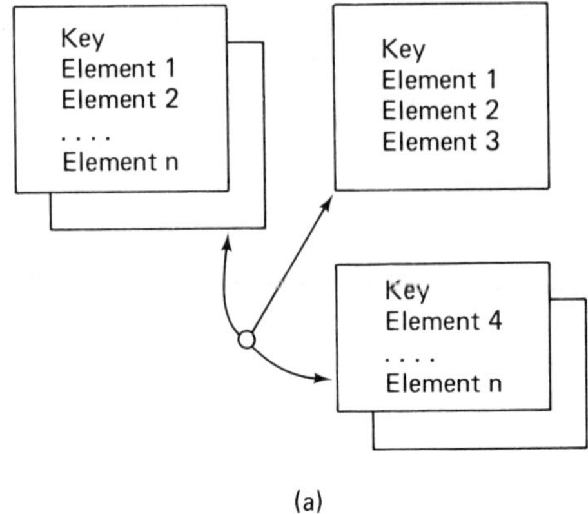

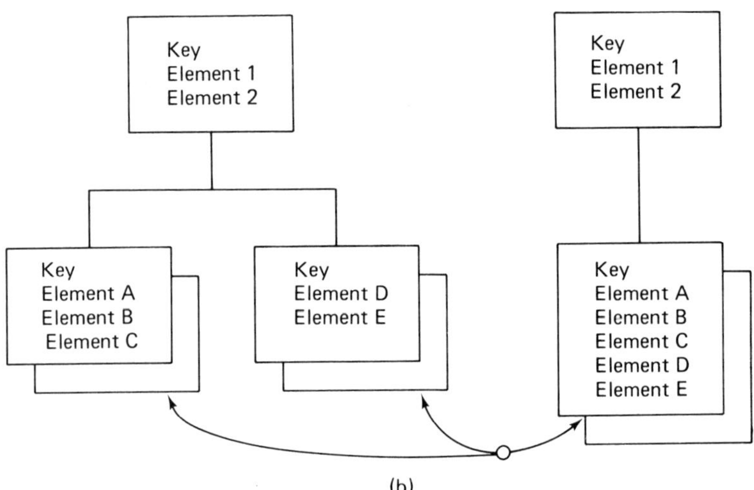

Figure 8.4 (a) In this case, a root segment is split into a parent/child relationship. (b) In this case, sibling segments are combined.

Even if these guidelines are followed, the splitting of a data base is a large undertaking. If there are many complex implicit relationships among the elements, the change may be very tedious.

OTHER TYPES OF RESTRUCTURING

Any hierarchical data structure can be flattened into a root-only structure. Of course, the advantages of a hierarchical structure are lost, but there may be some offsetting benefits from such a change. Flattening a

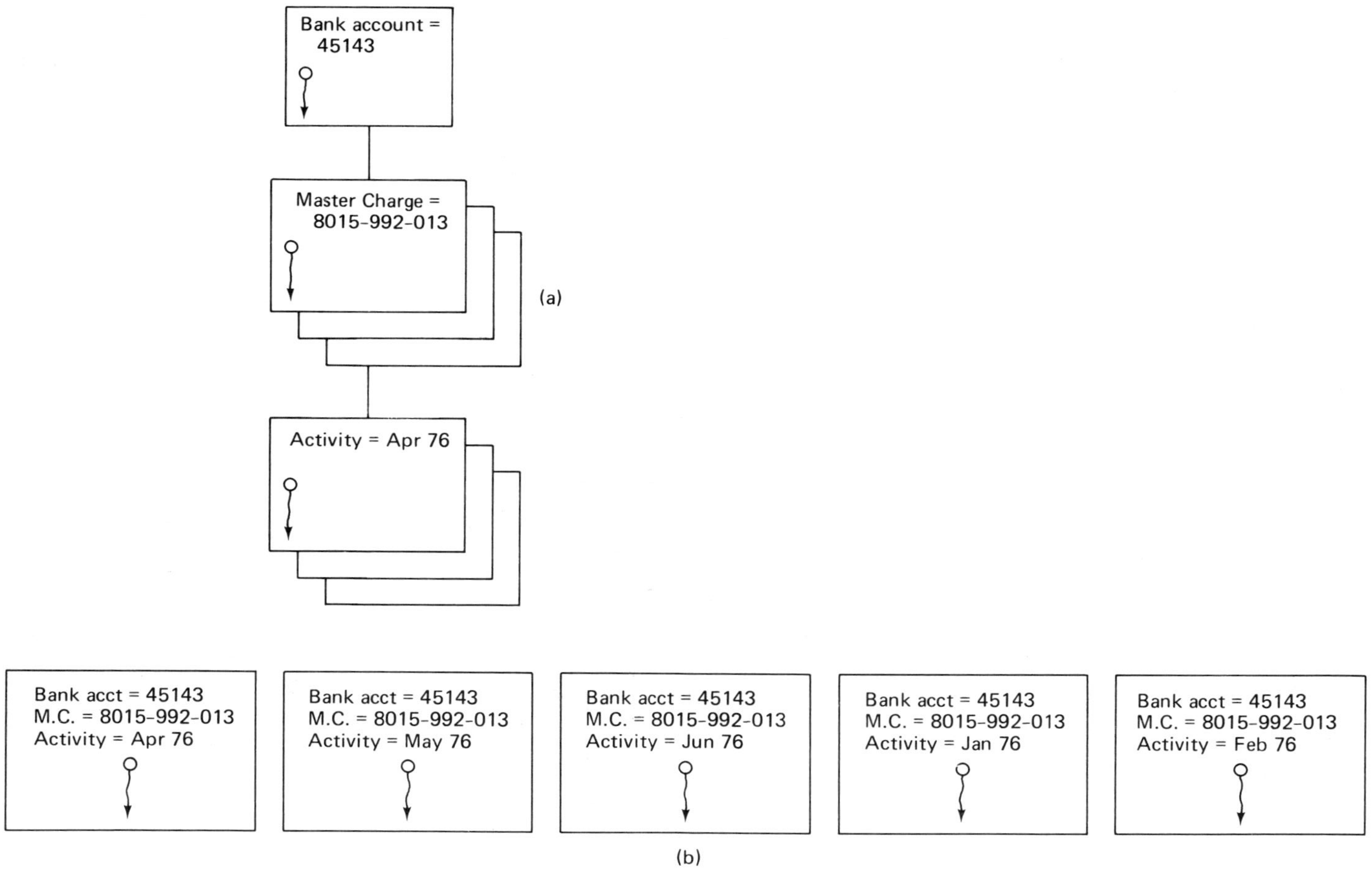

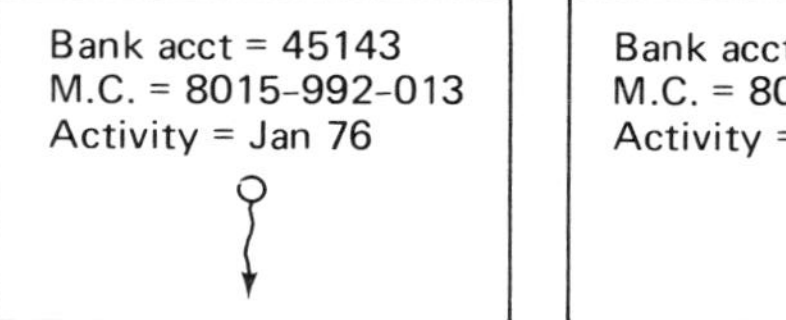
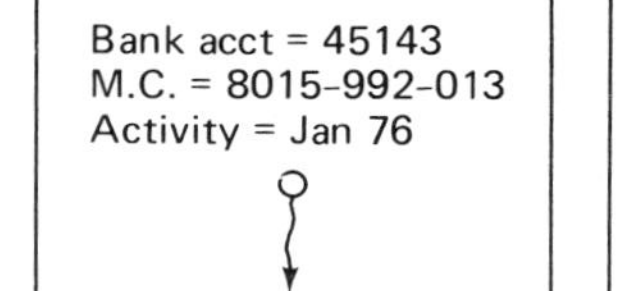

Figure 8.5 (a) This hierarchical data structure can be represented by this (b) flattened root-only structure.

data base is closely related to the process of "normalization" which comes from terminology associated with relational data bases. Figure 8.5 shows one way to flatten a data base.

When a hierarchical structure is flattened, space is wasted through physical redundancy and by reserving space for elements that may not exist for a given occurrence of the data but must semantically be defined. Great amounts of physical redundancy may occur because the key and data elements at all levels above the lowest level are repeated for each occurrence of the lowest level. Also, when a lower-level segment does not exist for a given occurrence of the data, and at least one segment in the same hierarchical path above it does exist, the root-only data base segment (that has been flattened to represent the multilevel structure) must represent the values contained in the lowest level as being null.

In most instances, it is not desirable to flatten a hierarchical structure. There are some advantages to doing so, however, and when the conditions are such that the penalties are not too severe, it may pay to create a root-only data base. A root-only data base is easy to access because retrieval requires a minimum number of calls to the DBMS. Furthermore, because of the way the data is organized, a call to a root requires less system utilization, since the roots are randomized or indexed.

Since all data, key and otherwise, is present in the segment, the root-only structure is versatile. As an example, suppose that an extract of data is to be done across the whole data base, and suppose the relevant data lies in the fourth level of a hierarchical structure. The extract must process down four levels of segmentation to determine whether or not the data is suitable for the extract. When the structure is flattened to a root-only data base, the extract can be done by looking at only one segment type.

Another lesser consideration concerning root-only data bases is that they are less prone to programmer error than are structures with several levels. The programmer has fewer opportunities to make mistakes.

DATA INVERSION

Just as data can be flattened, data structures (principally recursive data structures) can be inverted. In effect, the data structure undergoes a 90° rotation. This type of rotation may be appropriate for recursive data where unlimited recursive generality is not necessary. Consider the form of the generalized recursive structure shown in Fig. 8.6.

This simple form is used to build a recursive structure that can go to *n* levels of depth and allows the root of one substructure to be the child of another structure. The DBMS presents the logical view of the structure, not its actual physical implementation to the user. Figure 8.7 shows step by step how the logical structure is created from the physical structure.

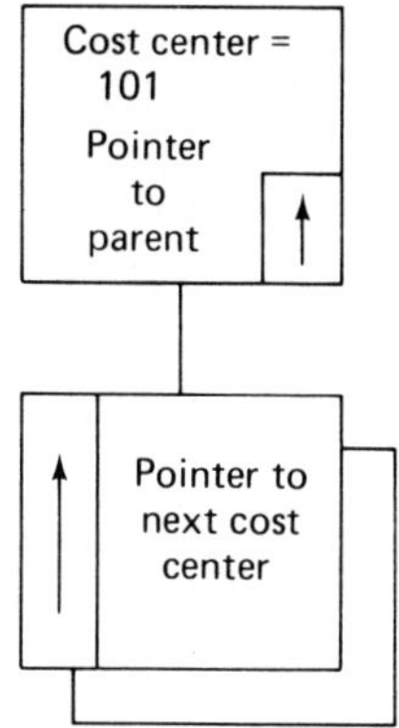

Figure 8.6

In this case, two retrievals (to the pointer segment and its target) are necessary to build one level of the logical recursive structure. The advantage of this type of structuring is that there is no limit to the number of levels of the logical structure. Another significant advantage is that any change (addition of a new element, enlargement of an element, etc.)

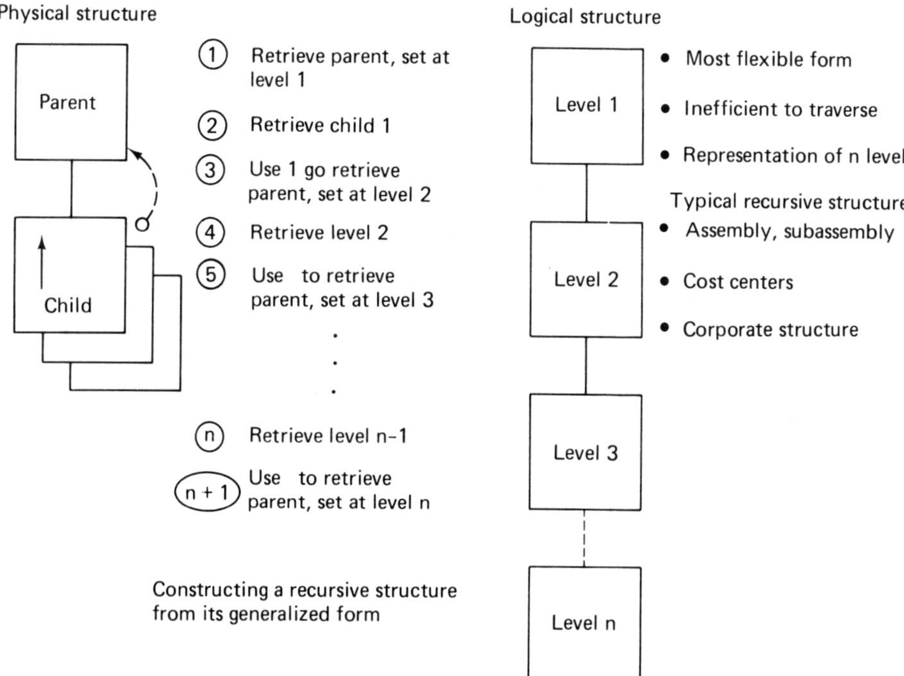

Figure 8.7 Restructuring Data Bases: Recursive Structures—Generalized Form.

modifies all levels of the logical structure. When recursive generality is required, this form of structuring is most suitable.

When the environment does not require a generalized implementation of a recursive structure, there are some other interesting possibilities. Consider Fig. 8.8. This type of structuring has limitations in that representation past a finite level (in this case, 4) is not possible. Another limitation that may not be obvious is the inflexibility of the data. Suppose that a new data element is needed to describe a cost center. The element must be added to every level, meaning that each segment type must be redefined to the DBMS, even though they are identical in form. If the structure were generalized (i.e., implemented by using a root and child pointer segment), the impact of the change would affect only one segment type. The impact of change is severe here.

There is an advantage to this type of limited recursive representation. Segments require less I/O to retrieve than in the generalized case. In the example presented, it requires only a simple search down the structure to the fourth level to retrieve the data residing there, whereas the generalized recursive structure requires four retrievals of the root segment and three retrievals of the child pointer segment. Furthermore, because the roots are probably scattered throughout the data base, the generalized set of calls requires four or more I/Os to occur, whereas the calls for the

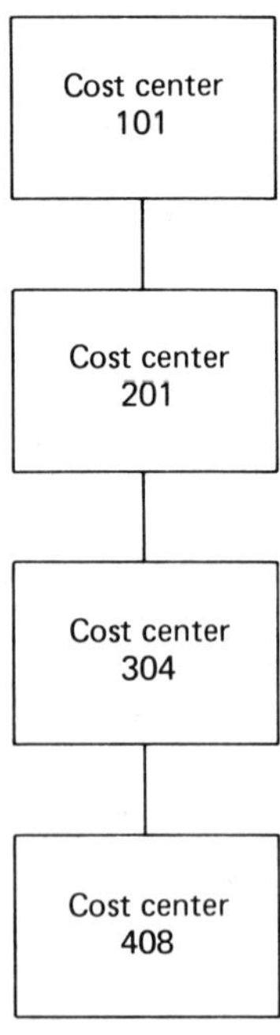

Figure 8.8 Limited recursive structure—physical implementation.

limited recursive structure require, on the average, a little more than one I/O.

There is another representation of recursive structures that solves some of the problems of the limited physical representation of a recursive structure. The method is to invert the limited physical data structure 90° into a root-only data base, where the key of the root is all that is needed to determine where the root fits into the logical view of the recursive structure (see Fig. 8.9).

This concatenated structuring of data is best implemented where the roots can be stored sequentially (as in an indexed organization), although strictly speaking it is not a requirement. The key of a root is simply the fully concatenated key of the logical structure down to whatever level the segment represents. This form of representation limits the extent to which the logical structure may be recursive (e.g., a root may not find itself able to be a child or grandchild of itself, as is possible in the generalized case).

An advantage of this type of representation is that a change to the root segment affects only one segment type as far as the DBMS is concerned. Consider the impact of change of the following situation. Suppose that a new segment needs to be added as a child to the root in a limited recursive data structure (Fig. 8.10).

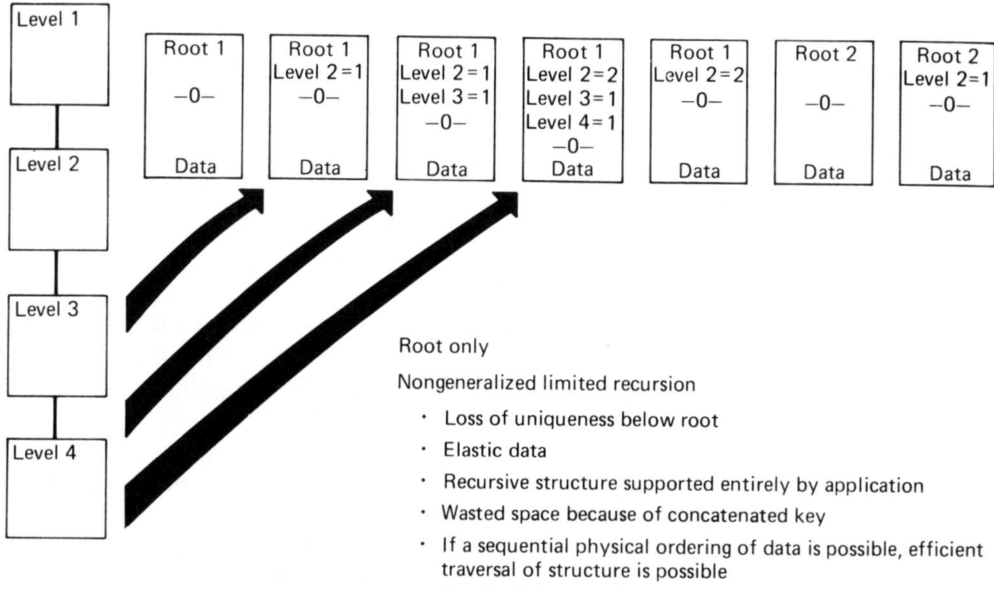

Figure 8.9 Restructuring Data Bases: Recursive Structures—Nongeneralized Limited Recursion.

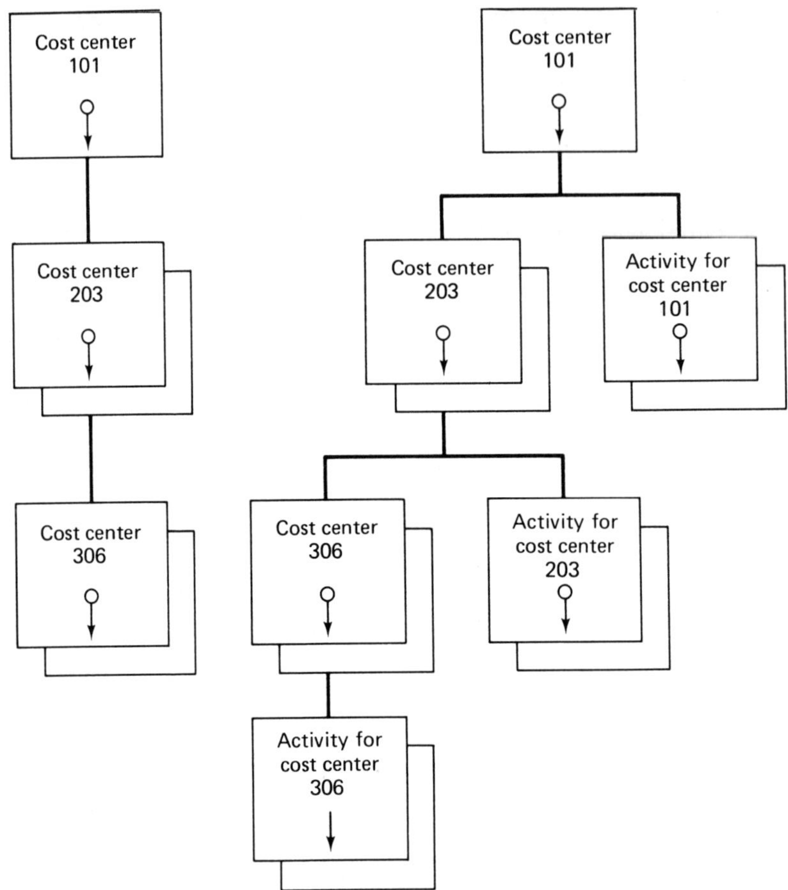

Figure 8.10 Adding an activity segment for each level of cost center is redundant and awkward when data is represented in a limited recursive form.

It is apparent that there are some distinct drawbacks to the flexibility of limited recursive representations of data. When the recursive relationship is represented by a root-only concatenated key implementation, adding a segment becomes a great deal easier, as in Fig. 8.11.

There are some disadvantages to representing recursive structures with a concatenated key. The DBMS does not support the logical structuring of the data—instead, the application program does. For example, it is possible to insert a root whose key reflects that it belongs on level 1 of the logical structure, then insert another root whose key shows that it belongs on level 3 of the logical structure, without having inserted a segment representing level 2 of the logical structure. A user attempting to use the logical form of the data would be distressed by the absence of the second-level segment, whereas the DBMS would never know the differ-

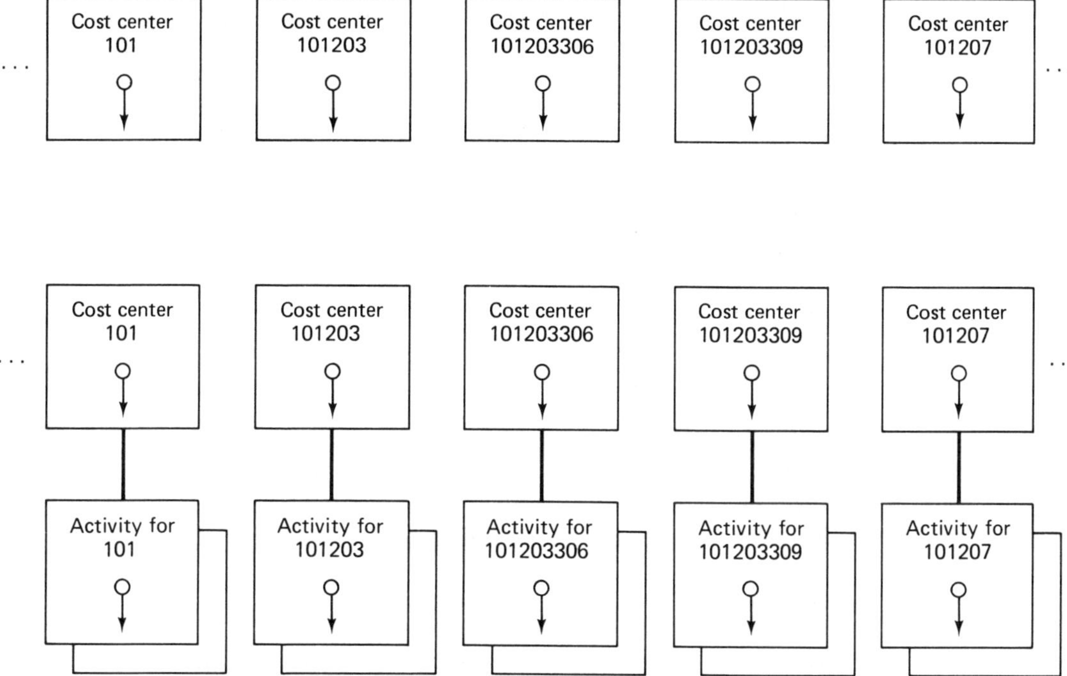

Figure 8.11 Adding an activity segment to an inverted limited recursive data structure is simple to do.

ence. Program logic must be written to ensure the integrity of the logical viewing of the data.

Another disadvantage lies in the concatenation of the key. If the length of the key needed to represent a single level of the structure is long, the concatenated key for many levels will be very long and, of course, space must be provided in each root for the fully concatenated key of the whole structure.

The real advantage of this type of representation is its flexibility and the accessibility of the data. This can be a big advantage if the structure is prone to environmental change or if massive amounts of sequential accesses are to be made (either for update or retrieval of data).

DISADVANTAGES OF NONGENERALIZED REPRESENTATIONS

There is one drawback to any representation of a recursive structure that is not generalized. Any node or segment (in the logical viewing of the data) loses its uniqueness. In a generalized representation, a node or segment can appear in more than one structure and may appear at any level.

Any nodes beneath it may be accessed by following the pointer segment. In a limited recursive representation, a node may appear at any level and more than once, but only when it is associated with a unique set of other nodes. This means that there is no single reference point to determine the location of a given node.

EXERCISES

1. Given an application, identify which programs and utilities are affected (and the degree of impact) by:
   a) A change in element size.
   b) Addition of a new element.
   c) Deletion of an element.
   d) Removal of an element from one segment and insertion into another.
   e) Redefinition of a programming algorithm that affects 12 data elements.
   f) Changing a direct pointer to a symbolic pointer.
   g) Changing a symbolic pointer to a direct pointer.
   h) Splitting a data base into multiple data bases broken as to key range.
   i) Splitting a data base into multiple data bases broken as to segment type.
2. In regard to restructuring data bases, give guidelines for the design of implicit relationships with regard to:
   a) Number of elements involved.
   b) Placement and complexity of the algorithm.
   c) Documentation of the relationships.
   d) Explanation to the user of the workings of the system (as the user sees it).
3. Given a difficult structural change, trace precisely the flow of activity from the time the decision is made to make the change until the change is implemented. Estimate the time and personnel required for each step.
4. When a recursive data structure is inverted by a 90° rotation, what are the implications of storing the data in a random organization?
5. In a nongeneralized recursive structure (one with a concatenated key), is it necessary to store the fully concatenated key or are there alternatives?
6. Does a structure have to be recursive to be inverted? If not, show how inversion can be done in a nonrecursive environment.
7. Give the data structure shown in Fig. 8.12. It is possible to construct another form of the data—that shown in Fig. 8.13.

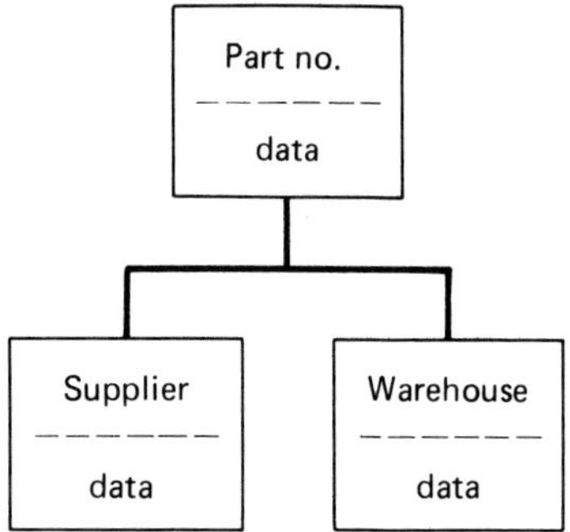

Figure 8.12

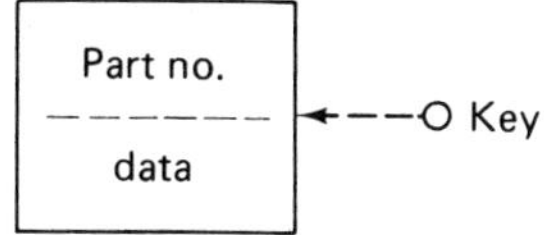

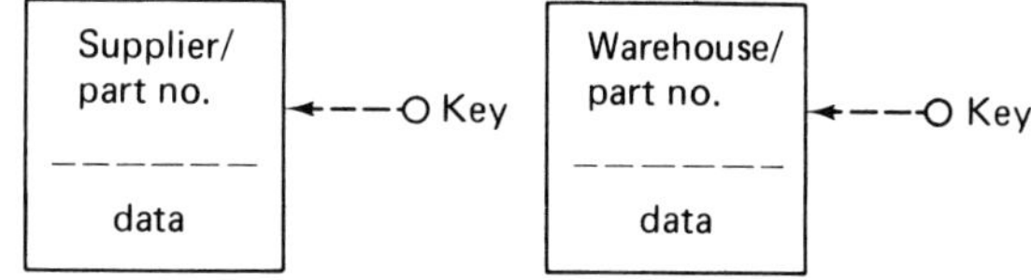

Figure 8.13

Discuss the two forms of structuring in light of:
a) Data availability.
b) I/Os per data access.
c) System flexibility.

NINE

DATA BASE DESIGN REVIEW

Acknowledgment is made to McDonnell-Douglas Automation Company (MCAUTO) and to IBM Corporation for their influence on the material in this chapter. In the following sections we outline their approaches to data base design review and demonstrate how their methodology is relevant to the effective design of data structures. MCAUTO's and IBM's approaches differ in scope and depth, but both are excellent.

DESIGN REVIEW—A METHODOLOGY

Design review is a process or methodology by which system designers enhance their chances of successfully building an effective system. Design review is aimed at identifying bottlenecks and rectifying them before they are programmed into the system. Weak and ambiguous aspects of the design are analyzed. Design review was born from the pains of discovering and correcting errors after the system was cast in concrete. The expense and effort that is necessary to correct a poorly designed system at that point justifies the arduous effort that a complete design review requires.

Design review is not a new technique. It is, and was, a valid technique from the earliest days of computer development. It becomes ever more appropriate and justifiable with regard to cost as the systems to be built become large, complex, and sophisticated. It is especially effective in the on-line environment because there are a multitude of variables that must be identified and successfully integrated before the system design is ready to be developed. A major difference between on-line and batch systems is that on-line systems offer greater exposure. When an on-line system malfunctions, it is obvious to the many users who actively depend upon it, while malfunctions in a batch system have less severe consequences. The essential reason why the design must be carefully controlled in the on-line environment is that the on-line system must be treated as its own precious resource. By its very nature, the on-line system will be shared, and this sharing means that every part of the on-line system must work in cooperation with every other part of the system—not at cross purposes to them. No part of the system should be allowed to waste resources, because all parts of the system are affected when waste occurs.

In the batch environment it is not difficult to isolate programs and data to the extent of being able to move whole applications to a separate machine if the need arises. For this reason, batch designers are not subject to as many critical variables as are on-line designers. The key to good on-line design is for each application to adopt the approach of constantly being aware of its impact on the system. In the words of MCAUTO:

"Control of application design and programming techniques is the key factor in achieving and maintaining on-line system performance."

MCAUTO

It is not possible to rely upon data base/data communications tuning after the system is built to ensure system performance. It is true that tuning a system should be part of the overall strategy in achieving system performance, but there is a finite limit to what can be accomplished. A poorly designed system cannot be tuned into producing good performance.

A very real risk in designing on-line systems with disregard for other users and without handling the resources of the DBMS with care is that the capacity of the computer may be exceeded, and with existing technology adding more hardware will not improve performance. The classical batch approach of adding hardware to enhance performance will produce only marginal results.

DESIGN REVIEW PARTICIPANTS

Anyone affected by the system being developed should participate in the design review. The involvement of an organization depends upon how it is affected by whatever the stage of development the system. The organizations usually include:

1. Data base management—people who are responsible for the use and performance of the DBMS and the overall maintenance of the DBMS. The concept of an on-line system as its own precious resource is at the foundation of data base management's involvement with design review. Becuase they are charged with protection of the DBMS and the applications run under the DBMS, data base management should have the right of rejection of any part of a design if that part of the system is going to adversely impact the other users of the on-line system.
2. End users—especially in the early system specification stages and then later in the testing phase, the end users should be actively involved. It is their responsibility to understand what is being built and to make sure that the end product will fulfill their needs. If the user involvement is minimized (especially at crucial times in the development process), there is a real risk that the system being built will not be very useful to the user. The crucial times are in requirement specification, system analysis, and in testing.
3. Development personnel—this category includes programmers, designers, and analysts. It is the responsibility of the development team to translate the user's requirements into a tangible system. Minimizing the involvement of development personnel may lead to a grossly complex or oversold and overburdened system. Development personnel should be especially concerned when the system goes beyond the boundaries of manageability.
4. Miscellaneous other groups—systems programming, technical support communications, auditing, and operational personnel should occasionally be involved with the design review. These groups need to know what changes will be occurring that will affect them. Where the impact is small or nonexistent, it is not necessary to involve these organizations.

DESIGN PRIORITIES

In the very earliest phases of design there are some fundamental issues that should be explicitly resolved. Failure to recognize and plan these aspects, and thereby allowing them to evolve in an uncontrolled manner, opens the door to some basic design flaws in the system. Two facts must be recognized: (1) the final product must execute efficiently, and (2) every system has a propensity for change and over time will change. A general philosophy that addresses these issues should be one of the very first discussions.

Another basic decision that should be made at the beginning of the design is the identification and proper placement of the complexities of the system. Where is the system design going to be complex and where can the complexities best be managed? Are complex system features best handled in the programs, the data structure, the DBMS, or in operational procedures at the user level? A written statement of objectives—a prioritization of goals concerning efficiency and flexibility and a plan for managing complexity—provides a framework for the next stage of design. As the system is being built, it will be necessary to refer back to these major decisions.

MCAUTO'S PROCESS

THE STANDARD WORK UNIT

The concept of the data base management system as its own precious resource in an on-line environment (which is central to the success of the entire on-line community) leads to the conclusion that applications running in the on-line system should be developed under stringent control. The content of the application and what it actually does is important only to the user. What is of importance to data management is how the applications processes operate within the DBMS. Each hardware/software configuration is different, so that it is not possible to define absolute standards into which all applications must fit. Because of differences in DBMSs, it is not possible to define all the criteria that go into the makeup of the standard work unit. However, typical measurements of the work unit are limitations on load module size, number of calls to the DBMS, CPU execution time per transaction, and amount of occupancy in the on-line region. In the batch environment work unit standards might include checkpointing, total run time, load module size, number of data bases used concurrently, and I/O usage. Standards for the batch environment are not as stringent as those for the on-line environment. On-line work unit standards can place a restriction on any aspect of a program that can impair the processing of any other program. Whatever standards are used must be quantified and published, and must be applied consistently. The goal of the design review, then, is to ensure that the transactions that will finally embody the design will fit into work unit standards.

PROJECT APPROVAL PHASE

The first phase of design review using MCAUTO methodology comes after the project has been approved and users and development personnel have some idea of the scope and intent of the system. At this point, data base management is concerned with the general nature and feasibility of the system and how it will mesh with other applications. If a required function of the new application appears to exceed the allowable standards of the shop in terms of resource utilization, it is up to data management to alert the users and developers so that alternatives to the offending part of the application can be considered. This is the ideal time to unmask system flaws since change of system design is cheapest now in terms of manpower and other development resources.

At this point of the design the structure of the data is quite ambiguous. A rough idea of what data elements are required and how they best fit together is the most reviewers can hope for as far as data structures are concerned. The only major consideration is whether data essential to the system will be difficult or awkward to obtain, or is unavailable. Identifying data unavailability here prevents redesign at a later stage.

SYSTEM SPECIFICATION PHASE

The second phase of design review of the MCAUTO methodology comes after system specification has been completed and exists as a formal document. The precise goals of the system are spelled out and interfaces with other systems are formalized. The processes of the system are perceived largely as "black boxes," but the input and output of each black box are defined. In short, the system specification phase is marked by the creation of a document stating the goals, constraints, and objectives of the system. Technical discussion shifts from what is feasible to what specific approaches and strategies are optimal for the processes at hand.

At that point the data bases are not entirely firm but, through a process of consolidation and review, they are taking shape. The actual shaping of data bases from elements and segments is begun and is influenced by the functional usage of the data and considerations of efficiency and flexibility.

The design reviewer has a rather solid idea of what the data structures will look like. He or she should make sure that no interface will be highly inefficient. All features that are out of the ordinary, such as indexes in a random data base, implicit or explicit relationships, exotic data bases, or application-supported substructures of data, should be justified. The reviewer attempts to weigh the cost of processing and maintaining these features against their utility.

END OF SYSTEM DESIGN PHASE

The third phase of design review occurs at the end of system design. At this point each black-box process has been well defined and is fit into a plan to work in conjunction with other black boxes. The questions—can the system work, will it work, and can it exist in the same environment with other systems—have been successfully answered, and the result is the specification for data base and programs. Central to the answering of these questions are accurate projections of the frequency of update, the volume of data to be managed, and statistics pertinent to the servicing of the data. Each process is reviewed in light of its impact on the system. As a process is reviewed, the data structures (which by now have a very firm shape) that are manipulated by the process are also reviewed. Changes are recommended based upon knowledge of the intricacies of the process being reviewed and the structuring and physical characteristics of the data. At this point bottlenecks are identified and rectified. An inadequate review here may allow a process to go into programming that will have to be modified later in the project. It is axiomatic that errors at this stage of system development are cheaper to correct than are errors in the programming stage. All internal and external interfaces should be investigated in detail. The specifics of each interface should be analyzed to determine if the interfaces will perform as intended, to make sure there are no previously unforeseen bottlenecks.

PRIOR TO PROGRAMMING PHASE

MCAUTO's next design review is done immediately prior to programming. By this time the data structures should be solidly established and the emphasis of the analysis is on the programming of the system. At this point all flaws previously discovered are reviewed and corrective action taken is discussed. The data structures are defined to the DBMS, space is allocated, and the data bases are ready for loading or conversions. All fine detail that has an impact on system performance is discussed, with detail pertinent to critical processes receiving the most attention. It is likely that even with a well-executed design review, a few details will escape attention. Minimizing the negative impact of these details is the single most important reason for doing design review.

Program specifications have been written and the call flow (to the DBMS) is extracted and analyzed. If any major errors are detected that cause large changes to the system, it may cause the design to regress to an earlier stage. The testing and implementation of the system is planned.

The result of passing this level of design review successfully is a complete set of program specifications and supporting data structures that have been thoroughly analyzed. If the design review has covered the appropriate topics, there will be no major inefficiencies or bottlenecks to surprise the user once the system is implemented.

LATE IN TESTING PHASE

The final phase of MCAUTO's design review occurs during final testing prior to full implementation. At this point tuning of programs and data can be initiated. Any program that does not fit within the system standards is identified. Corrective action is taken so that the program conforms to standards. If a program greatly exceeds system standards, it may be necessary to redesign the program by reducing its function or breaking its function into several subfunctions so that the subfunctions will fit into standards. Enforcement of standards will become a touchy issue, but data management must invoke its commitment by management to ensure future manageability of the on-line function.

Data structures are monitored to see how they perform. Unforeseen weaknesses may come to light at this time (e.g., unexpected long twin chains, awkward organization of data, greater volume of data than anticipated, misuse or misunderstanding of data by the user organization, etc.). Incomplete parts of the system are identified and plans are made to integrate them into the system when complete. An essential part of design review at this point is a review of the testing of the system. Performance is measured and future performance is predicted based upon projected growth of the system.

IBM DESIGN REVIEW METHODOLOGY

The MCAUTO design review covers the breadth of a project from approval through implementation. In contrast, the IBM design review covers in great depth the system specifications prior to programming. The IBM design review loses some of its effectiveness if done earlier in the life of the project. Each methodology shares many features with the other, and the end result is a system design with predictable bottlenecks identified and corrected, but there is a difference in the timing of the reviews.

The IBM design review attempts to produce a better design by predicting the performance or workability of a system, to make the customer aware of the bottlenecks, and to allow the customer to (quantifiably) select alternatives.

To conduct an IBM design review, it is necessary to have a working knowledge of the details of the DBMS. The review team should (collectively) know what the different and essential components of the DBMS are, how they interconnect, how to break the costs of using a component down to some common denominator, and what components can and cannot (and should and should not) be used in conjunction with each other. In a complex and generalized DBMS, this expertise is expensive to assemble.

The main thrust of the IBM design review is to break down system processes into detailed levels so that they can be compared with other processes at the same denomination. A typical measurement might be in terms of number of instructions necessary to execute a process, or the cost (in dollars and cents) based upon the charging algorithm of the installation being reviewed.

Once having established some base to which a process should be reduced, the design team is ready to analyze the system.

DESIGN REVIEW PROCEDURE

After the preliminary discussions concerning the goal and ground rules, the design review starts with an overview of the application. System specifications form the basis for this discussion. It is up to the user to inform the team of constraints, goals, and boundaries of acceptable and unacceptable performance. It does a disservice to the review team to withhold or omit information necessary for the making of good decisions. By the same token, it is wasteful to present irrelevant detail.

After the application is presented, the data processing overview occurs. In it, the general characteristics of the system are discussed. Typical run frequencies, program profiles, transaction volumes, and computer availability and capacity are discussed. The next topic is an analysis of the physical data structures. All relevant aspects are open to review—such as the ordering of the segments, the physical organization of the data, the occurrences of the data, and the profile of the data's activity. The next step is to select transactions that are representative of the bulk of the processing on the theory that a close analysis of one representative transaction will turn up problems common to all transactions. Other transactions selected for analysis are those that are critical to system performance and those that may be suspect prior to a detailed review.

Each transaction selected for analysis is then broken into a call flow of DBMS activity. Usually, the CPU utilization at execution is minimal for non-DBMS call activity. In the few cases where the transaction itself uses a high percentage of CPU time (away from the DBMS) the transaction should be scrutinized. Usually, this is not the case. The frequency of the calls to the DBMS are calculated; the probability that I/O will occur on a given call is calculated; and the index, overflow, and primary data base activity are figured into the program's activity. The final result of studying a transaction is a rough prediction as to how it will perform. By breaking a transaction down to this fine level, the customer is exposed to the real activity that is happening. The DBMS masks off many of the internal operations that occur, and it is not easy to understand design implications when the underlying economies are unknown. If a part of the design is going to be a bottleneck, alternatives can be analyzed, and since each process is reduced to a common denominator, the exact difference between the bottleneck and the alternative can be measured.

EXAMPLE OF IBM DESIGN REVIEW TECHNIQUE

All other examples and discussions in this book apply to hierarchical data bases in general. This discussion of necessity must refer to the specifics of a given DBMS–IMS. A design review that serves as a useful example must be reduced to the specifics of a given DBMS.

Suppose that a design team is considering building dependent segments beneath a root. The segments occur so that 10 twin dependents will exist beneath the root. There are only two data elements per dependent. A discussion of the relative merits of blocking the segments so that all 10 segments are contained in one physical segment leads to two points of view.

Since the segments are updated asynchronously (i.e., not all sequentially created in a single action), one designer argues that it will require more calls to retrieve the segment and replace it (in the blocked form) than it will to simply insert a dependent segment (in the unblocked form); therefore, there is no real argument for blocking the segment. Another designer claims that the efficiencies of retrieval are such that a single call (in the blocked case) will be much cheaper than one direct retrieval and nine sequential retrievals (as in the unblocked case). Furthermore, 90% of the activity in the system is retrieval and 10% is update. Without a further analysis, each designer could consider his or her own viewpoint to be correct.

A quantification of exactly what occurs inside IMS will shed light on the relative merits of each point of view. The environment they are running in (a hypothetical one) can be profiled by the following statements. The data base is HDAM with native OSAM organization. The size of the LRECL is such that all segments will fit into the same block. Byte limit count is not a factor. The size of the buffer pool and system activity are such that the buffer pools do not flush rapidly. The update and retrieval occur in an MPR (message processing region). Parallel IMS is not being run. The time to be measured discounts line time and formatting time to and from the MPR, since they will be the same regardless of the structure of the data base. The structure of the data and a rough idea of the pro-

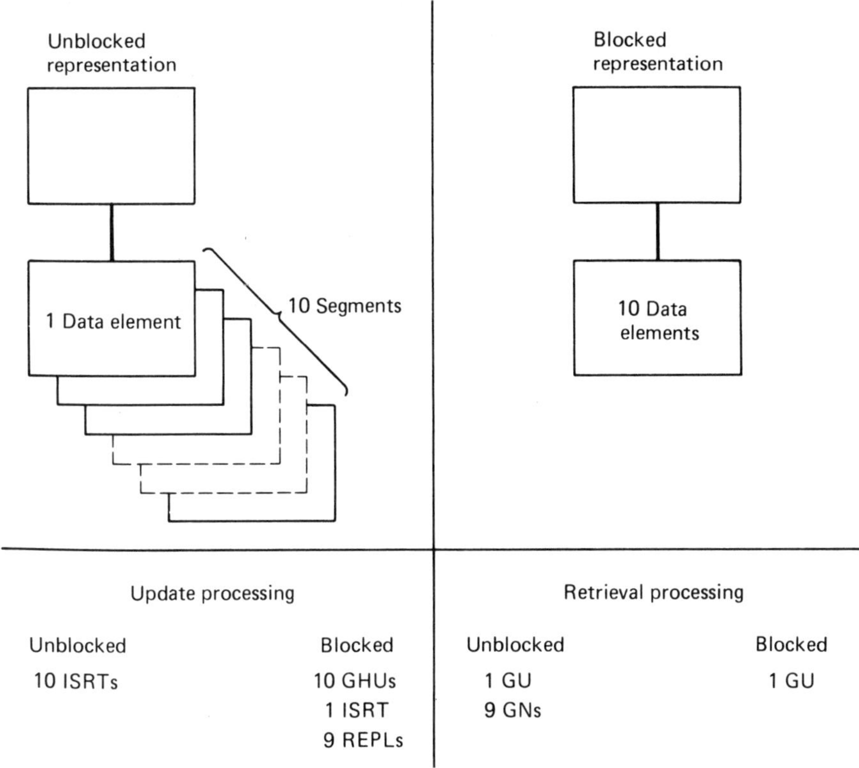

Figure 9.1

cessing is shown by Fig. 9.1. The process is broken into its respective call flows and the result is shown in Fig. 9.2.

Both designers agree that the processing external to the activity in the DBMS is unimportant for the sake of comparison. The call flows are broken into their respective components (GU, GHU, REPL, etc.) and the individual components are reduced to the basic levels of the DL-1 overhead, interregion communications, HDAM I/O activity, LRECL activity, and basic OSAM randomized read and write activity (Fig. 9.3). Each of these basic activities is translated into instruction path lengths or the number of instructions executed from the beginning of the activity to the end. (*Note:* These path lengths are hypothetical and may or may not bear a resemblance to actual IMS path lengths.) The frequency of each activity is calculated for one update and one retrieval. From the frequency, the number of times a function is invoked per call and path length per call, the total path length for a given function can be calculated. For instance, one complete update requires 10 inserts. The random I/O per insert is

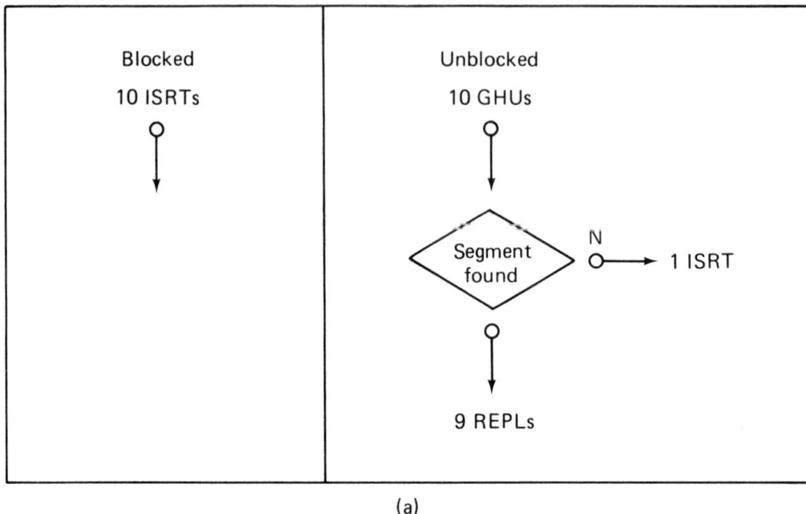

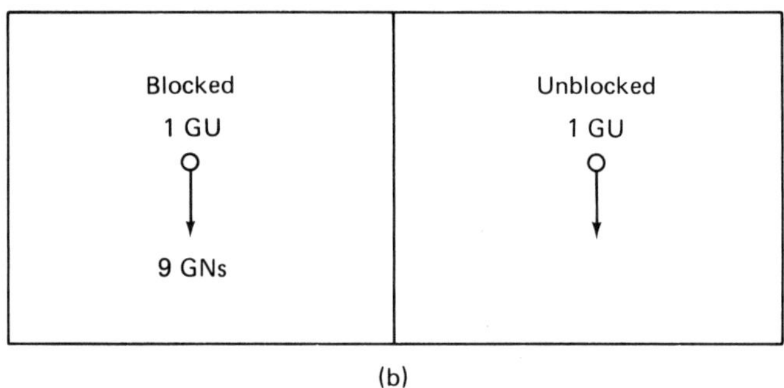

Figure 9.2 (a) Update call flow. (b) Retrieval call flow.

2 (one for the read, one for the write). The path length of a random OSAM insert is 4800. Therefore, the total path length for the update function is 10 X 2 X 4800 = 96,000 instructions. Combining all the necessary operations for the insert, the unblocked insert function (10 dependent segments done asynchronously) requires a path length of 179,300 instructions.

The same sort of analysis is done for blocked and unblocked retrieval (see Fig. 9.4).

ANALYSIS OF PATH-LENGTH CALCULATIONS

The designer who claimed that unblocked update was cheaper than blocked update is correct in this case. Equally correct was the designer

		Unblocked structure		Blocked structure				
	Path rate	Unblkd update	Path Lngth		Blkd update			Path lngth
Call	–	Isrt	–	GHU	GHU	Isrt	Repl	–
Frequency	–	10	–	1	9	1	9	–
D11/GU	1100	–	–	1	1	–	–	11000
D11/GN	940	–	–	–	–	–	–	–
D11/ISRT	1700	1	17000	–	–	1	–	1700
D11/REPL	470	–	–	–	–	–	1	4230
IRC	4500	10	45000	1	9	1	9	90000
HD Read RAP	250	1	2500	1	1	1	–	2750
HD ISRT	1500	1	15000	–	–	1	–	1500
HD REPL	1580	–	–	–	–	–	1	14220
OSAM Read IR	380	1	3800	1	1	1	–	4180
OSAM Rand IO	4800	2	96000	1	1	2	1	100800
Total			179300					230380

Figure 9.3

		Unblocked structure			Blocked structure	
	Path rate	Unblkd retrvl		Path lngth	Blocked retrvl	Path lngth
Call	–	GU	GN	–	GU	–
Frequency	–	1	9	–	1	–
D11/GU	1100	1	–	1100	1	1100
D11/GN	940	–	1	8460	–	–
D11/ISRT	1700	–	–	–	–	–
D11/REPL	470	–	–	–	–	–
IRC	4500	1	9	45000	1	4500
HD Read RAP	250	1	–	250	1	250
HD ISRT	1500	–	–	–	–	–
HD REPL	1580	–	–	–	–	–
OSAM Read LR	380	1	–	380	1	380
OSAM Rand IO	4800	1	–	4800	1	4800
Total				59990		11030

Figure 9.4

90% of system is retrieval, so relative cost of blocked vs. unblocked structuring of data structures is —

UNBLKD UPDATE PATH LNGTH + (9 x UNBLKD RETRVL PATH LNGTH) = UNBLKD PATH LNGTH

BLKD UPDATA PATH LNGTH + (9 x BLKD RETRVL PATH LNGTH) = BLKD PATH LNGTH

UNBLKD PATH LNGTH = 179300 + (9 x 59990) = 719210

BLKD PATH LNGTH = 230380 + (9 x 11030) = 284290

The total energy spent in support of the unblocked structuring of the data is significantly more than the energy spent for the blocked structure of data.

Figure 9.5

who claimed that blocked retrieval was faster than unblocked retrieval. However, since retrievals represent 90% of the activity against the system, the blocked approach is far superior to the unblocked approach. This is documented by Fig. 9.5.

Based upon the analysis of Fig. 9.5, it is obvious which approach should be chosen. However, it should also be obvious that there are many variables that must be taken into account that could have greatly influenced the outcome had their impact been different. Some of them are:

1. Ratio of update/retrieval activity—had the ratio been 90% for update rather than retrieval, the outcome would have been different.
2. Had parallel DL-1 been used, the IRC would be less than 4500, and this would have evened up the sizable difference between the retrieval ratios.
3. If the basic path length changed for a given variable, there would be some impact (i.e., suppose that OSAM random I/Os were reduced to a path length of 2000).
4. Suppose that the 10 segments were not entered asynchronously but were inserted all at one time.
5. Suppose that VSAM was used for the native data organization rather than OSAM.
6. Suppose that LRECL length were shortened, so that not all segments could physically be placed in the same block.
7. Suppose that byte limit counts were used, so that not all segments would be put in the same block if they happened to be inserted at the same time.
8. Suppose that the decision were made to change the data base to HISAM rather than HDAM.
9. Suppose that the release of IMS changes.

Any one of these issues has an impact on the outcome. In the particular example at hand, the impact is probably not going to affect the outcome. However, in other less obvious cases the outcome may indeed be reversed by single or multiple changes of variables—which points out one of the weaknesses of breaking a process down into detailed levels.

SCOPE OF DESIGN REVIEW

The scope of the IBM design review depends upon the size, complexity, and criticality of the project. For a small project the review will be small. This does not imply that small projects will be allowed to build transactions that will adversely affect the on-line system. There are economies of scale at work here. If a small project must be redesigned, the impact is on a small number of programs, a small number of users, and a limited amount of data. Large projects get the most attention, and deservedly so. As the size and scope of the system increases, its complexity and the interaction among its components increase. There is more at stake and a bigger payoff in doing a large design review than in the case of a small system.

DESIGN REVIEW FEEDBACK

The output of IBM's design review is a set of recommendations to better prepare the system for implementation and identification and analysis of critical processes. Predictable bottlenecks are uncovered and alternatives are suggested. Allowing the recommendations of the design review to go unheeded is usually costly. The organization that has the willpower to prevent one politically powerful user from adversely affecting all other users of the system stands to profit.

It is very easy for management to backslide against the prerogative of data base management to require that a user conform to reasonable standards. The argument usually is that the user has a particular need and "has to have" a particular feature. For this reason, it is absolutely imperative that management perceive the on-line system as its own resource. From this understanding of priorities comes the authority to enforce standards, which in the final analysis benefits everyone.

DATA STRUCTURES IN DESIGN REVIEW

In the early phases of design review, data structures and relationships are ambiguous, especially when many data elements and relationships are involved and different combinations of arranging data are possible. A good designer investigates these relationships, and, like a detective, juggles them together until he or she finds the most beneficial arrangement of data that fits the most needs. Typically, several people organize the data, each from a different perception.

As one viewpoint is compared to another, one particular arrangement emerges as having the most positive aspects and the fewest negative ones. At this point the data takes on a less ambiguous form and the processes that will use the data can be defined. As long as the form of the data is in a state of flux, it is difficult to speak of programs in any way except ambiguously. Once the structures are nailed down, the programs that use them can be specified. This phenomenon is easily seen in the steps that MCAUTO goes through. In each phase of design review up to and prior to programming, the data is less obscure than the programs.

The final sealing of the design process comes in the monitoring of the system as it is being used. At this point the statistics gathered by the designer and the designer's predictions are put to the test. A drastic miscalculation may cause a reworking of part of the system. If the design review has overlooked or miscalculated some important fact, it will surface here. If the system has been designed with flexibility as one of its parameters, the impact of change stands a good chance of being small. It may even be possible to tune the error so that it has no major impact. A minimum of surprises at this stage are the mark of a good review.

The techniques of design review methodology discussed here are in terms of IMS. IBM's methodology was designed for IMS and an explanation of it is necessarily appropriate at the implementation level, i.e., in reference to some of the specifics of IMS.

However, design review concepts are certainly not limited to IMS. The astute reader operating in an environment other than IMS should be able to get a flavor for the usefulness of design review and should be able to apply the concepts to his or her application.

One of the goals of design review is to reduce design decisions to a low enough level so that comparisons are objective, not subjective. Any application (in a non IMS environment) should be able to be reduced to a level of calls to DBMS, number of I/O's, or executable path length, if necessary. At this level, design alternatives can be reduced to a common denominator, and thus be evaluated objectively.

EXERCISES

1. Select a small existing data base application. Describe the application briefly in terms of user function, program specifications, and data base design. Select several programs (an update, report, and an inquiry transaction, for example). Translate these programs into strings of executable assembly language instructions. Breaking pro-

cesses down in this manner often unmasks the workings of the DBMS, and in doing so gives insight into the performance of the DBMS

a) Having broken the system into a fine state, make two lists:
   i) A list of insights into the workings of the DBMS gained by the analysis.
   ii) Detailed work that is irrelevant to understanding the internals of the DBMS.
b) Comparing the two descriptions of the system (the specification of user functions, program specifications, data base design, and the lists of executable assembler instructions), construct a list of design review questions that can be addressed by one or the other level. Include questions on search fields, secondary indices, data design practices, data base scans, and other appropriate topics.

2. For each of the items on the following list:
   a) Determine at what point in the life of the development process they should be considered.
   b) Determine whether or not a path-length analysis is necessary to measure trade-offs about:
      i. Data set organization—indexed, sequential.
      ii. Search fields.
      iii. Secondary index.
      iv. Fundamental system complexities.
      v. Capacity (CPU, storage, etc.).
      vi. Data base size.
      vii. Data base flexibility.
      viii. Call flow options.
      ix. System bottlenecks.
      x. Data redundancy.

TEN

STRUCTURAL ANALYSIS

Data bases and data structures portray objects and relationships that exist in the real world. As such, they are an abstraction of some aspect of the user's environment. A well-planned abstraction of data removes barriers, both in the present and the future, to the effective use of the data. Programmers find meaningful abstractions easy to understand and manipulate. Designers find that effective data structures are pliable and require a minimum of effort to change when change is necessary. Operations find that a carefully designed system (of which an integral part is well-designed data) is flexible and easy to manage, as opposed to running a poorly designed system. Often, there are so many variables that run at cross currents to each other that it is not easy to determine what is an effective data base design until the system is in operation, at which point it is expensive to correct mistakes.

There are no absolute rules for proper data base design. What is a poor practice in one instance may be optimal in another set of circumstances. To achieve the best results, the designer should consider how the system performs in light of the many parameters by which it can be measured, how flexible the system is, how difficult it is to construct, and how useful it is to the end user.

DESIGN PARTICIPANTS

The principal participants in the process of transformation of data from real-world entities into an explicitly defined data structure should be user representatives, system analysts, data base management, and program designers. The first step toward creating an effective system is to understand user requirements. An analysis that explores the following areas yields insight into the needs of the user:

1. Identify the components of operation. What are the basic units of operation and what are their boundaries?
2. Identify interactions and interrelations among the components of operation. How do the different units mesh together to form the system?
3. Identify the volume of activity, response requirements, availability of data, and constraints associated with the components of operation. What specific function does each unit perform and how is its work measured?
4. Based upon successful investigation of 1, 2, and 3, identify the critical aspects of the system. What processes are expensive to operate? What processes are time- and volume-sensitive? Where do the complexities lie?

Successfully answering these questions, as completely and accurately as possible, leads to a formal statement of user requirements and priorities within the system. It is the first step toward creating an effective data design and will serve as a foundation for future decisions concerning the system. Understanding the data conceptually from the user's perspective is the starting point of a well-planned abstraction of the user's environment.

After the requirements are drawn up, another question must be considered: What are the future needs of the system independent of current user requirements and what impact do these needs have on current design?

MESHING REQUIREMENTS INTO A DESIGN

Once the user requirements are documented, different alternatives for the construction of the system may be explored. It is desirable to investigate as many feasible approaches as possible. Examining many approaches opens the door quite naturally to alternatives if one approach is deemed undesirable. Also, exploring different possibilities of design helps shed light on the strengths and weaknesses of other approaches. Just as designing a system in a vacuum can lead to unacceptable results, implementing the first workable design without identifying and exploring alternatives can be equally disastrous.

At the point in time when the best overall approach is selected, the different arrangements of data structures that can support the plan should be investigated. All appropriate and likely arrangements of data should be examined and trade-offs between the different arrangements should be compared. The end result of this phase of design is a description of the chosen arrangement of data structures and a statement of how user requirements and future needs of the system are met by the design.

Prior to the formal definition of the data structures to the DBMS (which amounts to casting the design in concrete), there should be a final review of the data structures where the following suggested questions should be asked and discussed to possibly throw light on flaws that may have gotten through the design. Correcting errors at this point is inexpensive relative to the cost of correcting them later. The questions have no right or wrong answers. Instead, they are designed to initiate intelligent discussion of the design and, in doing so, to uncover errors. Often, merely raising the right set of questions at the right time prevents mistakes.

ANALYZING DATA STRUCTURES

1. Is the sequence field (key) of one data base duplicated in part or whole elsewhere? If so, what purpose does it serve?

In many cases, duplication of key values is useful. It can be used to break up data bases so that contention problems will be minimized. On the other hand, duplication of key values necessarily indicates redundancy and points to the problems associated with maintaining the data and keeping it synchronized (see Fig. 10.1). A bigger problem occurs when data that is used as a key in one place is represented elsewhere in a similar but not identical form. Key data usually implies that other data elements in the same segment relate to it, and if it appears in more than one part of a data base, there is a good chance that the data base contains redundancies of massive amounts of data. Allowing key data to exist in multiple places in a data base may indicate a confusion as to the real meaning of its abstraction, and, consequently, there may be wasteful and overlapping processing. This situation is ripe for error.

2. What implicit relationships exist? Why do they exist? Are they necessary? Is it worthwhile to maintain them?

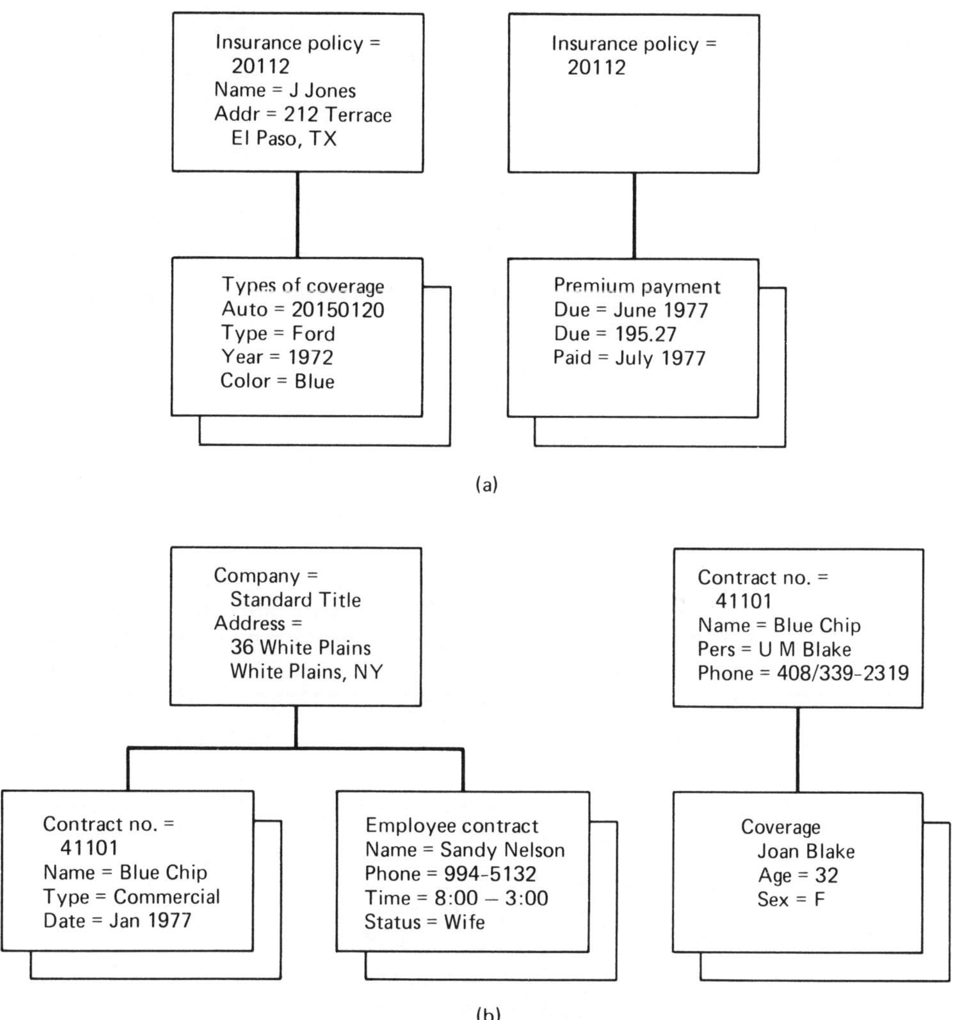

Figure 10.1 (a) In some cases, duplication of key information can lead to a beneficial separation of function. (b) In some cases, separation of a key into two data bases may indicate a need to consolidate data bases, depending upon the uses and environments of the data bases.

Implicit relationships can greatly enhance response time if used properly (Fig. 10.2). They can save unnecessary calls to segments, thereby minimizing DBMS activity. They can be used to package data in autonomous units so that a segment or data base is self-sufficient as far as the majority of the retrievals against it are concerned. The danger in using implicit relationships is that the burden of keeping the data tied together correctly may negate the advantage of having fewer calls to the DBMS or other

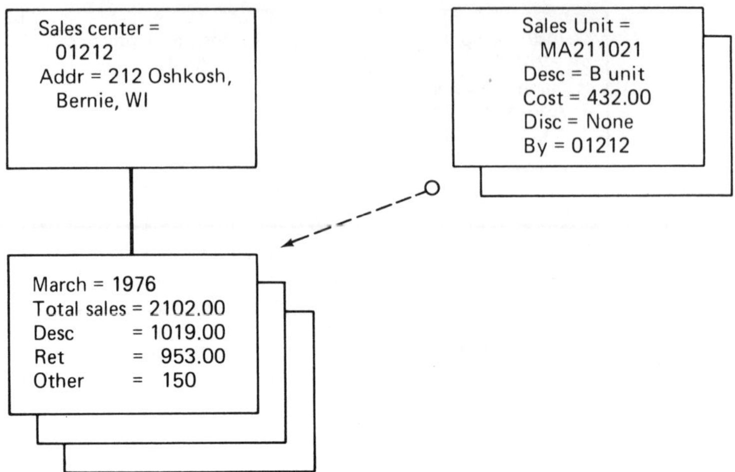

Figure 10.2 Sales are accumulated into sales center by month.

advantages that the relationship affords. Also, implicit relationships necessarily add a degree of complexity to programming and data base synchronization. Sometimes the level of complexity is so great that the relationship should be maintained or derived by some other means.

The least expensive implementation of implicit relationships occurs when batch runs are used to create and maintain the relationship, and later the on-line relationship is used for retrieval and display. Any other implementation may affect performance and should be closely scrutinized.

3. If two data bases are explicitly related:
   a) Is the relationship necessary?
   b) Will it serve the purpose intended?
   c) Will it need modification in the near future?
   d) Is it operationally sound?
   e) What alternatives exist?
   f) If malfunctions in the DBMS occur because of the relationship, what will the repercussions be?

Explicit relationships present a temptation to the designer to go overboard. Once the first explicit relationship works its way into the design, suddenly everything begins to be described in terms of explicit relationships and they begin to proliferate.

There is no valid argument for sophistication for sophistication's sake. If a function can be adequately and efficiently fulfilled within the boundaries of ordinary structural tools, there is no need to go beyond those boundaries unless special advantages are offered or research is the aim of the project.

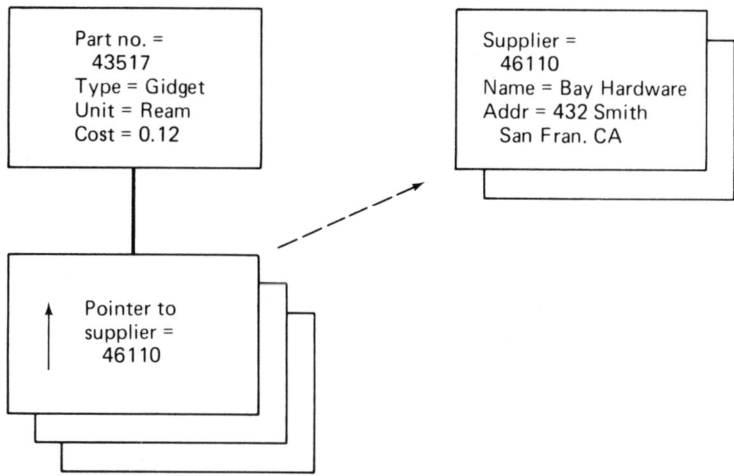

Figure 10.3 The supplier of a part can be found by searching the pointer segment of the part number data base.

Explicit relationships can save a great deal of processing when used properly (Fig. 10.3). There is an added dimension of risk in using them, however. The designer depends upon the DBMS to perform services somewhat beyond the primitive functions of segment insertion, deletion, and modification when the designer chooses to let the DBMS handle the explicit relationship. Because of this dependence upon the DBMS, the added exposure of system error must be calculated. This means that there may be moments of inoperability due to system malfunction. As a general rule, the less exotic the design, the less the risk.

Explicit relationships supported by the DBMS can become very complicated. The careful designer should rely upon the experience of other implementations that have built similar structures and should be especially wary of features for which no known successful application has been built. Vendors announce new features in support of explicit relationships from time to time, and there is a certain wisdom in not being the first to use the feature.

4. Is more than one segment an abstraction of the same or closely related object or relationship in the real world? If yes, why aren't they combined (Fig. 10.4)? What are the essential differences between the two abstractions?

There are legitimate instances where very similar segments are created and are not combined. Usually, they are separated because of differences in functional usage. In other cases, the volume of data and frequency of update warrant a separation. However, one hallmark of a poor data base design is many unjustified cases of redundancy. Such a design wastes

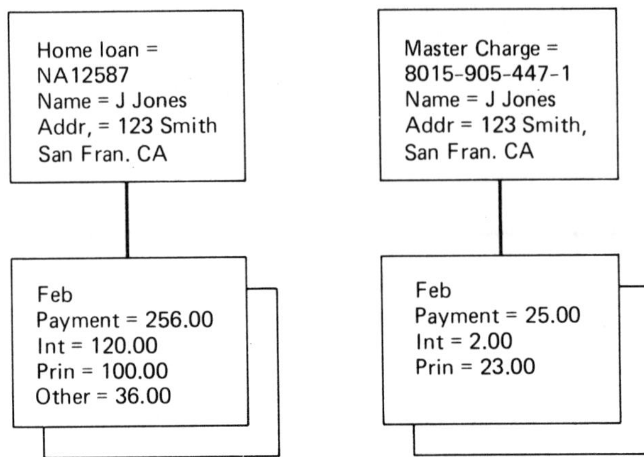

Figure 10.4 Example of closely related segments that might be combined.

programming effort and execution time, as well as short-circuiting future flexibility.

Surprisingly, if care is not taken to prevent its spread, redundancy creeps into a system quite naturally. Usually, it does so in the guise of data elements that are similar but have some small distinction. The difference between the elements lies only in the perception of the user or the analyst, not that of the designer, who must view the data objectively. It is the job of the designer to determine what data elements are intrinsically different from each other.

5. Is a data base made up of widely dissimilar data? If yes, why isn't it disseminated into several data bases (Fig. 10.5)?

In some cases it may be reasonable and desirable to combine diverse segment types. When a data base is used purely in batch and is infrequently updated, it may be advisable to congregate diverse data types into it. In other cases, it is probably a good policy to create a few more data bases, segregating like data elements into their own data base. (*Note:* Creating many data bases will cause problems with overhead. The DBMS must handle each data base separately, and some overhead is required for each data base. Splitting data bases so that each data base contains similar data types does not imply unnecessary proliferation of data bases.)

A major advantage of multiple data bases comes in the area of recovery and resource contention. It is always faster and cheaper to recover a small data base than to recover a large one. A large data base may be used exclusively in one environment while another environment is waiting on that data base for execution. In this manner, a large data base can become a resource constraint. Another advantage of grouping like segment types

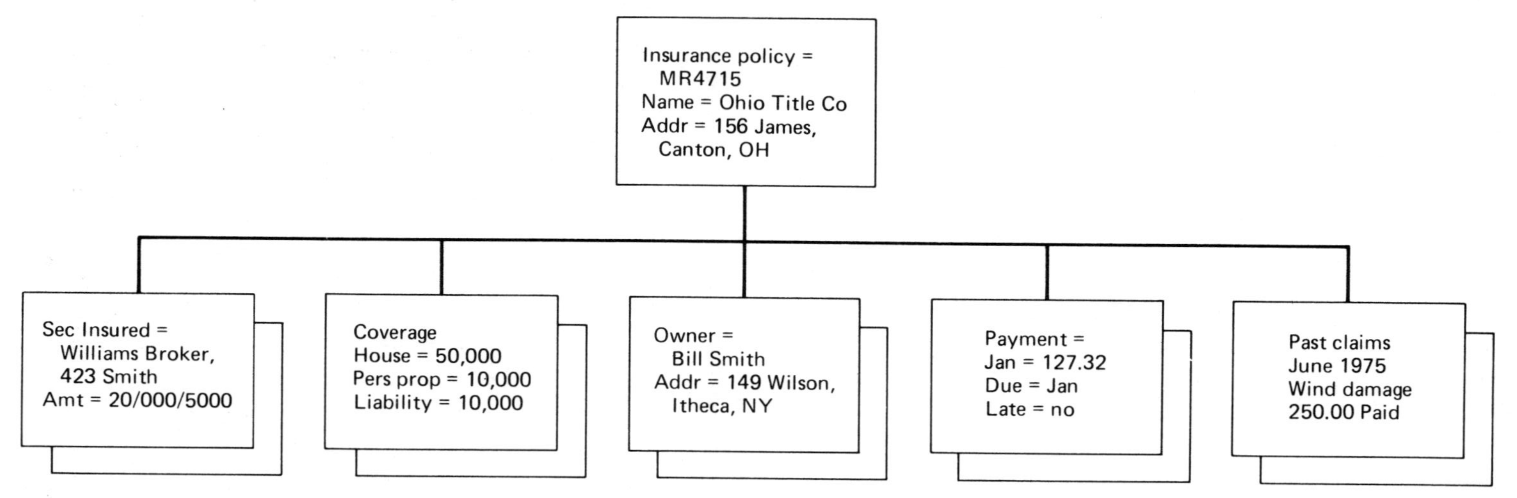

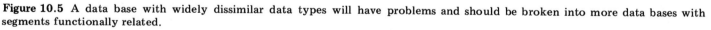

Figure 10.5 A data base with widely dissimilar data types will have problems and should be broken into more data bases with segments functionally related.

into their own data bases is that the impact of change is minimized. Less data is affected when a system malfunction occurs.

6. Is the system composed of many small interrelated data bases? If so, why aren't they combined?

There are, on occasion, reasons for creating many small, tightly interconnected data bases. Preparation for future growth or a diversity of function may be a valid basis for separating data. However, an arbitrary splitting of data bases has disadvantages. When there are too many data bases, the problems of updating them, keeping them synchronized, and bringing them together into a single retrieval program negate the advantage of splitting them. Also, many related data bases may be the sign of a design effort that has not been well coordinated. Typically, this is the result of several design teams working on a related problem but not communicating with each other and coordinating activities. Such an error leads to unnecessary resource consumption and reduces the effectiveness of the concept of data bases.

7. Is the system composed mostly of pointer and prefix data (Fig. 10.6)? If yes, is there a justification for it? Is more than 15% of the space occupied by the data base not used by the data portion of the segments?

In an effort to achieve data independence, the designer may be tempted to create many segments at many levels. In some cases, this may be worthwhile. In a batch-only environment, where data relationships are constantly changing, splitting a data base into many segments may have merit. In other cases, the segment length may justifiably be near the size of the prefix data. In a root-only data base, where absolutely fast access is necessary and no other data is relevant, it may be useful to have a very small data portion for the segment.

The valid cases in which the data area of a segment is small are very limited. Usually, when prefix data becomes a significant part of the total space of a data base, poor design is the cause. It is true that a high level of segmentation can reduce redundancy and save some space. However, the savings in space must be balanced against overhead necessary for the existence of any given segment.

8. Is it clear what a given segment (or data base) represents (Fig. 10.7)? Is it clear what real-world entity or relationship the segment is an abstraction of?

Consolidating data elements into a segment can be very beneficial. One of the methods to prevent oversegmentation is to put varying data elements into the same segment. If not done judiciously, however, one of the biggest mistakes a designer can make is to put data elements that are

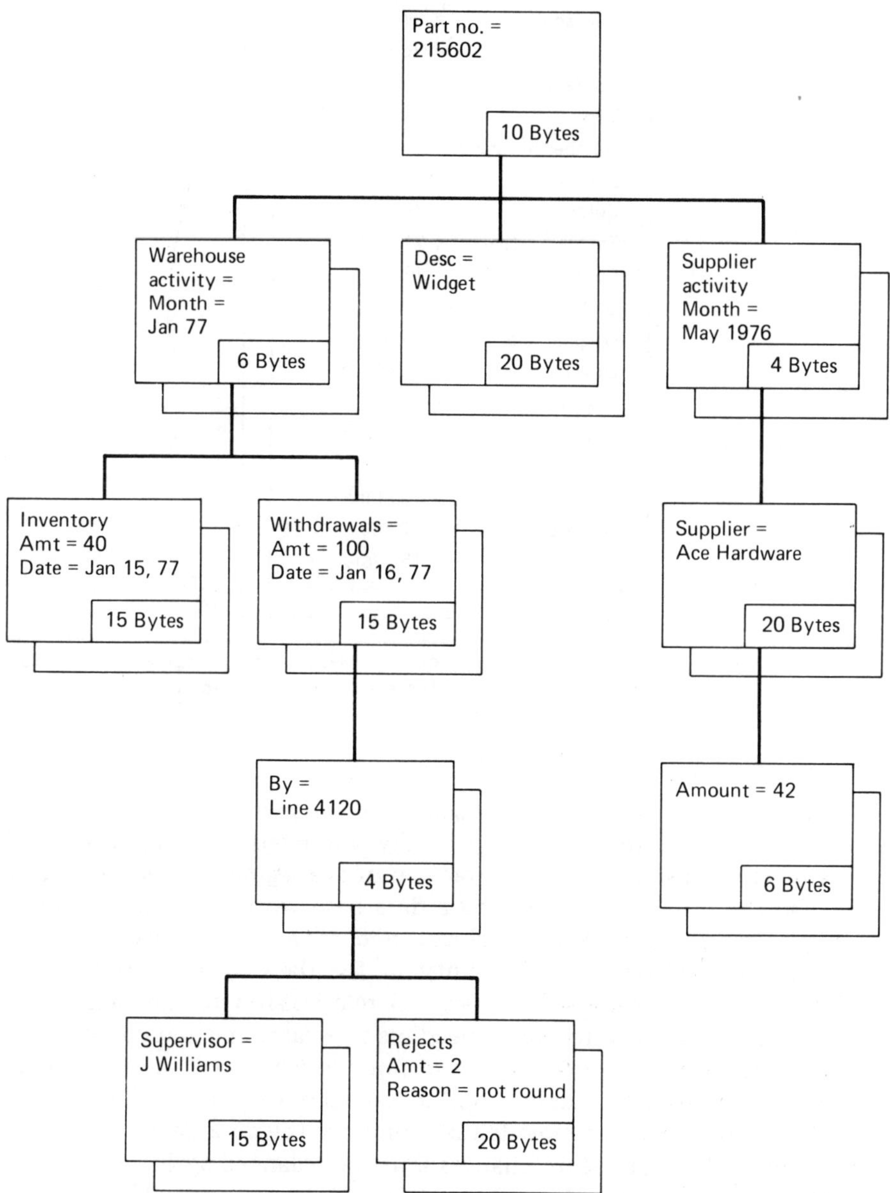

Figure 10.6 A data base that is oversegmented will have short data areas, a high percentage of the total of the data base will be prefix (overhead) data, and complex and multilevel calls will be needed to process the data base.

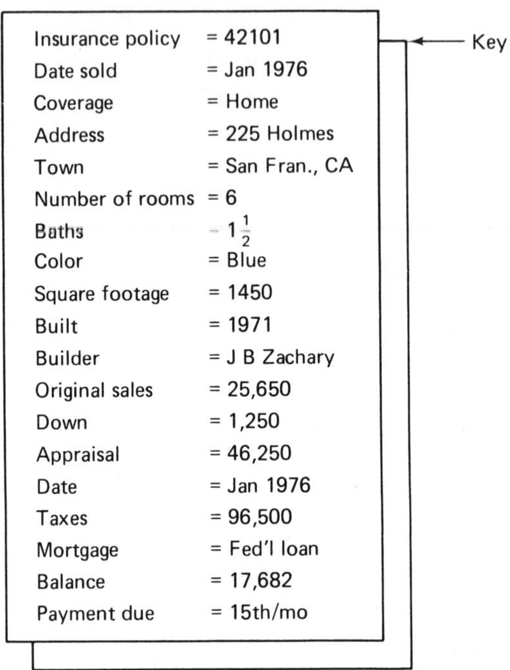

Insurance policy = 42101
Date sold = Jan 1976
Coverage = Home
Address = 225 Holmes
Town = San Fran., CA
Number of rooms = 6
Baths = 1 1/2
Color = Blue
Square footage = 1450
Built = 1971
Builder = J B Zachary
Original sales = 25,650
Down = 1,250
Appraisal = 46,250
Date = Jan 1976
Taxes = 96,500
Mortgage = Fed'l loan
Balance = 17,682
Payment due = 15th/mo
Key

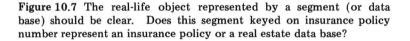

Figure 10.7 The real-life object represented by a segment (or data base) should be clear. Does this segment keyed on insurance policy number represent an insurance policy or a real estate data base?

only vaguely related into the same segment when there will foreseeably be a negative impact. Putting totally unrelated elements into a segment causes the meaning of the abstraction of the segment to become confused.

On the other hand, handling a data base with too many segment types means more logic, more overhead, and more complexity. Too few segments implies reducing flexibility of the data by impacting many data elements with changes that have no relationship to the element causing the change, and this results in needless programming and complexity. The fine line between good design and poor design is a thin one and is probably determined by making good decisions based upon analysis and understanding of the data elements that comprise the data base.

Preparation for future changes must be balanced against current performance criteria. Are data elements likely to change? If they are, oversegmentation may save quite an effort later. Otherwise, combining unlike data elements may actually be the best course. Is the data highly sensitive to performance? If so, undersegmentation may be the best strategy. From the perspective of the user, is the difference between data elements that reside in the same segment recognized? If not, the differences should be identified and discussed and the impact of putting a boundary around fundamentally different elements should be resolved. The cost of not recognizing and resolving a confused organization of data elements can be high, because future system flexibility is at stake.

9. Is there a significant difference between the structural abstraction of an entity or a relationship in a data base and the way that relationship is viewed in the real world (Fig. 10.8)? If so, is there a good reason for the discrepancy?

There are a few legitimate cases where the abstraction of an entity or a relationship may not coincide with the way the data is viewed in the user's environment. For example, in a recursive data structure the abstraction usually is not implemented the same way it is pictured by the users. (That is, the user sees a logical view of the data while the data physically exists differently. The DBMS can be used to interface between the physical implementation and the logical view so that the user does not have to change his or her perception of the relationship.)

In other cases, the designer may abstract the data so that its appearance is not similar to its real-world counterparts, allowing it to be manipulated more easily or quickly. Usually, the abstract form selected by the designer is a more powerful and flexible rendering than the end user's conceptualization.

The majority of the time, however, the abstraction of the data has a marked similarity to its real-world form. Whenever there is a major dis-

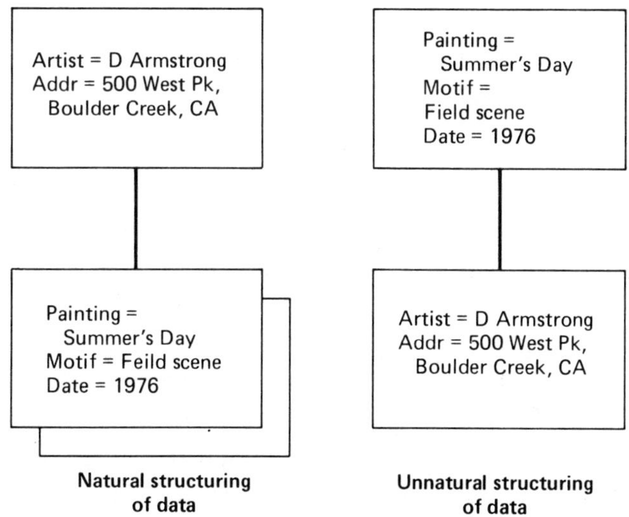

Figure 10.8 Data not structured in a fashion natural to its representation in reality may be redundant and limited in its applicability.

crepancy between the two, an investigation should be made into the differences. Often, a casual inquiry turns up major design flaws. Usually, the shortcoming of an abstraction of data that is not similar to its real-world counterpart is that the abstraction has inherent limitations.

10. Does the same data element appear multiple times in the data base? If yes, why?

Data elements that appear multiple times in a data base can be quite useful if used judiciously. Care should be taken, however. Even in the case where performance is enhanced by multiple occurrences of the same information, there are inherent inefficiencies in storing and updating the data.

Usually, when many data elements appear more than once throughout a system (over one or more data bases), it is a sign of sloppy design. Multiple occurrences of data elements may be an indication of an unrecognized recursive relationship that might best be represented by a true recursive structuring (Fig. 10.9). In other instances, multiple occurrences of data elements may represent a situation where segments should be consolidated. Every case of multiple occurrences of the same data element should be identified, documented, and justified.

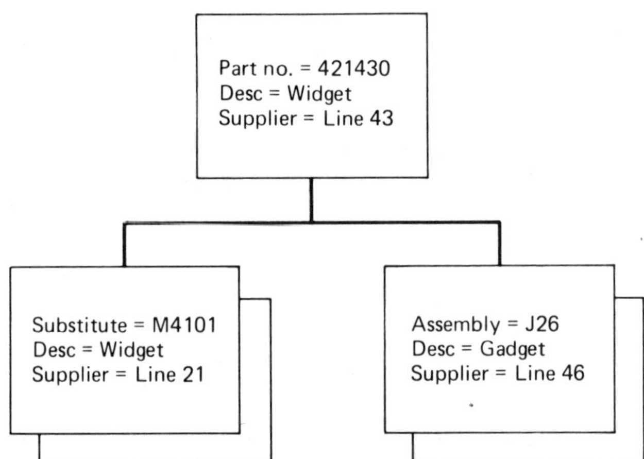

Figure 10.9 If the same or very similar data elements appear more than once in a data base, it may be an indication of recursive structuring done in an improper fashion or a simple redundancy.

11. Does the same (or very similar) internal structuring of data appear in more than one segment (Fig. 10.10)? If so, why?

(Note: In this case, internal structuring of data refers to relationships of data inside a segment, such as a table or the familiar COBOL record layout.)

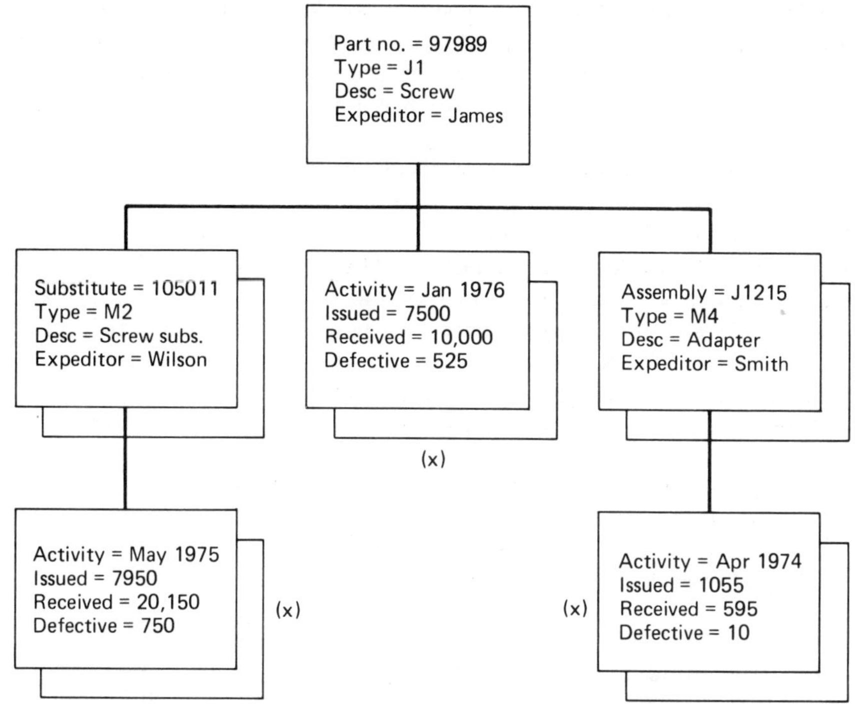

Figure 10.10 When duplicate data structures—that may not be exact duplicates are encountered, close examination should occur.

Even more important than identifying redundant data elements in a system is the identification of similar internal structures of data in a segment. For example, if a segment A contains a table with 12 entries, one for each month, and segment B contains the same table but with different data elements in it, A and B have a similar internal structure.

Redundant internal structures are more susceptible to change (and thus are more dangerous) than are redundant elements, because the internal structure involves both data elements and some relationship between those elements and, as such, is fragile. Furthermore, when change does occur, usually more than one type of data element is affected. Therefore, it is useful to identify duplicate internal data structures and justify their existence.

12. What alternative arrangement of data is feasible and will satisfy the system requirements? What advantage does the method selected have over the methods not selected? Why are the advantages of the method selected significant?

It is most beneficial to explore many different approaches to accomplishing the same result, and in the world of data base design there are a multitude of options, so that the designer is seldom forced to choose one method for lack of any other (Fig. 10.11). Each feasible approach will necessarily offer advantages over other approaches and will also have weaknesses that other approaches do not have. The effective designer explores as many approaches as he can so that the most effective system can be built with the least number of disadvantages.

Exploring different avenues illuminates areas that may have been considered to be closed issues. Many gross errors in design have been committed by unquestioningly implementing the first workable design or by always basing design decisions upon the tradition of "doing it the way it was done before." Looking at only one plan in depth leads to myopia (i.e., a designer begins to view the system only within the confines of the proposed design). Exploring other design alternatives allows the different problems the system presents to be seen with a new perspective.

13. How will future changes affect the data base design? Have ample "what if" questions been asked and successfully answered? Have all known future modifications and requirements been identified and allowances made for them?

Failing to investigate how future changes will affect the system can lead to a structuring of data that is brittle and will require massive efforts when the first change is encountered. Typically, some relevant questions are:

a) What happens when an element must be added? deleted? enlarged?
b) What happens when a segment needs to be added? deleted? enlarged?
c) What happens when a segment must be reordered (re-key-sequenced)?
d) What happens to performance when a data base grows large?
e) What happens when a data base used exclusively in batch suddenly becomes an integral part of an on-line system?
f) What happens when an interface between two or more data bases changes?
g) What happens when the relationship between data elements changes?
h) What happens when a segment (or data base) must be split into multiple segments (or data bases)?

The answers to these questions must be viewed from the perspective of the entire data base environment. The impact on programs, the DBMS, system resources, and other data bases must be considered. The penalty for not accounting for all aspects may be severe.

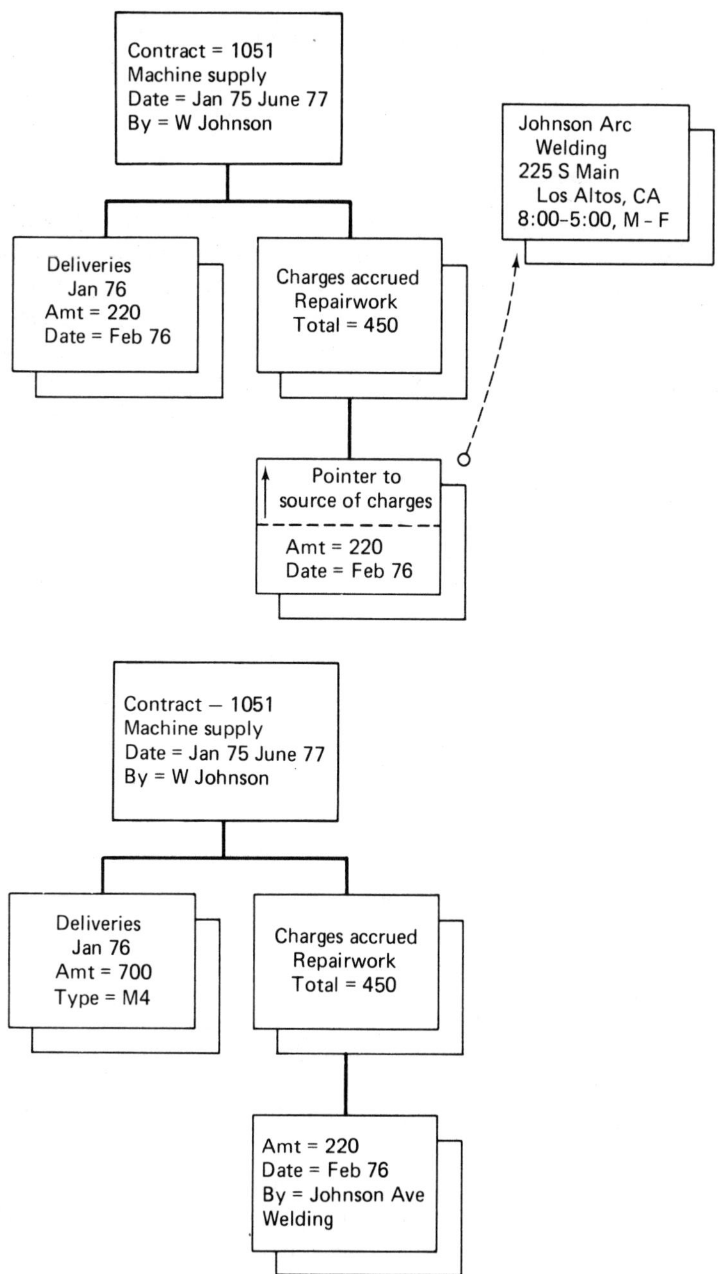

Figure 10.11. The choices between design options depend upon how the data is to be used, how it is maintained, and what interfaces to other systems will be necessary. Another relevant factor is the propensity for environmental change.

14. Is the data element being updated from more than one source? If it is, what techniques are available to determine how incorrect data got into the system? (In this case, "being updated from more than one source" implies that more than one program is updating the same data element, not that more than one clerk is entering data into the system.)

If at all possible, it is a good practice to have only one updating source for each data element. Otherwise, errors are difficult to find and fix when they occur (Fig. 10.12). Also, when more than one program updates a common element and change occurs, the program changes must be coordinated. In a highly controlled environment this may not present a problem, but when the system is large and many variables are involved, the complexity of coordinating multiple program changes can be taxing.

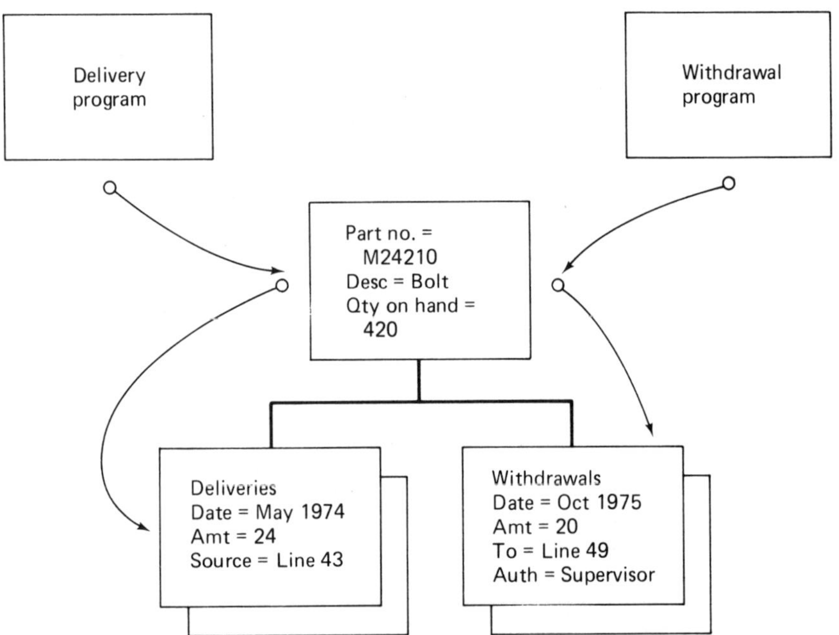

Figure 10.12 When values in the root segment are not correct, more than one program may be at fault.

15. At the initial design level, have all environments with which the data base interfaces been identified? Does the design meet the requirements for only the first phase of the development effort and is it perhaps inadequately prepared for future phases?

One of the most colossal errors that can occur is when the design of data structures does not take into consideration the full array of requirements for which the data structures are being built. When one phase has been successfully completed, it may be a shock to find that the next phase will require a significant redesign of data structures. The wary data designer makes allowances for more than the immediate needs of the current development effort.

16. What limitations are imposed by the design?

This question is always easy to answer after the fact. The importance of asking it as soon as possible becomes quite clear at that time, also. Once the design has been completed and the system goes into operation, the limitations of the system (planned or unplanned) begin to manifest themselves. Hopefully, the designer will have consciously planned the limitations so that constraints do not become an obstacle to user satisfaction. Following are some typical limitations:

a) Data retrieval is unacceptable and programs or data bases cannot undergo a tuning effort that will significantly improve performance.
b) Any change to the data structure affects many programs severely.
c) The data base must remain on-line for a certain number of hours, but there is also a need to access the data in batch during the same hours.
d) Data changes adversely affect other data bases that are related either explicitly or implicitly.
e) Data reorganization is a major task and cannot be scheduled frequently—at most once a year—for example.
f) Data base recovery is inherently a long, complicated process and will impose long periods of inoperability on the user.

Other limitations may exist that are peculiar to a set of circumstances. The careful designer guards against any really bad surprises by constructing (mentally or otherwise) a complete flow of how data goes through the system. Based upon the designer's concept of that flow, he or she can predict the location of weak points in the system. The more accurate the designer's understanding of the system and the DBMS, the better chance there is that major limitations will be uncovered. Not projecting the system and its working components prior to implementation invites a design that may have undesirable constraints that will not be discovered until it is expensive to correct them.

17. What is the real expense of maintaining a data structure (Fig. 10.13)? When special features are used, what is the total cost? Is that cost justified?

It is very easy to be myopic in misunderstanding the real cost of maintaining a data structure. A designer may view the cost of implementing a

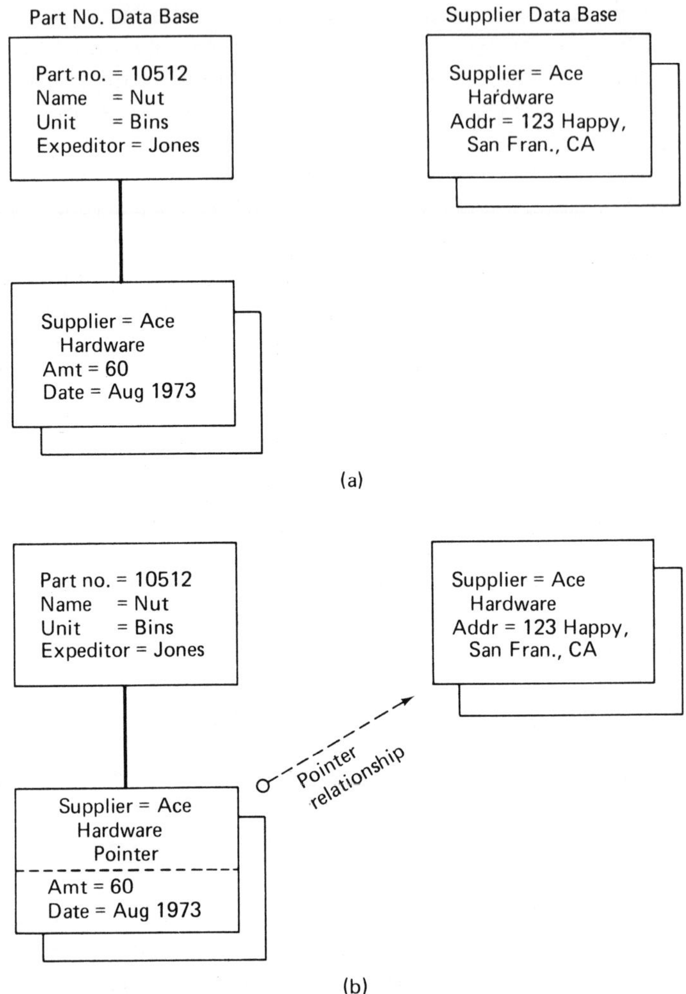

Figure 10.13 (a) If the relationship between the dependent segment of the part number data base and the supplier data base is infrequently traveled, it is cheaper to do separate calls to the data bases when the connections need to be made. (b) If the relationship is used frequently, it may be worthwhile to connect the part number data base and the supplier data base with a pointer.

feature such as an index as only what the feature costs when used. The designer neglects to count the costs of creating and maintaining the feature (Fig. 10.14).

If the cost of the index is viewed as only the resources that are incurred as the feature is being used, the index is beneficial because it uses 7000 I/Os a day as opposed to the direct-call relationships, which use 17,000

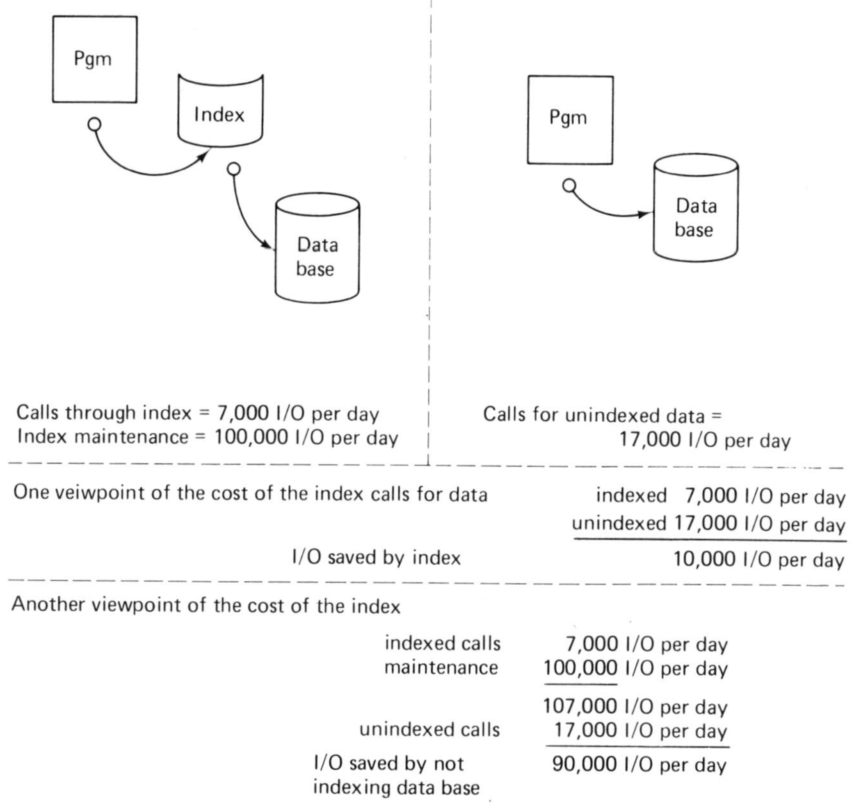

Figure 10.14

I/Os a day. However, when the total activity is taken into consideration, it is seen that support of the pointer is costly because normal maintenance of the pointer (100,000 I/Os) more than uses up its advantage. This analysis depends strongly upon the volume of data going through the system, the cost of maintaining the index, and the mix of transactions in the system. As these variables change, the analysis will change.

In any case, a knowledge of the workings of the DBMS and an awareness of what is really taking place is necessary to the understanding of what decisions are best.

18. Are there any control segments that are common to many transactions? Are there any data bases that are essential to the running of a large number of transactions?

There is a real danger in designing a control segment as an integral part of a system. The danger lies in data contention. While one transaction is executing, it may be holding exclusive control of the control segment that is necessary to the execution of another transaction. In this manner, transactions enqueue upon each other. There are enough barriers to smooth execution without inventing new ones.

Another case of data contention occurs when one data base is involved in the execution of many of the transactions within a system. In this case, when the data base has a malfunction, the system is brought to its knees and must be taken out of service. This is another way that a system may be stopped unnecessarily by an unsophisticated design.

19. If the occurrence of a segment beneath a parent has a relative frequency of 1, shouldn't it be combined with the parent? Unless there are extenuating circumstances, the segment should probably exist as part of its parent.

Normally, it does not make sense to create a segment when it will occur only once per parent. By its very nature, there should not be a great increase in redundancy if the segment were combined into its parent. In fact, there would be some savings because the overhead associated with the segment as a child would disappear. The only justification for such a design might occur when the segment was very large and it appeared, at most, once per root, not an average of one time per root. In this case significant data storage might be saved by separating the parent and child segment.

20. Do the data structures and the design they support fit into the mode of operations? Are the techniques used suitable for the data base environment?

Once data is structured and its native organization is decided, the designer can begin to use the data to its best advantage. The designer does this at the expense of reducing his or her options. Data optimized for on-line systems normally are not suited for much sequential processing. Similarly, data organized for sequential processes are awkward in an on-line mode. The designer does well to use the data in the manner for which it is best suited.

21. Is any data created, or created and updated, that is never used in any other capacity?

Data costs money to store and manipulate. Occasionally, data is designed into a system only, later, to have the reason for the system's existence disappear—but the data lingers on. If any amount of data behaves like this, energy will be expended unnecessarily.

In some instances the designer knows that future requirements will necessitate data that, under the current design, is not warranted. If the designer is confident of future requirements, he may be justified in designing data into a system that has no immediate usage.

DBMS AND ABSTRACTION ANALYSIS

Once the general framework of the design has been established and the data structures have been set, a final review of how the design will interact with the DBMS is in order. Appropriate questions might be:

a. Can the DBMS handle the designed structures? If not, why not? What alternative exists?
b. Can the DBMS meet the expectations of the user with the proposed design (in terms of response time, data capacity, system availability, and volume of transactions)? If not, what alternatives are there? What part of the design could have its requirements lowered?
c. Does any aspect of the design use untried features of the DBMS? If so, what is the assessment of the risk? What is the level of in-house expertise? What is the level of support and expertise available from the vendor?
d. How well is the DBMS equipped to handle all types of data base failures? Is system availability severely affected? What tools exist for correcting failures? What can be done to streamline the recovery process?
e. How does DBMS handle data reorganization? What will be the impact on the system when reorganization occurs? What will be the scheduled frequency of reorganization? What are the chances of unscheduled reorganization? To what extent is system performance impaired by having a poorly organized data base?
f. Is the design pushing the limits of the DBMS? Is there a good reason for this? What have other installations experienced in similar situations?
g. Is any one aspect of the design especially inefficient under the DBMS? If so, how critical is that aspect of the system? What alternatives exist?

EXERCISES

1. a) Select a large existing data base application. Analyze the application for key redundancy motivated by the following:
    i. Key redundancy to reduce data base size.
    ii. Key redundancy for data availability.
    iii. Key redundancy for on-line/archival data.
    iv. Key redundancy to reduce on-line data integrity conflicts.

   b) If key redundancy exists for other reasons, list those reasons.

c) Analyze the cost of key redundancy versus the benefits (i.e., the cost of extra storage and processing versus decreased data base size, etc.).

2. Given below are three types of implicit relationships:
   a) Within the same segment, a change in element A on occasion triggers a change in element B.
   b) Within the same data base, a change in segment A on occasion triggers a change in segment B.
   c) On occasion, a change in data base A triggers a change in data base B.

   Discuss the implications of using implicit relationships based on these examples in terms of:
   i. System performance.
   ii. System flexibility.
   iii. Data reorganization.
   iv. Program design.
3. Identify the impact on operations caused by explicit relationships. What difference does it make if the relationship is direct or symbolic? When data bases need to be recovered, what is the impact?
4. Discuss the advantages and disadvantages of the following types of explicit relationships. Use examples if at all possible. Include the viewpoints of:
   a) The user.
   b) The designer.
   c) The data administration.
   d) The programmer.
   e) The operator.
      i. Direct relationships within the DBMS.
      ii. Symbolic relationships within the DBMS.
      iii. Direct and symbolic relationships (concurrently) within the DBMS.
      iv. Symbolic relationships external to the DBMS.
5. Select an existing application. Relate each element, segment, and data base back to its origin in the user's environment. If it is unclear what any segment or data base represents, determine the degree of elasticity of the data structure. Be especially wary of data bases that contain extremely dissimilar data types.
6. Determine how much of a given data base comprises prefix data. Analyze the data base physically; do not rely on design estimates or anything not directly tied to the physical existence of the data base.

   If over 15% of the data base is comprised of prefix data, analyze the data design and determine whether or not there is a misuse of space.

   Discuss the available existing software as a tool in analyzing percentage of prefix data. Discuss writing tailor-made software.

7. a) Give examples of the following cases of elemental redundancy:
   i. Wholesale elemental redundancy.
   ii. Sparse elemental redundancy.
   iii. Elemental redundancy within a segment.
   iv. Elemental redundancy within a data base.
   v. Elemental redundancy over more than one data base.

   b) What percentage of elemental redundancy is healthy?

   c) Give examples of elemental redundancy disguised as very similar elements with small distinctions (e.g., HOURS-WORKED-MONDAY, HOURS-WORKED-TUESDAY, HOURS-WORKED-WEDNESDAY, etc.).

   d) Discuss the motivation for legitimate elemental redundancy.

   e) Discuss the causes of harmful elemental redundancy.

8. a) Design a data structure to illustrate each type of internal structure:
   i. A table of values.
   ii. An internally blocked segment.
   iii. A "natural" ordering of data.

   b) Discuss the considerations of performance in regard to the internal tables.

   c) Discuss the considerations of flexibility in regard to the internal tables.

9. An application with 50 update transactions and 7 data bases is designed so that any activity is recorded on an *audit* data base.

   a) What happens when the audit data base fills up or is unavailable due to an error?

   b) What happens when the transaction rate causes enqueues to occur (by transaction) on the audit data base?

   c) Is it necessary to have only one audit data base?

ELEVEN

TIME-DEPENDENT DATA STRUCTURES

Representing data as it changes over time is a common problem. There are many diverse applications that require tracing the changes of the contents of a data element as time passes. Historical records, future projections, and current status of variables all present problems to the designer to preserve information accurately and efficiently. Although the applications where time-dependent data is found are greatly varied, there is a rather standard way to handle them.

GENERAL FORMS OF TIME-DEPENDENT DATA

Time-dependent data can be represented in two basic forms. It can be organized into *time-span* segments, where each segment has, explicitly or implicitly, a beginning and an ending time associated with the segment. The data elements that are contained within the boundaries of time have the same value for the length of time continuously defined by the begin-

Beg date = June 1, 1976 End date = Aug 13, 1976 Employee status = Trainee Salary = 450/mo Supervisor = J Grey Location = 225 Clark, San Fran., CA	Beg date = Aug 14, 1976 End date = July 5, 1977 Employee status = Clerk Salary = 508/mo Supervisor = S Wright Location = 225 Clark, San Fran., CA	Beg date = July 6, 1977 End date = Dec 31, 1977 Employee status = Clerk Salary = 508/mo Supervisor = B Johnson Location = 225 Clark, San Fran., CA

Figure 11.1 Time-span segments depicting an employee's work history.

ning and ending values of the segment. Figure 11.1 illustrates time-span segments.

Time-dependent data may also be represented in a *discrete* fashion. In this case a segment serves as a "snapshot" of the value of data elements contained within the segment for some point in time. Instead of defining the value of data elements from a starting to a stopping point as a time-span segment does, a discrete segment defines an instant in time at which one or more elements have their value recorded. This is shown in Fig. 11.2.

TIME SPAN REPRESENTATIONS

The data elements that are represented by time-span segments must necessarily be nonvolatile, because a change in the value of any of the data elements within the segment can cause one or two new time-span seg-

Bank acct	= 41102
Date	= Jul 1976
Demand dep	= 43.02
Savings	= 1211.00
Master Charge	= 0.00
Cert dep	= 2000.00
Car loan	= 1531.32

Bank acct	= 41102
Date	= Aug 1976
Demand dep	= 256.13
Savings	= 1211.00
Master Charge	= 26.98
Cert dep	= 2000.00
Car loan	= 1467.69

Bank acct	= 41102
Date	= Sept 1976
Demand dep	= 196.13
Savings	= 1315.42
Master Charge	= 0.00
Cert dep	= 2000.00
Car loan	= 1389.40

Figure 11.2 Discrete representation of data—the data is captured for the closing day of the month. Nothing is said about the data for any other point in time.

ments to be created as well as modifying the existing segment. Figure 11.3 shows how changes affect time-span segments.

Time-span segments should contain closely related elements for another reason as well. As the number of data elements within the segment increases, the probability of change of value of one or more of the elements increases; hence more segments are needed to describe the elements over time. If there are many elements within a segment and those elements are only loosely related to each other, it is probable that there will be many time-span segments representing only short periods of time. If the elements are closely related, changes that occur to one element may also occur to other elements at the same time, so that no new segments will be needed to describe the elements over time, thus reducing the total number of segments needed.

Each time-span segment must have (either explicitly or implicitly) a beginning and an ending unit of time associated with it. The time span is explicitly defined when both units of time are contained within the segment. If either (but not both) a beginning or an ending unit of time is not present in the segment and must be algorithmically derived, the time span is defined implicitly. The unit of time should be appropriate to the data. For example, representing contract dates for a union down to the second would normally be wasteful, as would representing changes in the flight of an airplane in units of days. In general, the unit of measurement should go down to the lowest meaningful level appropriate to the elements within the segment. Needless to say, it must be uniform through-

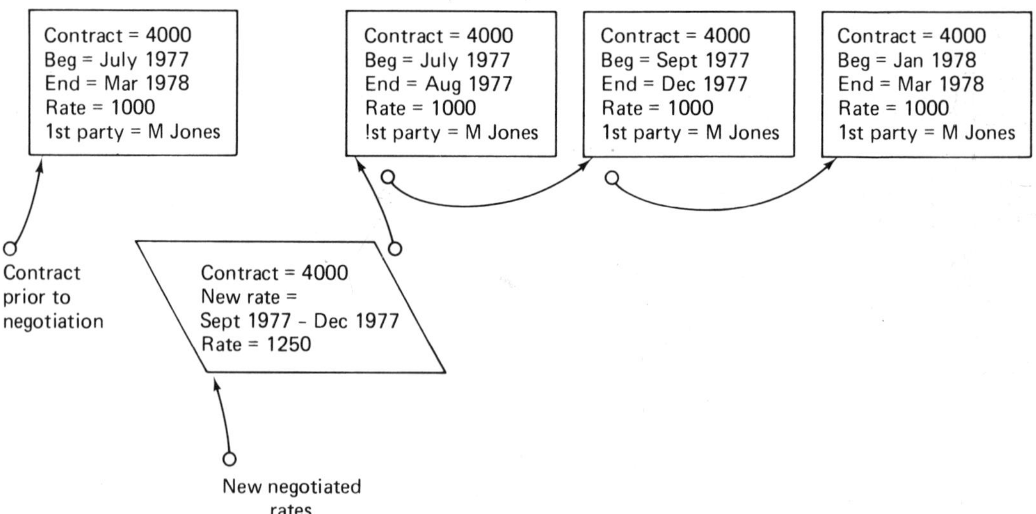

Figure 11.3 When applied to the old rates, more segments are needed to represent the contract.

out all segments of the same type. Typical units of measurement are Julian date, calendar date, absolute date, end of month, hour of day, and so on. The time unit is most convenient when stored in an all-numeric form so that comparisons are straightforward and calculations may be performed. In some cases it may be useful to store the units of time in 9's-complement form. This can be useful when normal update activity to the segments causes overflow to occur.

A time-dependent segment may be at the root or *n*th level of a structure and may have a key of data elements and unit of time or just unit of time. In any case, the low-order portion of the key must be the unit of time. Two examples are shown in Fig. 11.4.

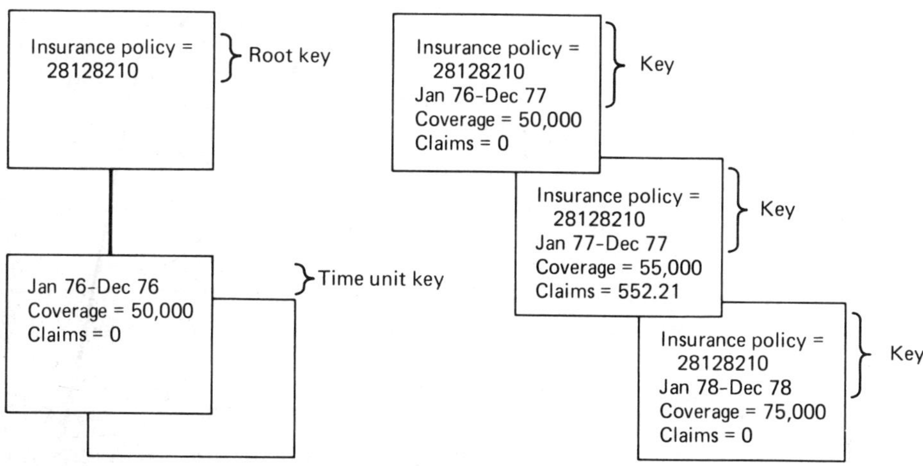

Figure 11.4 The unit of time must be the least significant part of the key of the time-span segment.

In a very few cases it may be useful to store either (but not both) the beginning unit or the ending unit of time in the segment. In this case it is necessary to access two segments to determine what the full time span of the first one is (an implicit span of time). For example, suppose that only the beginning date is stored in a segment. Suppose that the first segment is read, retrieving Beg Date_1. Now the next segment is read, retrieving Beg Date_2. The time span of the first segment is determined to be Beg Date_1 to Beg $\text{Date}_2 - 1$. There are some valid instances where this technique will save space and will not cause inefficient processing. As a matter of course, however, it is not a good practice. This organization of data is shown in Fig. 11.5.

Time-span data may be continuous, noncontinuous, or overlapping as far as the time span defined by two or more segments is concerned. The

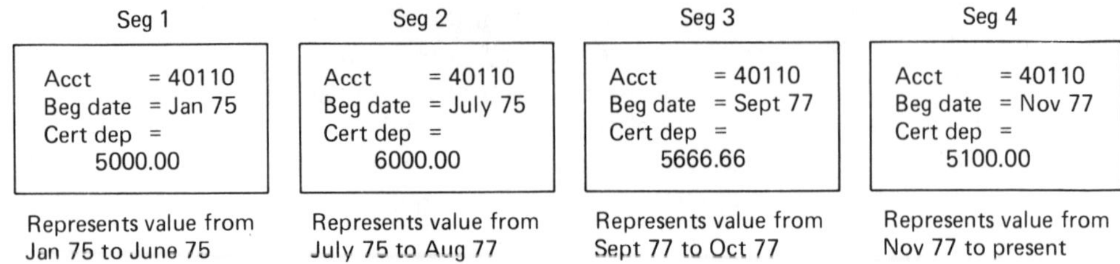

Figure 11.5 To determine the value of a certificate of deposit for December 76 for account 40110, it is necessary to read segment 2 and segment 3. There may, however, be certain operational advantages to structuring segments without both beginning and ending dates.

most useful general form is continuous, but there are occasional cases where noncontinuous or overlapping representations are appropriate. A continuous ordering of data is one where the ending unit of time is one less than the beginning unit of time of the next segment. In a noncontinuous form, this difference is greater than 1. The interpretation of a unit of time is such that the unit (beginning or ending) is contained within the segment, so that where a continuous ordering of segments is called for, no point of time is left undefined (see Fig. 11.6).

It is often useful to allow the beginning or ending unit of time to have a value that can be interpreted as infinity or negative infinity. When an ending unit of time has an "infinite" value, it means that the last segment represents a time span from the beginning date into the future. When the beginning unit of time has a "negative infinite" value, the segment is defined for all previous time up to the ending date of the first segment. Of course, in a continuous ordering of data, no segment may precede a segment beginning with negative infinity or may follow a segment ending in infinity. Using this interpretation, indefinite periods of time may be represented. As an example, see Fig. 11.7.

A necessary part of the algorithm for the building of time-dependent segments is a plan for determining default values when a segment is being created and there is no value entered as part of the instigating transaction. The algorithm may then use a calculated value, a predefined value (default value), or a value found in an adjacent segment (see Fig. 11.8).

Time-dependent ordering of segments is designed for quick and straightforward access, especially when both units of time are specified explicitly in each segment. Searches to determine the value of a given data element at some point in time are easy. Data is thus optimized for retrieval. The complexity arises in the algorithm necessary to build and maintain time-dependent structures. As an example of what one such algorithm might look like (in terms of primitive insert, delete, replace functions), suppose that the designer wished to construct a continuous, nonoverlapping, infinite-ending-date, single-keyed (by beginning date) data base containing

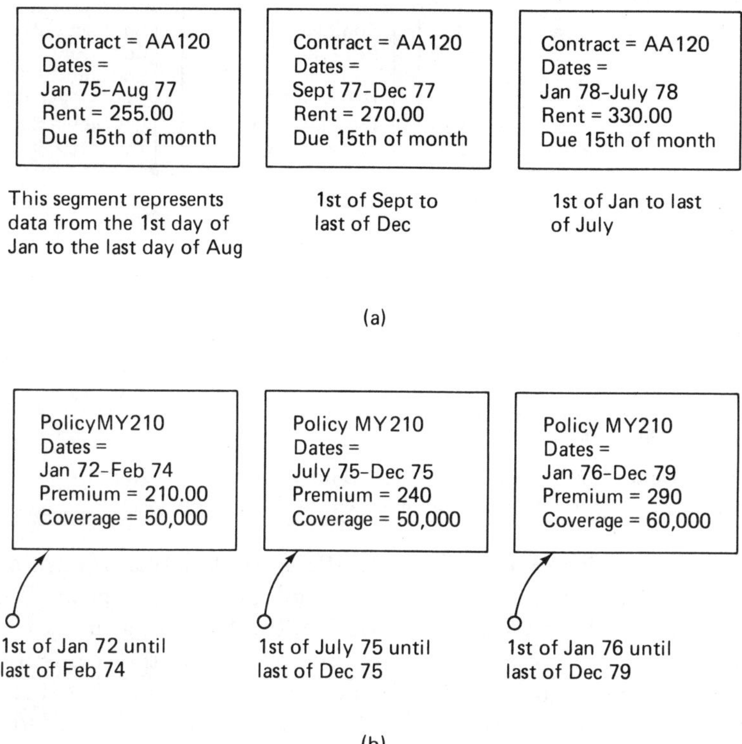

Figure 11.6 (a) This data representation is continued for the time span January 75 to July 78. At any point in time, there is a value and due date. (b) This representation is noncontinuous. The policy lapsed between March 74 and June 75, when it was renewed.

ending date as a nonkeyed data element in the segment. This example represents a common set of criteria for time-dependent data structures. The possibilities of updating a data base record versus a transaction are shown by Fig. 11.9.

In this algorithm the data base is to be scanned sequentially from the

Law no. = US2101	Law no. = US2101	Law no. = US2101	Law no. = US2101
Beg = $-\infty$	Beg = Feb 45	Beg = Apr 49	Beg = Aug 54
End = Jan 45	End = Mar 49	End = Jul 54	End = $+\infty$
Min wage = 0	Min wage = 1.50	Min wage = 1.65	Min wage = 2.10

Figure 11.7 In this continuous, infinitely defined data base, for all occupations under Law US2101, the minimum wage prior to January 45 was 0; the minimum wage from August 54 thereafter was 2.10, and at any time between those dates was defined.

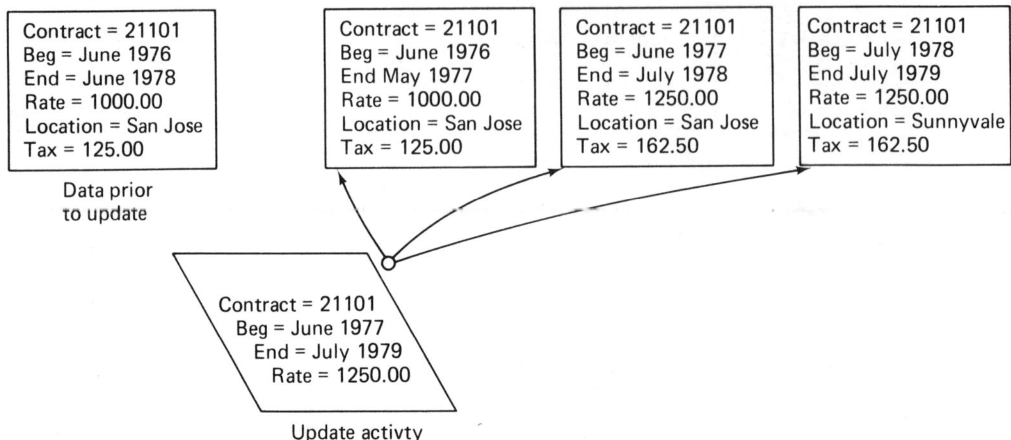

Figure 11.8 Default value for location is Sunnyvale unless otherwise specified. Tax is calculated from a table based on the value-of rate.

earliest segment to the latest (Fig. 11.10). Four variables determine what activity is to transpire: TXBEG, the start time of the transaction; TXEND, the stop time of the transaction; DBBEG, the beginning unit of time in the segment; and DBEND, the ending unit of time in the segment (it will equal all 9's or logical infinity for the last segment). The algorithm makes the assumption that the transaction has been successfully edited and is ready for activity.

As an example of how the algorithm works, consider the very small

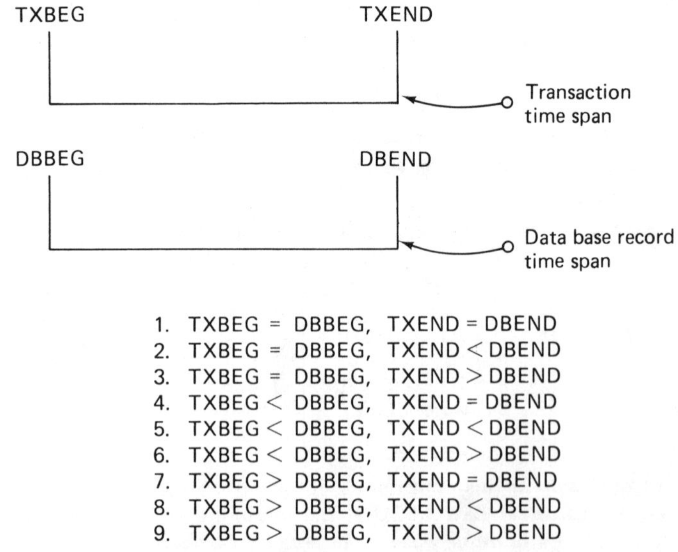

Figure 11.9 The nine possible cases for relationships between a transaction and a data base time-span segment.

[1] Sequentially get a base segment where TXBEG ≤ DBEND, if there are no segments, create a segment using TXBEG, ∞, and stop.

[2] (Case 1) If TXBEG = DBBEG and TXEND = DBEND, change data in segment from transaction, replace, and stop.

[3] (Case 2) If TXBEG = DBBEG and TXEND < DBEND, create a new segment from TXEND+1, DBEND using existing data from segment, change the existing data from transaction, set DBEND to TXEND, replace, and stop.

[4] (Case 3) If TXBEG = DBBEG and TXEND > DBEND, change the existing data from transaction, replace set TXBEG to DBEND+1, and return to [1].

[5] (Case 4) If TXBEG < DBBEG and TXEND = DBEND, create a new segment from TXBEG to DBBEG−1, change the existing data from transaction, replace, and stop.

[6] (Case 5) If TXBEG < DBBEG and TXEND < DBEND, create a new segment from TXBEG to DBBEG 1, change existing data from trasaction, set DBEND to TXEND, replace, create a new segment with the original values of data (at time of retrieval) from TXEND+1 to DBEND, and stop.

[7] (Case 6) If TXBEG < DBBEG and TXEND > DBEND, create a new segment from TXBEG to DBBEG−1, change existing data from transaction, replace, set TXBEG to DBEND+1, and return to [1].

[8] (Case 7) If TXBEG > DBBEG and TXEND = DBEND, set DBEND to TXBEG−1, replace, create a new segment from TXBEG to TXEND using existing data and transaction data, stop.

[9] (Case 8) If TXBEG > DBBEG and TXEND < DBEND, set DBEND to TXBEG−1, replace, create a new segment from TXBEG to TXEND using existing data and transaction data, create a new segment from TXEND+1 to DBEND using original valued in segment, stop.

[10] (Case 9) If TXBEG > DBBEG and TXEND < DBEND, set DBEND to TXBEG−1, replace, create a new segment from TXBEG to TXEND using existing data and transaction data set TXBEG to DBEND+1, and return to [1].

Figure 11.10 Time-Span Data Base Update Algorithm.

data base shown in Fig. 11.11. Suppose that the transaction shown in Fig. 11.12 is run against it. The situation can be depicted as in Fig. 11.13.

An examination of the dates used in the example shows that case 8 of the algorithm applies. The transaction is brought into the program, the data base is read, and a comparison is made using the dates in the data

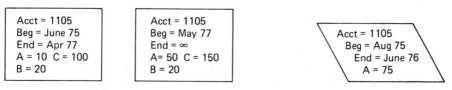

Acct = 1105
Beg = June 75
End = Apr 77
A = 10 C = 100
B = 20

Acct = 1105
Beg = May 77
End = ∞
A= 50 C = 150
B = 20

Figure 11.11

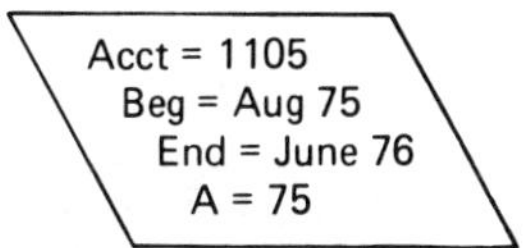

Figure 11.12

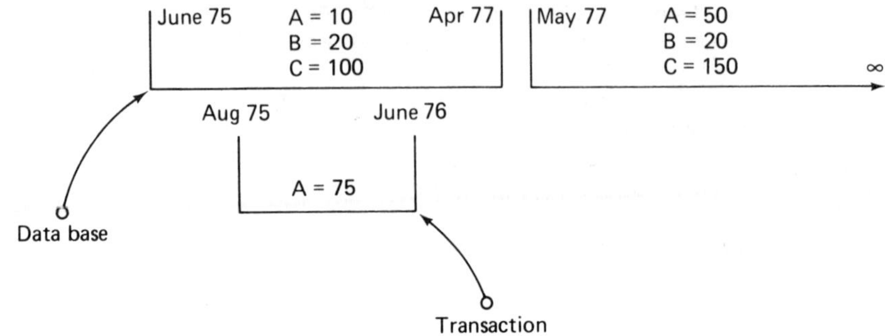

Figure 11.13

base and the transaction. Following the program to case 8, the ensuing activity occurs. The existing segment has its value of DBEND set at TXBEG - 1. Then a new segment is created, spanning time from TXBEG to TXEND, merging the data from the data base and the transaction. In this case the value of A is set to 75 in the newly created time span. Then

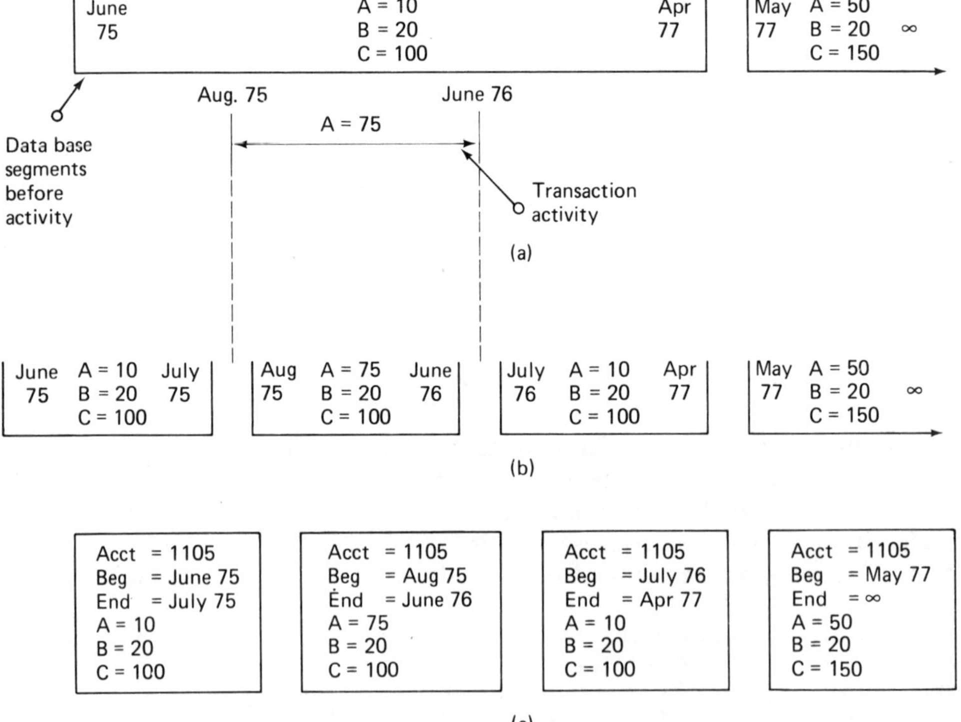

Figure 11.14 (a) Data base prior to activity. (b) Data base after activity. (c) Data base after having been acted upon by transaction and processed by the time-span algorithm.

another segment is created from TXEND + 1 to DBEND using only the values originally found in the data base (see Fig. 11.14).

Data Fracturing As activity occurs, the data base grows in size. When data becomes volatile, the time spans in the data base represent smaller and smaller amounts of time. This can be a problem if the data base is large at the outset. There is a possibility of updates occurring so that an unnecessary fracturing of data occurs. By this it is meant that the values of all data elements of two or more adjacent segments are identical. In this case it is convenient to merge the two segments. Figure 11.15 shows how two segments might be merged.

There are at least three basic approaches to solving the problem of overfractured data segments.

1. Periodically run a batch program that scans the data base looking for this condition. This means that from the time the overfracturing occurs until the batch run is made, there will be an exposure, which, if detected, may be confusing to the user.

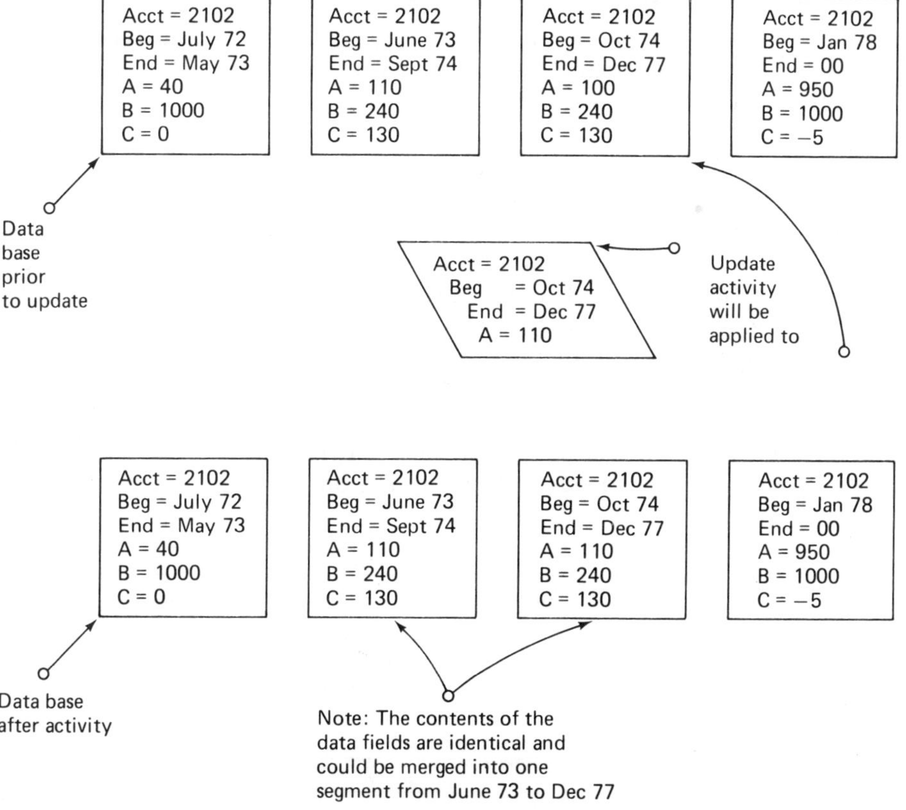

Figure 11.15

2. Check for overfracturing each time an update occurs. This means that at least one extra call to the DBMS must be made each time an update to the data base occurs. Where on-line response is a consideration, this extra bit of overhead may be costly.
3. Ignore overfracturing. Where the data is not volatile, there is only a small chance that overfracturing will occur. If the user is made aware of the possibility of the condition and elects to live with it, then ignoring overfracturing is the cheapest alternative. The data is still correct insofar as the data elements yield the appropriate value for any query for any point in time, even though more segments than necessary are used to store the data.

DISCRETE REPRESENTATION OF DATA

When data is described for only a single instant rather than over a time span, it is discretely represented. It provides, in effect, a snapshot of the value of one or more data elements and says nothing about the data at any time prior to or after the snapshot. Data that is highly volatile is usually maintained discretely. It is often convenient to capture the value of many data elements at the same time. The bulk of the work to be done involves preparing for the snapshot, storing it, and so on, so that the overhead of measuring many variables at the same point in time amounts to a fraction of the total effort. Discretely described data can be created from time span data, but it is not possible to accurately create time span data from discrete data. Figure 11.16 illustrates an example of discretely organized data.

A discrete segment may exist as a root or as a dependent segment, and the unit of time for which the snapshot applies may be all or part of the key of the segment, as in time-span segments. If the key contains data elements other than the unit of time, those fields must precede the time unit, so that the time unit is the least significant portion of the key.

Like time-span data, the unit of time selected should be appropriate to the data elements within the segment. It does not make sense to discretely measure the speed of a car by a monthly unit of time, nor does

Bank closing Feb 1, 1977	Bank closing Feb 2, 1977	Bank closing Feb 3, 1977
Savings = 1,527,243.20	Savings = 1,574,192.46	Savings = 1, 575,019.24
On loan = 561,293.21	On loan = 568,173.21	On loan = 571,241.42
Cert dep = 10,110,211.60	Cert dep = 10,110,211.60	Cert dep = 10,125,630.00
Dem dep = 261,197.32	Dem dep = 274,261.32	Dem dep = 296,562.41
Interest paid = 27.62	Interest paid = 37.42	Interest paid = 18.62
Interest earned = 1,291.45	Interest earned = 1,421.31	Interest earned = 989.61

Figure 11.16 Example of discrete representation of data.

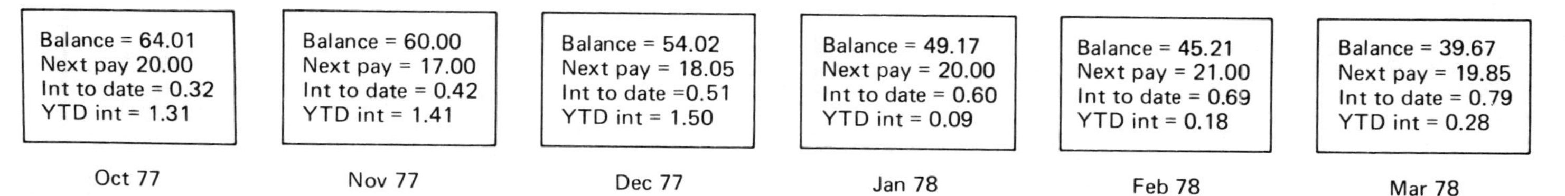

Figure 11.17 Knowing where the segment for October 77 is means that the address of the segment for January 78 can be calculated.

it make sense to measure the amount of money a bank has at a single point in time in milliseconds. The unit of time must be small enough so that meaningful changes in the value of the data elements can be captured and large enough so that huge amounts of meaningless data are not recorded.

The unit of time should be consistent for all segments of the same type. The difference between the units of time may or may not be uniformly distributed. For example, a bank may want a snapshot of its accounts taken on the last working day of the month (a uniform distribution), whereas an industrial engineer doing time and work studies may want to record findings as he or she randomly samples an assembly line (not a uniform distribution).

As a general rule it is not possible to interpolate values of data elements from one snapshot to the next. Suppose that a savings account has $100 in it on March 1 and $110 on April 1. It should not be stated that on March 15 the account had $105 in it. A deposit of $500 may have been made on March 2 and a withdrawal of $490 made on March 25, so the balance on March 15 would be far from $105. In some cases, if specific properties about the data are known, it may be possible to interpolate, but in general interpolation is not possible.

If the unit of time is distributed uniformly, it is possible to treat the data as if it were a table (and, in fact, the data or selected data elements may be brought into storage and accessed like a table). It may be useful to store data elements sequentially without a key. At least one snapshot has a point in time associated with it, so that the snapshot associated with other points in time may be calculated as an offset from the established snapshot. This technique is shown in Fig. 11.17.

A common practice when updating a discrete data base is to add segments sequentially at one end or the other of the string of segments. It is unusual (although certainly very possible) to insert a segment between two segments already in existence. For this reason, updating a discrete data base is a simple task and the data lends itself nicely to sequential processing.

INTERFACING DISCRETE AND TIME-SPAN REPRESENTATIONS

If a time-span ordering of data is continuous, it can be reduced to a discrete representation over the period of time for which it is defined. To do this, the unit of time and the distribution of the discrete organization is selected. The time-span segments are then sequentially scanned, and a discrete segment is created for the appropriate unit(s) of time covered by a given time span.

On the other hand, it is not possible to accurately produce time-span data from discretely ordered data, because the discretely ordered data is not continuous. (Because of the nature of data elements in a discretely ordered segment, it probably would make no sense to measure the elements in a continuous fashion, in any case.) Only in the case where special assumptions can be made about the data elements in a discrete segment can a time-span representation be generated from discrete data.

A surprisingly difficult problem arises when it is necessary to match discrete data and time-span data. (For example, at some point in time, what is the value of a discrete data element and, for that same instant, what is the value of some other data element in a time-span segment?) The difficulty lies not in the simple mechanics of searching the segments, but in not wasting resources in the search. If the problem involves matching the two types of data arrangements for only a single point in time, only two calls to the DBMS are needed. However, if there are many points in time for which information is needed, the number of calls to the DBMS and the amount of processing escalates. Conserving the amount of resources consumed is greatly enhanced by following a few simple rules:

1. Design the data structures so that time-span and discrete data are ordered in the same direction (i.e., from earliest to latest, or vice versa).
2. Arrange the points in time for which information is necessary in a sequential order compatible with the time-span and discrete data bases.
3. Each time a "hit" is made on a time-span segment, store the segment in core so that the next iteration of retrieving a time-span segment will begin with examining the previous segment. In this manner, unnecessary calls to the DBMS will not be made.

AGING TIME-DEPENDENT DATA

Often, time-dependent data loses its utility after some passage of time. When this happens, the data can be aged (removed from the data base). This is usually done by sequentially scanning the data base and removing all segments prior to a predetermined point in time. Care must be taken to maintain the logical consistency of the data base. For instance, if a time-span data base was continuous prior to aging, it should still have the properties of continuity after the aging process has been completed. As the aging program marches through the data base, it may be convenient to have it perform other tasks, such as check for overfracturing or gather statistics about the data base.

It may be useful to create a historical file with the data that is being deleted rather than merely discarding the data. Even if no current use is seen for such a collection of information, the mere fact that the data exists in a neatly time-stamped form means that capturing it will be easy to accomplish and storing it will be cheap.

EXERCISES

1. Design a data base that will hold the monthly wages, taxes paid, and hours worked by an employee of the Jones Corporation. Record all data elements in a single segment type for a given employee for a given month.

   Design a personnel data base for each employee, showing starting date, termination date, job classification, and rate of pay. Build one segment for each job classification/rate of pay.

   Write a program that will calculate average actual wages paid for a job classification. Account for overtime, lost time, sick time, and regular time. The program will process each employee's segment for job classification/rate of pay and will find the corresponding data in the monthly wage data base to calculate the necessary details.

   Assuming these data bases serve no other function:
   a) Should the monthly wages data base be randomized or sequential?
   b) What should the key structure of the personnel data base look like?
   c) Should the monthly wages data base be continuous?
   d) Should the personnel data base be discrete?
   e) Should the personnel data base be continuous?
   f) From a performance standpoint, should the sequencing of the data bases be the same as far as recording time? (That is, should both data bases record their segments in ascending or descending order in terms of time?)
   g) Should the personnel data base contain both the beginning and the ending date in the segment? How much space could be saved by omitting one or the other? How much time would be required?
2. Translate the time span data base update algorithm into a program (PL/1, COBOL, etc.)
3. How would the time-span data base update algorithm change if:
   a) The data base was not continuous?
   b) The last segment of a given time span did not end in infinity?
   c) The data base was sequenced in reverse order (i.e., the first segment retrieved the oldest, the next retrieved the next oldest, etc.)?
   d) The transaction was discrete?
   e) The data base was discrete?

f) The first segment of a given time span started with negative infinity?

4. In a few cases, the effect of overfracturing data bases in a continuous environment can be observed in a discrete environment. Identify conditions under which this might happen and suggest some alternatives. Why isn't overfracturing of data normally a problem in a discrete environment?
5. Design a single data structure in which discrete and continuous representations exist simultaneously. Allow for overlaps of time and discontinuity. Based upon the design, determine the limitations of the structure.

TWELVE

STRUCTURAL AUDITING AND DOCUMENTATION

The usefulness of documentation becomes apparent when a crisis (such as a data base failure) occurs or when design decisions have to be made that affect an existing data structure. Whenever an error occurs that affects a data base (I/O, program error, etc.) and all or part of an application ceases to function, documentation that is accurate, concise, organized, complete, and easily obtainable will greatly expedite the solution of the problem. In such situations, time is of the essence. The first line of defense is usually people who have a working knowledge of the application, but dependency on people has several shortcomings. When a system is large and complex, no one person may know enough about the application, the DBMS, and the host computer system to solve the problem. The system may have changed unbeknown to the person making decisions. In short, human fallibility can compound problems at a time of great vulnerability.

The other time when good documentation is a real asset is when design decisions are to be made. Information about the use and contents of the data base is particularly useful. The criteria pertinent to design decisions as the data base was transformed from the information model to the storage model may also be useful.

Another indirect service documentation can provide is as a learning tool. As a system is being designed, many decisions are made based upon projections. It is a good exercise to review those decisions and projections once the data base is up and running so that inaccurate projections can be identified. Knowing the strengths and weaknesses of past design decisions can greatly enhance an organization's effectiveness by bringing to light areas that need to be considered more carefully.

It is an arduous task to keep documentation current. It is difficult to keep track of certain changes, such as a change in the physical characteristic of a data base or in programs that manipulate the data base. The larger and more complex the system, the more difficult (and important) it is to keep track of changes. Yet in a moment of stress (such as the on-line system being rendered inoperable), those very facts that are difficult to keep current loom as the most important to the solution of the problem.

The following represents a list of certain aspects of data base design that will be useful at one point or another in the life of the system. Some things will be documented once, then never changed, and other information will be quite dynamic. All are central to the task of operationally maintaining a data base and supplying needed information to designers.

1. Native data organization—The native data organization should be documented. All physical data bases and indices that participate in the organization should be identified. Any nonstandard characteristics should be explicitly stated (e.g., secondary index, data set groups, sparse indices, etc.). The person doing the documentation should not assume a prior knowledge of native data organization by the reader. A logging of all changes that affect the data organization should be maintained. It is worthwhile to state why the designer chose the particular native data organization and how it has advantages over other organizations.
2. Randomization—If a randomizer is used, the designer should specify what it is and why it was chosen. Any unusual features should be documented.
3. Physical structuring of the data—A layout of what each segment looks like (down to the finest level) should be kept current. Two views of the data should be maintained: what the programmer sees as he or she accesses the segment through the program and what the segment looks like to the DBMS. This last view includes the data portion of the segment and all other prefix, control, or physically existing overhead. This information will be very useful if recovery must be done external to the utilities of the DBMS. The

number of occurrences of each segment should be kept here. It is useful to keep a record of the projected number of occurrences from the design stage and the actual frequency of occurrence from time to time after the data base is in existence.

4. Blocking of data base records—The proposed and actual blocking of data should be documented. When changes occur, the rationale behind the changes should be noted. This information is useful for future data base tuning and to look back and tell how successful past tuning efforts were.
5. Physical data set names—The actual names of the data bases should be documented. If there are multiple copies with different names, they should be identified and the differences between the copies should be noted. If there is an aging scheme or substitution, dummy, test, or initialized data bases that are all compatible, that should be recorded.
6. Data base size—The amount of space allocated for the data base, how it is used, and which segments use which space should be documented. As changes are made, they should be logged and the reason for the change should be registered. A periodic statistical profile of the size and general shape of the data base may be very helpful for the tuning and design effort.
7. Narrative of the meaning and function of a data base—A description of the function of the data base from the application standpoint should be included. Especially interesting will be the relation of data within the data base: what is critical, what is not, and so on. The information may be useful to the person doing data recovery or prioritization of resource allocation.
8. Description of the relationship to other data bases—Both implicit and explicit relationships should be described. The precise form of explicit relationships should be spelled out (e.g., symbolic or direct pointers, prefix information, etc.). The nature of the implicit relationship and the algorithm that binds the data should be clearly stated.
9. Structural changes—All changes should be recorded. The form of the data before and after the change may be of interest to the analyst gathering information about the evolution of the data base. The motivation for the change should also be recorded.
10. Recovery procedures—Of particular interest to operations and data management personnel responsible for keeping a system on-line are recovery procedures. Each of the tools that is available for recovery and has been tested should be documented. It is very important that these procedures be available and up to date. It should

be noted which situations require which procedures. There is normally a wide variation in approaches to recovery, based upon the criticality of data, sophistication of the user, amount of preparation made for recovery, and other factors. It is difficult to standardize procedures because of these differences.

It is also useful to document each recovery problem after it has happened. What caused the problem, how it was circumvented or solved, any mistakes during recovery should be noted. Keeping track of the past recovery problems helps in two areas: (a) it gives a clue to the data analyst as to what might be wrong when a problem has to be solved, and (b) it can be compiled into a list with other recovery problems to alert management of difficulties.

11. Update information—A cross reference of segments in the data base and programs that access them is useful. This function may be provided by a data dictionary if one is being used. This information is especially useful for programmers as they debug a problem and for designers as they determine the impact of changes to the system.
12. Schedule of data base usage and availability—Operations benefit by carefully planning the schedule of data base activity. Data management also benefits if a decision must be made quickly concerning the data base. The manager can better plan strategy knowing the requirements of the data base.
13. Archival listings—Certain listings are appropriate to the documentation of a data base. Initial allocation, initial loading of the data base, the most current activity against the data base, and current statistics regarding the profile of the data base are always useful to have available for a number of reasons.
14. System costs and miscellaneous data—Including the costs of running the system, response time, the volume of transactions, the transaction rate, computer usage, and so on. This information is of interest to management during the life of the system and to the designer in the planning stages of other systems. This data should be collected on a periodic basis and charted so that trends can be identified. Another set of figures of interest is in the comparison between the projections of the system designers and how they were realized. Any large discrepancies will be worth investigating so that the same mistake need not be repeated in other designs.

It is also worthwhile collecting information appropriate for tuning on a regular basis even if a tuning effort is not on the immediate horizon. At such time when tuning becomes an issue, there will be a backlog of information available to determine what a "good" day and a "bad" day look like.

15. User interface—An up-to-date list of appropriate user interfaces should be made. The hours of availability and phone numbers should accompany the list.

STRUCTURAL AUDITING

The programs used to perform structural audits may be vendor-supplied and/or tailored to an application by a user program. There are disadvantages and advantages to both approaches. Vendor-supplied programs are readily available and (hopefully) free of errors. They may take advantage of special system features that may not be available to the application. Their disadvantage lies in the fact that they are inflexible. If a vendor-supplied program does not serve the particular needs of an application, there may be no suitable way to modify the program. Also, the vendor's program may perform time-consuming functions that are not wanted or needed.

The advantage of a user-written structural audit program is that it can be tailored to meet a specific need. It should not be written with any great amount of generality. Since the specifications are application-dependent, they can only completely meet the needs of the designer. The program can be modified over time as changes occur. The problem with user-written structural audit programs is that they require resources to write, debug, and maintain. If the program is written internal to the DBMS, certain structural features that are masked by the DBMS may not be auditable. If they are written external to the DBMS, the audit program is subject to change every time a new release of the DBMS is applied—certainly a fragile situation. However, writing a structural audit program external to the DBMS allows the programmer total freedom to audit all aspects of the data base.

AUDITING STRUCTURAL INTEGRITY

Auditing the structural integrity of a data base validates the mechanical components of the data base. A structural audit is especially useful when a data base malfunctions due to an I/O error, software error, and so on. It may also be useful as a periodic check to determine the usability of a data base and certain physical characteristics, such as degree of disorganization of the data base. Some of the criteria of a structural audit are:

1. Validation of all prefix information (pointers, counters, etc.)—Specifically, the audit program should determine if there is a

pointer to a segment that does not exist or if a segment exists that should be pointed to but is not. The usual technique is to extract all segments that point to another segment, extract all segments being pointed to, and match them. All pointer types should be checked. This includes pointers that support the physical structure of the data and internal pointers that support explicit relationships. The program(s) will be severely affected by a large data base, because the volume of data and the way it is handled will necessarily be time-consuming.

2. Selective audit—It may be useful to have a program that will audit only a specific set of pointers, a specific key, or a range of keys in the data base. The usefulness of this program depends upon the level of confidence the data manager has in manipulating the data base. Such a program unquestionably executes more efficiently for a specific operation than does a generalized program, but may miss an error that exists in the data base when the error is beyond the scope of the program. Where the data manager is very experienced at data base recovery, a selective audit program can be a very effective tool.
3. Physical verification—The physical characteristics of a data base may be checked (such a check probably has very limited applicability). This entails verifying for consistency the physical characteristics of prefixes, segments, records, and blocks. This type of check may uncover an I/O error or logic error.
4. Data base statistics—Whenever it is necessary to scan the entire data base, it is usually inexpensive to keep track of information uncovered incidentally, such as percent of free space left in the data base, number of records in overflow, how many segments are in the data base, how they are distributed, what segments are logically deleted but still physically present, and so on. These numbers are useful to data management in determining when to reorganize a data base or in deciding when to allocate more space for the data base. Other information that may be useful is the length of pointer chains and index organization.
5. Implicit relationships—Implicit relationships that exist between data bases or within the same data base are entirely supported by application programs and as such are highly vulnerable to error. Auditing an implicit relationship must be done by a user-written program, not a vendor program. The structural impact of an implicit relationship can be as important as an explicit relationship or may not be as critical, depending upon the data involved. The audit program is based upon the algorithm that binds the data together.

EXERCISES

1. In light of the requirements for documentation of an application, what services can a data dictionary provide? Given the current state of the art, what role do data dictionaries provide? Why is there a discrepancy between the potential of a data dictionary and the actuality? What suggestions for improvement can you make?
2. Given the following criteria, define the area of responsibility between data administration and applications:
   a) On-line system availability.
   b) Data base design.
   c) Data base recovery procedures.
   d) Data base tuning.
   e) Selection of a DBMS.
   f) Prioritization within the DBMS.
   g) Response–time optimization.
   h) Batch window availability.
   i) Application design review.
   j) User system effectiveness.
3. Data bases should be audited for more than structural integrity. Suggest some of these criteria and how they can be accomplished. To what extent are they tied to an application?
4. How should archival listings (or copies) of data bases be stored? How long should they be stored? Who should have access to them? What kind of archival backup should be done? Should archival data bases be used in a "disaster" situation? Discuss archival data bases based upon these questions.
5. Given an existing data base application, in a noncritical environment, force an error (e.g., by loading data past the physical capacity of storage) and practice backup procedures. Pay careful attention to:
   a) Length of time needed in backup.
   b) Data bases affected.
   c) Timing considerations (e.g., proper backout of offending transaction).
   d) Data integrity exposures.
   e) Impact on on-line system.
   f) Potential for operator error.
   g) Impact on user's environment.

THIRTEEN

QUERIES, REPORTS, AND DATA STRUCTURES

Information is normally taken from a data base in one of two forms: a query or a report. A *query* may access the entire data base, a subset of the data base, or a single segment in the data base. It is usually done by an end user or a programmer and designed to be easily accomplished. Queries tend to be nonrepetitive in nature. A *report* normally uses all or large amounts of a data base and involves sequential processes and sorting of data that has been extracted from the data base. It is normally run on a scheduled basis or on request as a production function. Reports are repetitive in nature. Each type of information-gathering process has its own measures of success.

QUERIES

A query is designed to be easy for the user to accomplish and, in relation to reports, performs a minimum of calls to the DBMS. A query can be for on-line or batch data bases. An on-line query may search across several data base records or be keyed to a single record. When it is directed at a single unit of information, it is called a *retrieval*.

The query may be preprogrammed or not. When it is preprogrammed, it can be accomplished with a transaction or with a query language. In this case the user enters some parametric information that is translated into an intelligent gathering and display of data. A data base can be optimized for processing a predefined query if the major function of the data base is so suited. Some of the methods of tailoring a data base to suit a planned set of on-line inquiries includes organizing search keys in an advantageous manner, organizing many data types into the same segment type, and simplifying the data structure.

The query should be limited in scope insofar as the interface between the user and the data base is concerned. This usually means accessing a single segment or a limited number of segments for each set of parameters entered by the user. It may entail a limited search by key range or other criteria. It does not involve a complete scan of the data base or searching for a segment that cannot quickly be located by a key or an index.

REPORTS

Reports in a data base environment are best done off-line. Systems analysts and designers who are migrating from batch systems to on-line systems must be weaned from the practice of designing long sequential reports that are derived from an on-line data base. In an on-line environment they should reshape their thinking from the sequential mode into the interactive, direct-access mode. On-line data bases will incur scheduling and other resource contention problems when sequential activity over large amounts of data is required.

Reports require a scanning of all or sections of the data base. Generally, these reports are predefined so that application programs can be written to support them. Reports typically involve accumulations, lists, subtotaling, key-change breaks, and processing data in an order different from its physical sequence. Such processing requires an extraction of data and rearrangement into the desired order. Obviously, an extract is not necessary if the data physically exists in the same order as required by the report.

Since the formats of reports are predefined and do not need to be recompiled for each execution, and since it is expensive (both in terms of CPU cycles and by occupying a resource exclusively) to access a data base for an extended period of time, it makes sense to limit the number of extract programs that will be run against a data base (Fig. 13.1).

Some of the other generalizations that hold true for reports are that logical chains that exist in the data base should not be followed if possible

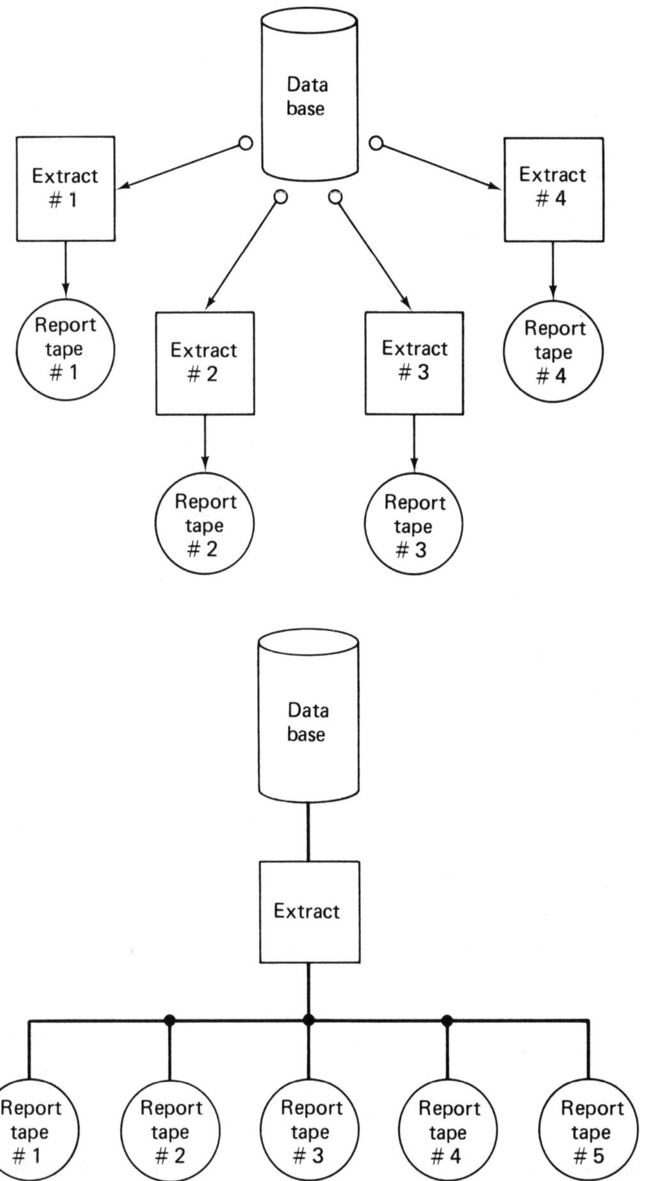

Figure 13.1 It is usually a good practice to extract sequential report data sets from one program, not many.

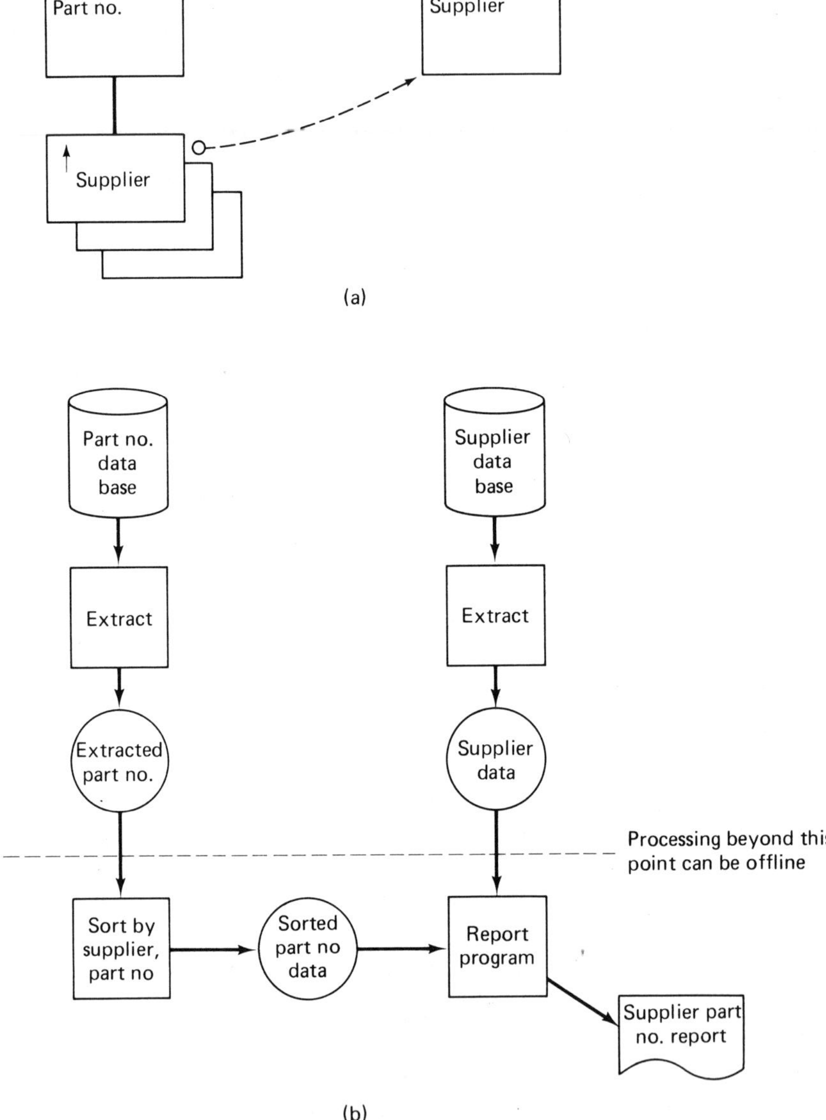

Figure 13.2 (a) For large amounts of data, it is expensive to extract data using explicit relationships. (b) Matching pointer chains by extracting data, then sorting and merging, is cheaper than producing reports by following pointer chains.

when extracting data. This is so because it is expensive to follow pointers, and the chain can be reconstructed cheaply by a sequential pass of the data and an accompanying sort and match program (see Fig. 13.2).

It is usually not a good practice to build too many implicit relationships among data elements to accommodate reports. In unusual circumstances this may be acceptable or in the case of a periodic "sweep" program, data relationships of this type may be justified. Accumulating or relating large amounts of data leads to inflexible data structures and wasted updating resources.

The disadvantage of building implicit data relationships at updating time is that the number of calls to the DBMS is increased substantially, unnecessary space is used, and program complexity is increased. The advantage is that when it is done and an update occurs, all related data elements contain valid values. The advantage of maintaining an implicit relationship by a program external to the updating process is that it is done independently and can be put off-line. The disadvantage of an external algorithmic supported implicit relationship is that the data must be related each time it is used, not each time it changes. Furthermore, the data does not explicitly exist anywhere.

A third approach for noncritical data is to maintain the implicit relationship on a periodic basis (nightly, weekly, etc.). This may not impact on-line performance but does mean that for some elements for some period of time there is an incorrect relationship. The sweep program is run and corrects the relationship at a convenient time. These approaches are shown by Fig. 13.3.

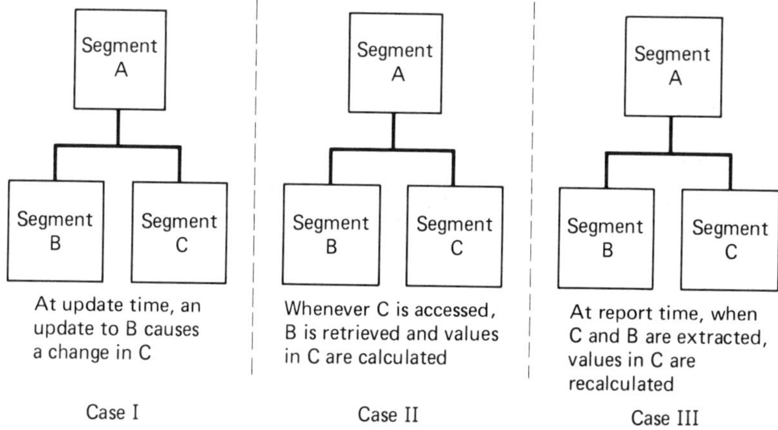

Figure 13.3 Maintenance of an Implicit Relationship. Case I—Values in B and C are always correct, but unnecessary I/O may be done. Case II—Values in C are recalculated only when accessed, causing unnecessary I/O when multiple access is made to the same segment. Case III—No unnecessary I/O is done but values in C may be synchronized with values in B for all occurrences of B and C.

DATA STRUCTURES FOR QUERIES AND REPORTS

Data structures that are designed for queries should be flat, simple structures. This enables application programs to handle less structural logic and places fewer levels of segmentation between the user doing the inquiry and the data needed for retrieval. It may be a good idea to have a few appropriate elements of redundant data, but it is usually a symptom of poor design when large amounts of data are redundant.

In the case where data structures are being built for queries that are not predefined, it is a good practice to carry an excess of data elements, especially those that might be needed for control purposes. The strategy is to sacrifice a little space in the data base to prepare for future unknown needs. Data structures for reporting purposes should be simplified, as in the case of structures optimized for query, but can still contain sophisticated substructures. Usually, report requirements are reasonably well defined early in the life of the design of the system. For this reason, data structures supporting reports are not subjected to the same degree of risk of change as data structures that support queries. Also, because extracts can be done off-line (and therefore have minimum impact), structures supporting reports are not as fragile as those supporting other functions.

QUERY LANGUAGES

There are several query languages designed to extract and display information from a data base. The biggest selling point of a query language is the ease of usage and consequent savings of programmer time. A brief description of some languages and their strengths and weaknesses follows:

1. GIS/VS—IBM's GIS/VS is a query language that has evolved from its early origins as a report writer. GIS operates in an IMS environment, both batch and on-line. GIS's strength is its report-writer capabilities, although it can be used for data retrieval on-line. GIS is versatile and flexible. The major weakness of GIS is its inability to be controlled in the on-line environment. Also, users claim that GIS appears to be more of a high-level PL/1 than a user-oriented language.
2. MARK IV/Query DC—Informatic's MARK IV/Query DC language can operate in a sequential mode or in conjunction with several data bases. MARK IV is a report-writer language. Its architecture is such that a data base (or data bases) is scanned once and an extract is performed for every identifiable criterion. The extracted data is sorted and merged to produce the desired reports. The on-

line counterpart of MARK IV/Query DC is a user-oriented language that is translated into MARK IV code, and then is assembled and executed.

MARK IV is a proven product with a stable track record. Its weakness is that in the on-line mode, it is not as sophisticated as it might be and is somewhat limited in scope compared to GIS.

3. QBE (Query-by-Example)—A relative newcomer is the language created by Zloof—QBE. QBE is oriented toward the end user and is easy to learn to use. The data is supported by a relational model. One interesting feature is that no programming is necessary. Criticism of QBE is that (currently) it runs under a limited set of software (VM-CMS), its handling of large data bases is suspect, and many people view it as an untried product. With these criticisms in mind, QBE offers solutions to problems that other languages have.

Other inquiry languages aimed at quick retrievals are ASI-ST, by Applications Software, and INQUIRY/IMS, by CGA Associates. These languages typically have limited report-writer capability but can access selected amounts of data quickly. These languages serve ad hoc requests best.

DATA BASES FOR QUERY LANGUAGES

It is common practice to produce a subset of a data base for use exclusively by a query language. This approach provides the capability of using data without disturbing them in their original form and means that the original data base does not have to be manipulated whenever a request is made. There are some fallacies in depending entirely upon extracted data. The data is not truly on-line: that is, after it is extracted, any further updates to it will not be reflected until the next extract occurs. Also, an extract usually copies some portion of the data—all or several selected segment types or all segments within some key range. If a need for data not covered by the extract arises, there is a conflict. Either a new and/or expanded extract must be performed on the data and must be retrieved from the original source, which may be awkward if the source is on-line or is otherwise allocated.

Another problem arises in using query languages when multiple data bases contribute to a single query. This is shown by Fig. 13.4. It may be difficult to coordinate the data retrieval from the different sources, especially where implicit relationships are involved. Query languages may be more difficult to use in this situation than are native languages.

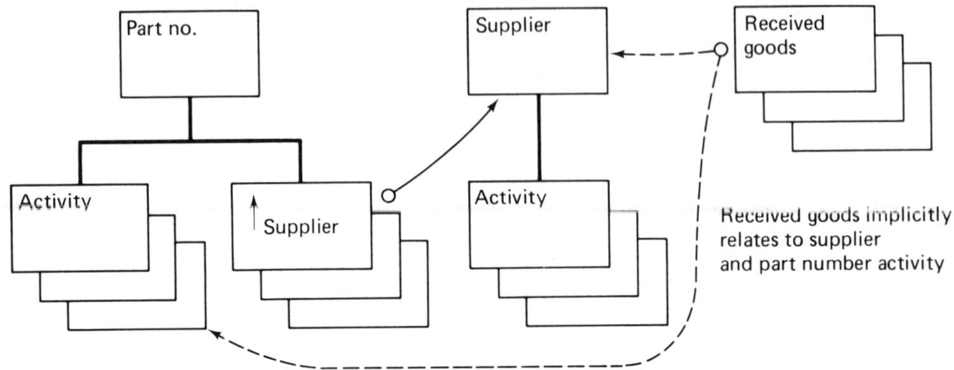

Figure 13.4 Retrieving data across multiple data bases can involve complex logic.

DATA BASE ENQUEUE PROBLEMS

When queries run against large amounts of data, it is possible to encounter enqueue problems. An *enqueue* problem occurs when one program accesses a segment and other programs want to access the segment concurrently and cannot because of integrity considerations. Depending upon the sophistication of the DBMS, the problem may be superficial or profound. The data designer can bypass the problem entirely in some cases by separating unlike data types into different data bases. This technique is illustrated by Fig. 13.5.

The problem of enqueue is particularly acute for queries that reach across many segments. The chances of an enqueue problem rise quickly as the scope of the search increases.

INDICES AND REPORTS

There is a temptation for the novice designer to use indices to produce a secondary sequencing of data for reports. In nearly every instance this is costly and should be avoided. Indices that resequence a data base are best suited for single on-line retrievals or limited entry into the data base. The efficiencies involved are shown by comparing the amount of I/O (direct and sequential) that is necessary to produce a report. Compare the two cases discussed in Fig. 13.6.

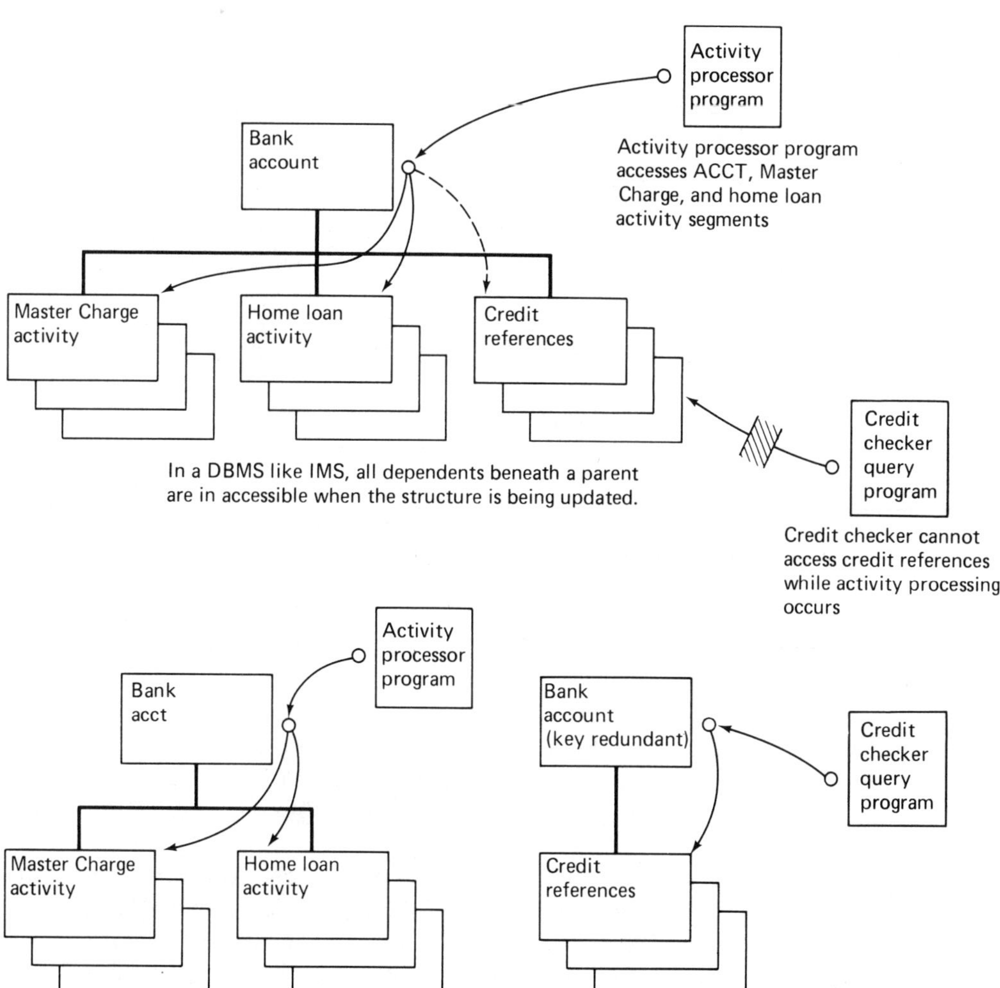
Activity
processor
program
Bank
account
Activity processor program
accesses ACCT, Master
Charge, and home loan
activity segments
Master Charge
activity
Home loan
activity
Credit
references
Credit
checker
query
program
In a DBMS like IMS, all dependents beneath a parent
are in accessible when the structure is being updated.
Credit checker cannot
access credit references
while activity processing
occurs
Activity
processor
program
Bank
acct
Bank
account
(key redundant)
Credit
checker
query
program
Master Charge
activity
Home loan
activity
Credit
references
By separating (physically) the data bases, the designer has averted a potential
enqueue conflict.

Figure 13.5

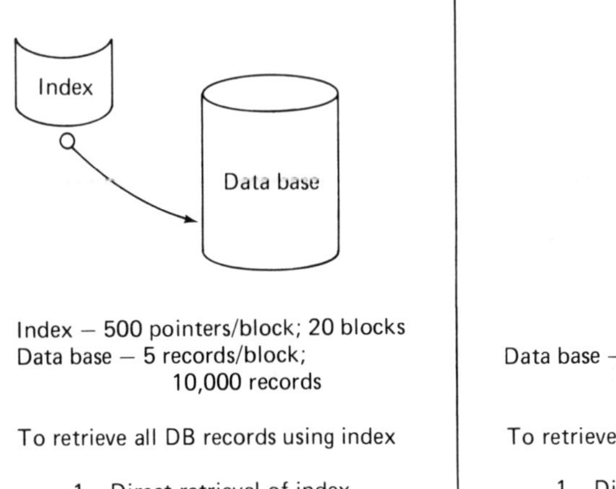

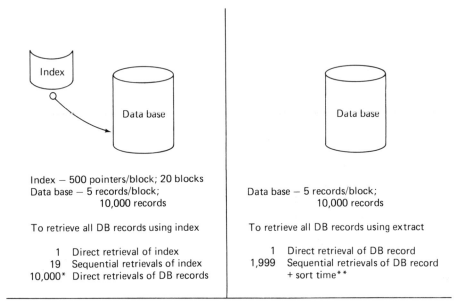

Figure 13.6

Furthermore, the energy needed to support the index at updating time is not calculated. Adding in maintenance time further tips the balance toward not using an index for reporting purposes.

EXERCISES

1. Why should queries be nonrepetitive in nature?
2. What general classification of data leads itself to queries? To reports? Why is there a difference? Should that difference impact the design of data?
3. What features does a DBMS have to prevent reports from being done on-line? What features does a DBMS have to protect itself when queries are external on-line (e.g., how can the DBMS prevent a query from executing too long while on-line)? Is there a graceful way for the DBMS to stop a runaway query?
4. Create two data bases connected with a logical twin chain with an average of 100 twins on the chain. Write two reports, one that accesses all the data in both data bases using the twin chain, and one that reads both data bases independently, producing two sequential data sets and then sorting and matching the two data sets together to produce the same report. Analyze the total amount of CPU and I/O necessary to accomplish the task.

FOURTEEN

EXAMPLES OF DESIGN—DATA BASE VERSUS LIST MATCH PROGRAM

There is great usefulness in examining problems associated with data base design as they happen in practice. Issues and questions that may not have been previously considered will surface as the problem is solved. Observing the problem-solving process in its entirety rather than a piece at a time ties together the different sets of considerations appropriate to recognition, analysis, and resolution of a problem. Often, the novice learns more when theory meets practice than from many passive observations of "how to" lectures.

The following example of a problem in an IMS batch-processing environment is taken from a real application. It illustrates the recognition of a problem, suggests several solutions, and analyzes the disadvantages and advantages of each solution. Two general approaches (with minor variations) are discussed: one a natural, intuitive approach and the other a rather awkward, unintuitive approach. A careful analysis shows that for a general solution the intuitive approach is very costly. The unintuitive approach for most conditions is shown to use the fewest resources.

PROBLEM DESCRIPTION

A program in a batch environment is to be written in which a data base with a secondary index is to have massive sequential updates made against it. The secondary index points to a second-level segment (Fig. 14.1).

A list structure of data internal to the application program is created so that its key has as its least significant order the value of the key of the index (i.e., the ordering of the internal list is by list key/index key); see Fig. 14.2.

There are 250,000 index entries and there are approximately 250,000 first-level segments. There is an average of one second-level segment per first-level segment and the median value is 3, so there are many first-level segments with no dependents. There are an average of five third-level segments per second-level segment.

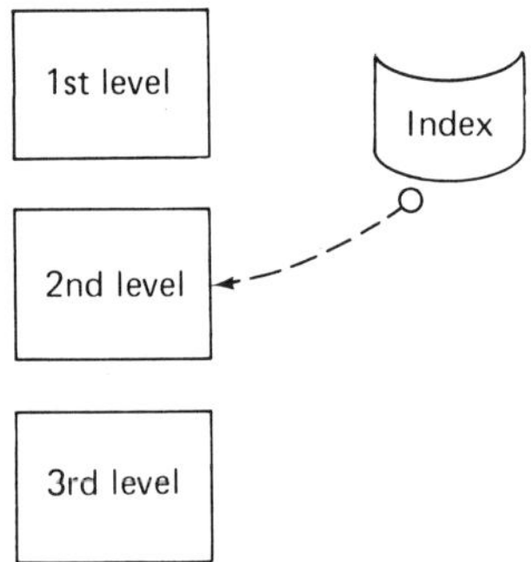

Figure 14.1 The basic form of the data base consists of three levels with an index pointing into the second level.

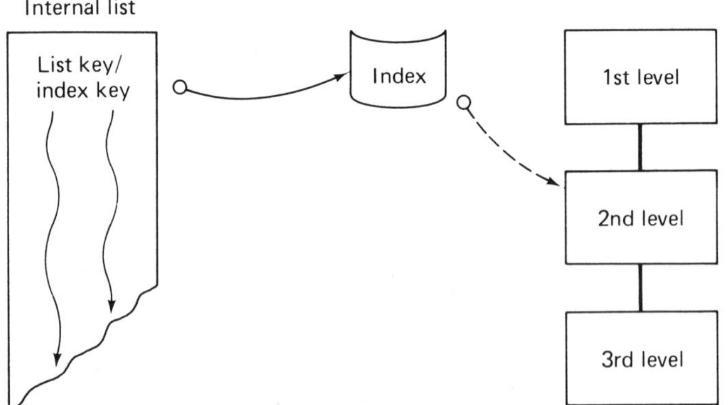

Figure 14.2 A list of all items needed to be updated is created internally, linking the list to the index of the second level.

The volume of update activity against the data base has a wide variation. When an update is to be done, an entry is made into the internal list structure. In most cases the list contains a maximum of 2000 entries with an average of 500. Occasionally (during the worst case), the list contains 225,000 entries. The difference between the worst case and the average case is very large. The worst case cannot be dismissed as an infrequently occurring event. It is a predictable, regularly occurring phenomenon.

When an update is to occur, an entry is made into the list which indicates that activity must occur to segments at the first, second, and third levels. Multiple segments at the second and third level may require update.

ORIGINAL DESIGN

The original approach to the design was done by a person unfamiliar with the handling of data bases or the trade-offs involved with designing programs that utilize data structures. The main consideration of the designer was "will my design work?" not "how well will my design work?"

The original approach (see Fig. 14.3) was to:

1. Sequentially travel down the index.
2. Using the index found in Step 1, search for it in the list.

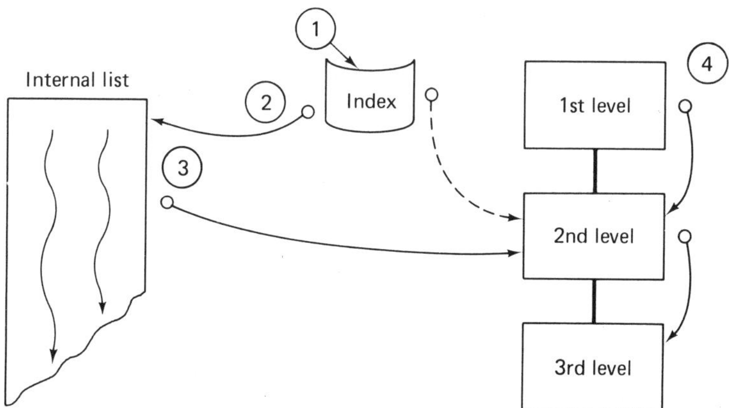

Figure 14.3 Original processing specifications: 1. Sequentially retrieve an index segment. 2. Using the value retrieved from the index, search the list. 3. If found, retrieve the appropriate second-level segment. 4. Using data from the second level, retrieve the first level segment, then all the second- and third-level segments beneath it. 5. Replace segments after update.

3. If found in Step 2, retrieve the second-level segment via the pointer from the index into the second level.
4. Using the second-level segment found in Step 3, use the physical parent pointer to locate the first-level segment that is the parent.
5. Retrieve all second- and third-level segments beneath the root.
6. Perform the changes and replace the segment.

The interesting thing about the original solution is that it works at all however complex and circuitous. As long as there is a small number of entries in the internal list structure, this solution is not (operationally) too bad. Once the list grows to any size at all, the glaring inefficiencies of the program become apparent. A startled programmer found that in the first large test case the program ran for 7½ hours, and this was not representative of the worst case. In the test case only 20,000 or so entries were made onto the list. Rightfully so, the programmer worried about how long the program would take when more than 200,000 entries would be made to the list, as he knew would occasionally happen.

The programmer expressed concern and it was decided to analyze the program with a data base designer (up to this point the system had been developed without benefit of review by data base designers). The following represents some of the ideas discussed.

INTUITIVE APPROACH

The review team decided to simplify matters by comparing the list and the data base to a list of words that needed to be looked up in a dictionary. Intuitively, it seemed logical to take the list and look up each word on the list. This idea is especially appealing if there are not many entries on the list. This would be the equivalent of sequentially searching the internal list of data and directly accessing the data base for each entry in the list. The implementation of this idea would involve a similar logical path as did the original plan. In fact, the only difference is that the index is not read sequentially (Fig. 14.4).

1. Sequentially process the list, entry by entry.
2. Using data from the list, access the index.
3. Using data from the index, access the second-level segment.
4. Now access all three levels of segmentation.
5. Perform the changes and replace the segment.

As long as there are not too many entries in the list, the intuitive approach is acceptable. However, an analysis of what really takes place when I/O occurs shows that for many entries in the list the intuitive approach is a poor performer.

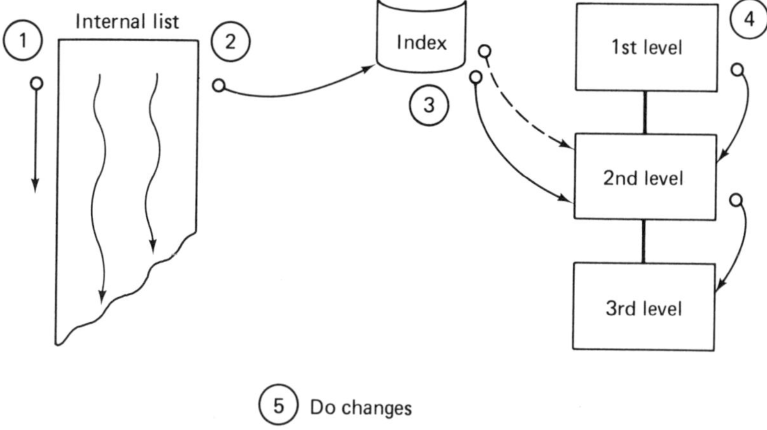

Figure 14.4 Intuitive approach.

I/O activity will occur about 99% of the time the index is accessed. It will also occur about 99% of the time the index is used to point to the second-level segment, and will occur a smaller percentage (e.g., 20% of the time) when all three levels are accessed. If there are 1000 entries in the list, there will be 990 I/O events used to access the index, 990 I/Os to access the second-level segment, and roughly 200 more to access the three levels in the data base. It is clear that as the number of entries in the list increases, the number of I/Os grows proportionally.

UNINTUITIVE APPROACH

Another approach was suggested. Using the analogy of a list of words and a dictionary, it would normally not make sense to sequentially search down the dictionary, scanning each word in the dictionary, then searching to see if that word was in the list. Under real-world conditions, such a technique would be very tedious. Thus, if the technique was applied to the computerized environment intuitively it would seem to be a very poor approach. However, the economies of the real world are not the same as the economies of the computer. The technique amounted to sequentially reading the root segment, then all second-level segments. Upon retrieving a second-level segment, the list was scanned to see if the entry existed in it. If the entry did exist, the third-level segments were read and processed. The steps are (see Fig. 14.5):

1. Sequentially access all the root segments and second-level segments.
2. Scan the list.

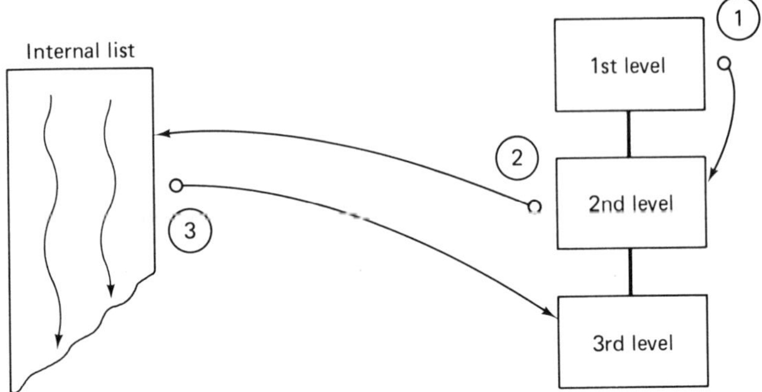

Figure 14.5 Unintuitive approach.

3. If on the list, retrieve the third-level segments.
4. Perform the change and replace the segments.

Some interesting facts come to light when analyzing the I/O done in the unintuitive case, especially in the worst case, where some 225,000 entries exist in the list. Sequentially accessing the data base (for all segments) costs roughly 5000 I/Os, because the roots exist in blocks with an average 50 root second- and third-level segments per block. Scanning the list requires some work, but not as much energy as an I/O. When a hit occurs, the third-level segment will be read. Because of the internal arrangement of data, an I/O will occur only about 10% of the time when it is necessary to read the third-level segment. In the worst case there will be 25,000 hits on the list, so about 22,500 I/Os will occur.

A comparison of the two approaches (the intuitive and the unintuitive) points out the expense (in terms of I/O) of each method (Fig. 14.6).

Intuitive approach		Unintuitive approach	
Average case —			
1,000 reads—index	990 I/Os	250,000 reads root, second level	5,000 I/Os
1,000 reads—second level	990 I/Os	1,000 hits, third-level read	100 I/Os
1,000 reads—three levels	200 I/Os		
	2,180 I/Os		5,100 I/Os
Worst case —			
225,000 reads index	222,750 I/Os	25,000 reads root, second level	5,000 I/Os
225,000 reads second level	222,750 I/Os	225,000 hits, third level	
225,000 reads, third levels	45,000 I/Os		
	490,500 I/Os		27,500 I/Os

Figure 14.6

In the average case the intuitive approach performs more than twice as fast as the unintuitive approach. But in the worst case, the unintuitive approach is far superior, to the extent that the intuitive approach should never be used for processing large volumes of update.

OTHER CONSIDERATIONS

It is obvious that there could be some savings made by sorting the list prior to processing. In the intuitive case, a sort by secondary index key would save considerable I/O when the list is matched against the index, since a sequential search could be used rather than a random search. In the unintuitive case the sort would allow the scanning of the list to be done sequentially so that processing time would be saved (no I/Os would be saved).

Another type of modification that might be considered would be the altering of the data structure. In reality this was not considered, because other applications required the data to remain in its current form. A change that was considered but was rejected was to put some data in the root segment that would have allowed the index to point to the root, not the second level (Fig. 14.7). This was rejected because (1) the change would add a new level of complexity, (2) it would not buy that much, (3) it would be awkward to add an element to the root level, and (4) extra processing would be involved to keep the new element up to date.

A more fundamental change would have been to create two data bases—one with the given root and a pointer segment beneath it and the other data base containing the second- and third-level segments now as their

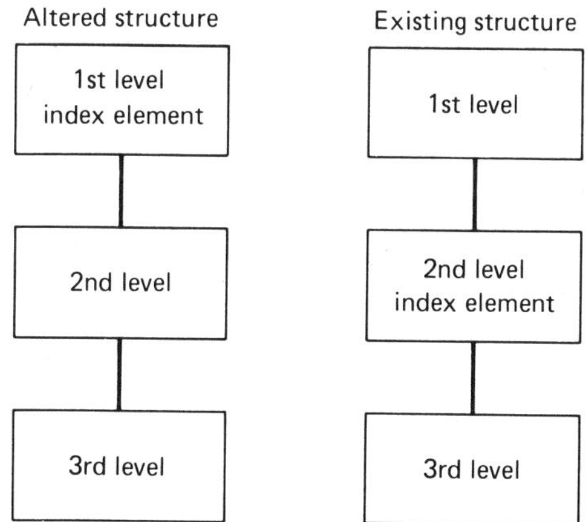

Figure 14.7 Moving the element pointed to by the index from the second level to the first level would have smoothed the processing of the data at the expense of creating more complex programs and affecting the processing time of other programs.

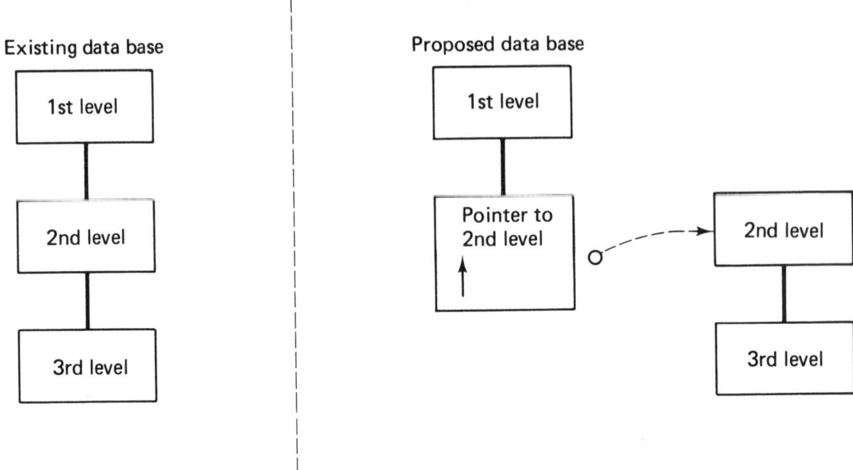

Figure 14.8 One alternative was to change the physical organization of the data so that two data bases were created from the original. This would optimize the particular process being examined at the expense of all other processes that used the data base.

own data base (Fig. 14.8). The pointer of the original root data base points to the second-level segment (now a root in its own data base).

Creating two data bases out of the original one allows the second-level segment to be accessed sequentially. If the order of the segments is properly arranged, this removes the need for an index. There is more than meets the eye to this modification, however. In all other applications where these data bases are to be used, to traverse from the first-level segment to the second-level segment (second level of the original data base) requires at least one extra I/O than in the original design, since the pointer segment must be used to connect the two data bases.

If these data bases are not used elsewhere or are only used in a very limited environment, it may be worthwhile splitting the two data bases; otherwise, the split will increase the cost of normal processing wherever else the data bases are used. This is a good example of how overoptimization of one process can cause a decrease in total system energy expended for a small part of the system at the expense of all other parts of the system.

FINAL SOLUTION

In practice the solution adopted was that of the unintuitive approach. The user was willing to pay a higher price for average processing so that when the worst case came about he would not be left in an inoperable state. The changes were made to the program and the desired results were achieved.

There was one other solution that was discussed but not implemented. In practice, it would have been optimal because it would have combined the best parts of both the intuitive and unintuitive approaches. Simply stated, as the list is being built internally, the program keeps track of the number of entries. Then upon the end of loading, the number of entries determines which approach is to be invoked. For example:

1. Load list, count entries.
2. If entries <= 2000, then:
   a) Sort entries by index key.
   b) Reload list.
   c) Process list sequentially.
   d) Retrieve index until all indices are processed.
   e) Retrieve second-level segment.
   f) Retrieve first-level, second-level, and third-level segments.
   g) Perform change and replace.
3. If entries >= 2000, then:
   a) Sort list by second-level segment interface.
   b) Reload list.
   c) Read first, second-level segments sequentially.
   d) Determine if second-level data is in list (use binary search).
   e) If found in list, retrieve third-level segment.
   f) Perform the change and replace.

This algorithm incorporates both strategies and uses less total system resources than either approach done separately. However, it was not selected, because it was more difficult to program than the unintuitive approach. To save progamming and test time, the user was willing to accept the extra overhead in running normal processing. The most influencing factor in deciding not to use the dual approach was the added complexity.

Complexity is a difficult factor to assess. Adding a new level of complexity has several undesirable implications. It makes the program larger and more fragile. What happens when the average large workload (2000) creeps above what it is projected to be? What happens when the data structures change? What happens when the process changes and a new programmer has to modify the program? All of these factors must be considered when raising the complexity of a process. The designer chose to minimize those problems at the expense of extra processing time.

FIFTEEN

EXAMPLES OF DESIGN—ON—LINE MESSAGE SYSTEM

Trade-offs between speed and storage exist in the on-line environment as well as the batch environment. The essential difference between on-line and batch is that the designer has a much greater exposure when manipulating the trade-offs. The very essence of the on-line system is that it is up, operational, and responsive. When it is not, it is obvious to everyone who regularly depends upon it, whereas in batch there is a margin for error if there is a malfunction of the system before users begin to be affected.

Because of the exposure in an on-line environment, the optimal solution for a given problem may not be implemented if it is complex or will take a great deal of time. The more options a designer has when a system malfunctions, the better the chances are of being able to quickly effect a solution. The data designer allows himself or herself more options by keeping the design simple with clean interfaces with other systems. When data recovery is involved, it is important to have well-defined and straightforward interfaces.

When the on-line data designer encounters a problem and then sets about to resolve it, the solutions usually are classified by how quickly they can be implemented. Solutions can be stopgap (or temporary), short range, or long range. It is usually more important to have some quick solution than it is to have an optimal solution that requires a long time to implement. The accepted practice is to effect temporary solutions immediately while long-term solutions are concurrently being worked on. The result is a phased solution to the problem.

Another phenomenon the on-line designer encounters in many forms is that of *threshold response* (Fig. 15.1). Threshold response is commonly referred to as "critical operational point," "saturation point," or "breakpoint." Because there are so many variables that are complexly interwoven, it is difficult to determine the cause of threshold response. As an example, an on-line's system buffer pool has eight buffers and has performed successfully for an extended period of time. In normal running circumstances, eight buffer pools are quite adequate. Then one day almost inexplicably the buffer pools begin to flush at a very high rate. One or more variables in the workload of the system has caused it to go past some "threshold," and instead of experiencing a gradual increase in buffer flushing, the effect is violent. A saturation point or critical operating point has been reached.

This phenomenon occurs in many places in on-line systems. The critical point may be reached because of many subtle shifts in variables. Transaction volume may not be an appropriate measure of workload at all. Variation in such factors as transaction mix, resource utilization, resource availability, or changes in the SCP may well cause the threshold

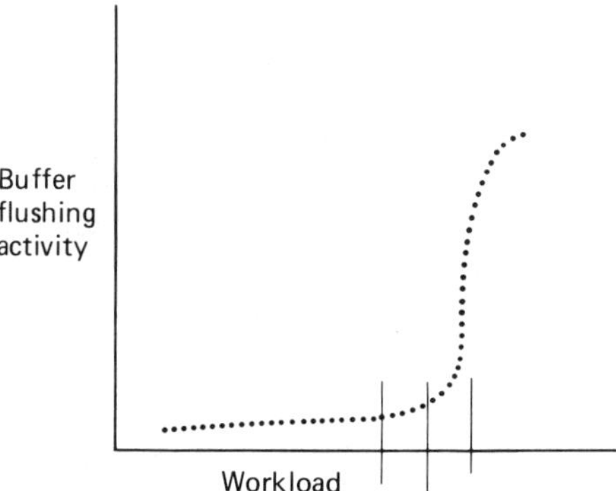

Figure 15.1 In time slot A, as the volume of transactions increases, the activity in the buffer marginally increases. In time slot B, the increase in the buffer flushing activity is entirely disproportionate to the increase in the workload. This phenomenon is caused because a threshold or saturation point (or critical operational point) has been reached.

to be reached with no increase in transaction volume. One way the on-line data manager can begin to understand and control a system is to keep records of the vital operating aspects of the system over time. Records of system parameters while the system is operating satisfactorily are as important as those while the system is performing poorly. The problem presented in the on-line discussion illustrates some of the considerations of short-range and long-range problem solution and threshold analysis.

PROBLEM DESCRIPTION—ON-LINE ENVIRONMENT

The facility for sending and storing communications between terminals in an on-line system is achieved by a data base with a root segment for each terminal and a dependent segment to hold the message that has been transmitted to the terminal (Fig. 15.2).

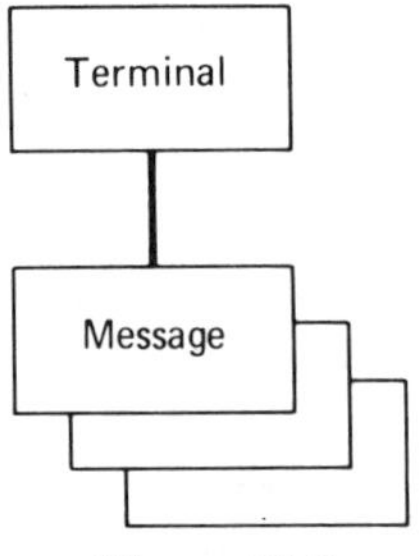

Figure 15.2

Not only does each root associate with a terminal, but each root may also be associated with a class of terminals. For example, a root may belong to a class of terminals on a specific line or all terminals belonging to the western sales region of a company. Communications can be sent to the root by its individual name or by addressing all terminals in its line or all terminals in the western sales region. A single message sent to a class of terminals arrives at the root of all terminals in that class. This circumvents having to send the communication multiple times.

The message segment (beneath the root) is stored one line at a time as it is entered into the system. One option the user has is to store messages below the root in FIFO or LIFO order. Another option the user has is to determine the length of time the message is kept. The user predetermines the retention period, and that value is stored in the root segment. As messages are received, the retention date is calculated by adding the current date with the retention period. The calculated date is stamped on the message. There is a cross reference between the sender and receiver so that future communications can reference a specific message.

SYSTEM OPERATION

The messages are not directly displayed to the terminal for which they are destined. The operator of the destination terminal must initiate action to view the messages that are queued beneath the root segment. This communication replaces many long-distance phone calls and telegraph communications. In addition to displaying the messages sent to him or her, the operator can send his or her messages to hardcopy if written documentation is desired.

Every night when the on-line system is brought down, a batch run is made against the message queue segments and all segments where the retention date is less than the current date are deleted.

TRANSACTIONS

The transactions that support the on-line message facility are (see Fig. 15.3):

1. TRANSMIT transaction—up to full screen (approximately 2000 bytes) or a string of data from a teletype can be sent to the root of a terminal or class of terminals. The average length of a message is about 9.4 lines per message or about 750 bytes per transmission.

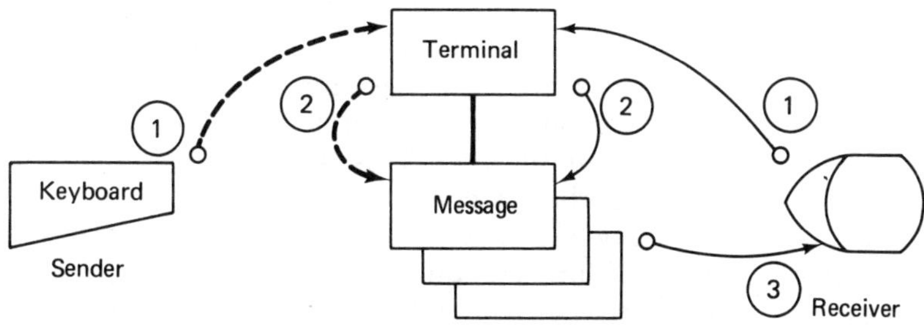

Sending

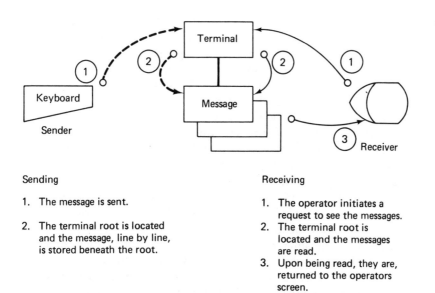

1. The message is sent.
2. The terminal root is located and the message, line by line, is stored beneath the root.

Receiving

1. The operator initiates a request to see the messages.
2. The terminal root is located and the messages are read.
3. Upon being read, they are, returned to the operators screen.

Figure 15.3 Operation of the on-line message communication system.

2. LOOK transaction—the LOOK transaction examines the messages queued up for the terminal for the user entering the LOOK request. All messages are fetched in the order in which they were stored. The user has the option to not look at any more messages after seeing what he or she wants to see. The user exercises this option by depressing a special key that erases all the messages left in that transmission. In any case, the messages remain in the dependent segment beneath the root regardless of the number of LOOK transactions run against the messages.

ON-LINE PROBLEMS

For an extended period of time, the system has run with no errors and very little maintenance activity. Then one day the space available for queueing messages fills up and the system ceases to function. The data base is monitored on a monthly basis and the prior month's statistics show that ample space existed. In fact, for the life of the system there has been a consistent record of space availability. In conjunction with the filling up of the message data base, it is noticed that the LOOK transaction is running about 100% longer than it ever has before. Even though the LOOK transaction represents a small fraction of system transactions, it is beginning to degrade overall system performance. The smooth flow of transactions through the system is broken up by the occasional long-running LOOK transaction.

Very quickly, all concerned parties met to discuss the problem. The organizations represented at the meeting were data management, programming, user liaison, and system design personnel. The first question discussed was why there was suddenly a problem after a long record of successful and uneventful operation. This led to a discussion of what factors have changed within the system.

At least three factors which happened to coincide were discovered. The time of year of the failure was during the peak business cycle. The day the problem occurred was the day books were closing for the month. The messages flowing through the system were essential to the business of the company. The second factor that contributed to the problem was that a large new division had just been added to the message system and the staff was just learning to use it. The third factor was that users all over the system were becoming more sophisticated and were using system features such as transmission to classes of terminals rather than to single terminals. This lowered the number of transactions but increased the number of messages in the system. All these factors happened at the same time and produced a workload the system had not previously experienced.

After the problem-solving team satisfied themselves that they knew the cause of the problem, they discussed possible solutions. The situation was not relaxed because overall system performance was being degraded at a critical time. Also, communications passing through the system at that particular time were very sensitive to the running of the business. Thus data management could neither take the message system down entirely to enhance overall system performance nor could they allow it to perform at its current level.

SOLUTIONS TO THE PROBLEM

Even though time was of the essence, the problem-solving team took the luxury of listing and investigating (at least on a cursory level) some of the possible alternatives before one or more schemes was chosen to alleviate the problem. They did not make the mistake of hastily embarking upon the first possible course of action without understanding what the alternatives were and what trade-offs were involved. Because the critical expertise had been gathered in one place and was focused on solving the single problem at hand, the time to enumerate and evaluate the alternatives was not long. The proposed solutions were:

1. Reduce the number of messages kept in the data base by entering a new value into the root segment for each terminal for the retention period. This would cut the number of messages processed by the LOOK transaction by approximately 35%. It would not speed up the TRANSMIT transaction, but it was not in a great deal of trouble anyway. This solution, recognized as being short-term, was desirable because it could be implemented almost instantaneously, as the parametric changing of the retention date required no program change and a small amount of data entry. The drawback was that it cost the user some reduction of function. Frequently, users would browse over communications that had transpired over the past week. This solution meant deleting some percentage of data that was useful.

2. Enter default values on the LOOK transaction so that only messages for the current and prior day would appear, instead of all messages in the user's queue. An additional parameter could be entered with the LOOK transaction so that all messages would appear. This parameter would default to a null value. The problem with this solution was that it would require program changes, not reduce the total number of messages in the system, and would speed up only the LOOK transaction. The program changes were simple and were estimated to take 2 days.

3. Shut down the LOOK transaction at certain peak hours of the day. This solution would require no programming changes and could be implemented immediately through the facility of the DBMS. It would reduce the strain on the system at critical periods. However, it would mean

a significant loss of function to the user and would increase his or her frustration with an already straining system. This solution, of course, was only temporary.

4. Block the message segments. The segments would be stored and transmitted half a screen at a time rather than line by line. This would require a little more space, since some fraction of the message segment (on the average) would be unused. However, the insert activity would be cut by approximately a factor of 10, as would retrieval activity. This represented a long-term significant solution to the problem. The number of messages in the system would not change, but the work necessary to handle them would be significantly cut. The number of segments in the data base would be reduced, however.

The problem with this solution was that it affected programs throughout the system. Principally affected were the TRANSMIT and LOOK transactions, as well as other programs and transactions that accessed the queued messages. Furthermore, the transaction changes were not simple. Changing the blocking of a segment intuitively seemed to be a simple change, but a closer investigation showed that there were many intricate details that were involved that had to be handled delicately. It was felt that this solution offered the best real solution but would take a minimum of 2 weeks to implement if all went well.

The size of the blocking of the segment was arbitrarily set to hold 12 lines of text (Fig. 15.4). This meant that any communication with greater than 12 lines would require two physical segments to hold the data. The average communication was 9.4 lines, so it seemed reasonable to choose 12 lines per segment for blocking.

5. Restrict transmission options. This plan would restrict operators from sending messages to classes of terminals and/or limiting the number

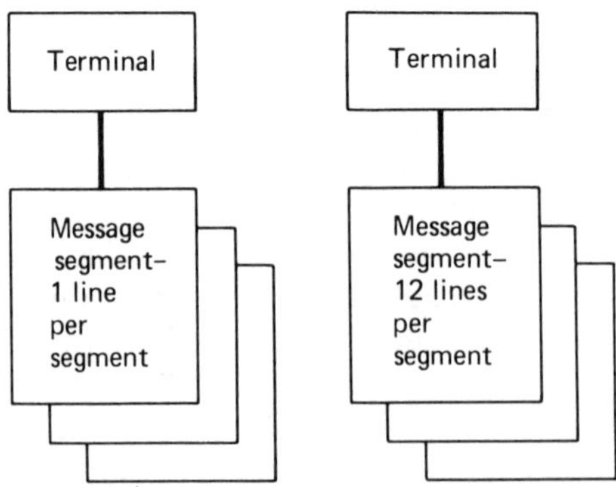

Figure 15.4 Proposed data base change to alleviate problem of message transmission. Blocking 12 lines per segment would save time in insertion, deletion, and retrieval.

of lines per communication. A program change would be made to the TRANSMIT transaction. The change would be simple and it was felt that it could be completed in 2 days or less. The problem with this solution was that it would reduce the user's functional usage of the system. The user liaison felt that this loss of function was so severe that it was not considered further.

6. Ask users to send shorter communications. A note would be sent to all operators explaining briefly what the problem was and requesting that they minimize the use of the system. As an extra incentive, shorter communications would be charged less than lengthy communications. The solution could be effected immediately and would require no program changes but would be enforced only voluntarily, since the system could not restrict message size without some alteration. Another consideration was that a new division had recently been added to the system and it would be psychologically unsettling to ask that user to restrict use of the system.

7. Compact the message. Another alternative was to increase the message space and compact it, since there were usually long series of blanks in the message (Fig. 15.5). The compacted message would be expanded upon retrieval. This solution would require tedious changes to be made to the LOOK and TRANSMIT transaction. Furthermore, data compaction would introduce a new level of complexity within the system. It was felt that 2 to 3 weeks would be necessary to implement this change. Another disadvantage was that at execution time more instructions are required. However, the benefits of compacting the data would be derived by having a decrease of activity in the DBMS.

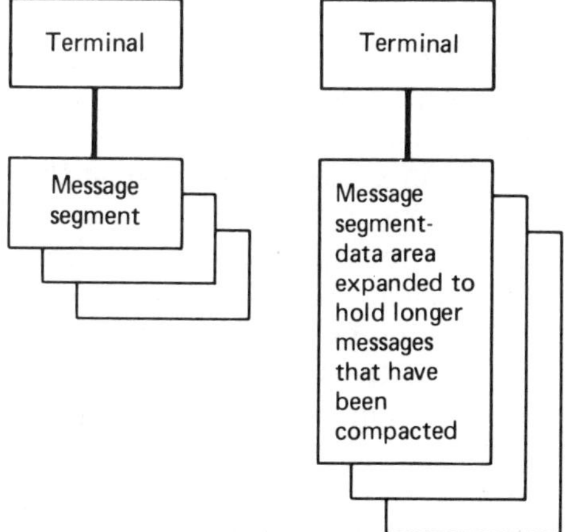

Figure 15.5 Proposed data base change—enlarge the message segment and compact the data as it is entered.

PLAN OF ACTION

Once the alternatives and trade-offs were discussed, it was decided to implement several actions concurrently. The short-range solution was to reset parameters inside the root segment so that messages would be retained for a shorter amount of time. This reduced the user function, but it was agreed to by the user liaison because of the critical nature of the situation. The first step was taken immediately. The next part of the plan was to reprogram the transactions to block the message segments.

Even though it was begun immediately, it was recognized that it would not have an effect on the system for 2 to 3 weeks. It was looked upon as the best long-term solution to the problem. As an intermediate step, the LOOK transaction had default parameters placed in it to limit the number of messages sent to the screen. This change, which was concurrent with the others, took 1 day to implement. The other alternatives were shelved for future implementation if the communication system began to suffer problems at some future time.

IMPLEMENTATION

After discussion, implementation of the plan was immediate. The communication system was already down. More space was allocated for the data base. The appropriate system utilities were run off-line and the data base was readied for action. It was brought up and, before any users could access it, the parameters were reset in each root to hold less data and were then purged of data beyond the retention date. The system was then brought up.

At the same time, one programmer modified the LOOK transaction (not the production version of the transaction) to retrieve only 2 days' worth of messages unless otherwise requested, and tested it. It was a very simple change and was put into place so that when the on-line system was brought down and then brought up, the new version of the transaction was used. This took 1 day to implement, as the on-line system was not brought down until the normal midnight stopping time. This change reduced the resources used by the LOOK transaction by about 25%.

The third change, blocking the data, took 2 weeks to implement. Once tested and set into production, it reduced system resource usage by a factor of 7 (i.e., the LOOK and TRANSMIT functions used one-seventh of the resources they formerly did). The user never knew that a conversion took place except that response time suddenly improved dramatically. After all program changes were made, the retention period in the root segment was reset to its value prior to the problem.

GLOSSARY

ADABAS — A data base management system (by Software AG).

Archived Data — Data removed from the main storage of a system to a medium suited for mass storage (and usually sequential access). Typically, data selected for archiving is inactive, old, irrelevant, or redundant.

Audit Procedures — Programs or techniques to ensure data validity or existence.

Backup — A procedure used to "freeze" a data base in a usable form at a given time. Data can be restored to a point in time when the backup is run.

Backward Pointer — Pointer maintaining the reverse (collating or hierarchical) sequence of segments.

Batch — Computer environment in which programs (usually long-running, sequentially oriented) exclusively access data and user activity is not interactive.

Blocking of Data by Application — Insertion, deletion, update, and retrieval of multiple, distinct units of information in a segment controlled by an application program (as opposed to a system function). To an extent the application program accomplishes some of the functions of data management.

Block Size — The number of bytes into which one or more logical records may be placed. One of the basic units of data transfer.

Boundary — Logical and/or physical unit of groups of data elements.

Child — A segment that has a parent; a dependent segment. A child has only one physical parent. It may occur zero or more times per parent.

Compression — Removal of unnecessary or repetitious character strings for the purpose of reducing data transmission and storage utilization. Upon retrieval, data is decompressed.

Concatenated Key — The keys of the first to *n*th segments down a hierarchical path laid in order from top to bottom. The concatenated key of the root level is the key of the root. The concatenated key of the root and a dependent is the key of the root plus the key of the dependent, and so on.

Conceptual Model of Data — Abstraction of data as it exists in the user's environment. May include multiple environments and interfaces. Operated on by conceptual processes.

CPU — Central processing unit.

Data Administration — Administrative function encompassing or embracing data base design, system availability, system security, data dictionary, and so on.

Data Availability — Ease of access and capability of change of data (both semantic and physical). (*Note*: This term as used here is not standard common usage.)

Data Base — Collection of data in one or more physical files controlled by a data base management system.

Data Base Concept — Integration, organization, and control of data for use in different ways in multiple environments.

Data Base Record (IMS) — The root segment and all its physical dependents. IMS tries to store (unless specifically told not to) a data base record in one physical block.

Data Bases Tied by Transaction — When a transaction accesses two or more data bases so that data in both depends upon the execution of the transaction, when the transaction is unavailable, both data bases are affected. Even worse, when one data base goes down, both are affected.

Data Dictionary — Software for the semantic definition and control of data, principally data elements, but also including structures, data bases, relationships, and so on.

Data Driven Process — A process whose resource utilization depends on the structure and occurrences of the data being operated on. For example, a root has on the average 2 dependents but has one case where there are 1000 dependents. Any process accessing the root and all dependents will be data-driven (i.e., behaving nicely 99% of the time, and awkwardly 1% of the time).

Data Element — Basic unit of semantic definition of data. The definition of the physical embodiment of some entity in the user's environment.

Data Group (also, Group of Data Elements) — Usually thought of as part of the conceptual model, a group of data elements. As the conceptual model takes shape, in IMS it is equivalent to a segment.

Data Integrity — Protection of data values and their relationships with one another from uncontrolled, external factors such as logic errors, system failures, power failures, and so on.

Data Relationships (Implicit or Explicit) — Logical connection of data elements or segments to each other. Explicit relationship: supported by the physical existence of a pointer. Implicit relationship: supported by application programs.

DB/DC — Data Base/Data Communications.

DBMS — Data Base Management System: Software that facilitates the development and operation of systems under the data base concept.

DBMS Language Interface (DB I/O Module) — Software that applications call, which in turn call the DBMS. By making the interface to the DBMS indirect, several benefits will derive, such as standards enforcement, standard error checks, and so on.

DC Monitor — Software that marries the networking, message handling, and on-line considerations with the data base software. In IMS, an internal trace facility.

Delete Segment — To remove a segment from the data base—a physical delete—the segment cannot be accessed physically. In a logical delete, the segment cannot be addressed logically. (*Note*: Physical delete may not mean that the segment is actually removed from DASD.)

Dependent Segment — A segment with a parent.

DL1 — Data Language/One.

Encoding — A shortening or abbreviation of the physical representation of a data value. For example, male = M, female = F.

Environmental Change — A semantic change to a data element. For example, pay is defined as 8 bytes and must be changed to 9 bytes, or order number is to be moved from one segment to another.

Exclusive Usage of Data — Occurs when a process is accessing data and will not let any other process concurrently access it. Data can be controlled exclusively by data base, data base record, or by segment.

Exit — User-defined program exit. Software in selected places allows users to write and execute their own code as a part of the larger software package.

Explicit Relationships — Data relationships implemented by means of a physical pointer.

FIFO — First in, first out—a fundamental ordering of processing a queue.

Flow of Data — The progression of data as it enters a system, is manipulated, is retrieved, and finally is deleted.

HDAM — Hierarchical Direct Access Method—a basic IMS access method.

Hierarchical Structure — An organization of data composed of segments and parent/-child relationships.

Holding Data Base — A data base temporarily used to store data.

Image Copy — A utility in which a data base is physically copied to another media for backup.

Implicit Relationships — Data relationships supported only by application programs.

IMS — Information Management System—IBM software product for data management and data communication.

Inoperative Data — Data not accessed by a program, system, and so on.

Insert Segment — Physical placement of a segment in a data base.

Internal Segment Redefinition — Occurs when a segment has multiple data definitions within the application program.

Internal Structuring of a Data Base — The ordering of segments within a data base.

Internal Structuring of a Segment — The ordering of data elements within a segment.

Intersection Data — A feature of IMS logical relationships in which data relevant to the logical parent and physical parent is stored in the logical child.

I/O — Input/output; also, the activity of executing an input or output operation.

IPL — Initial program load.

IRC — Interregion communication.

ISAM/OSAM — Indexed Sequential Access Method/Overflow Sequential Access Method.

Key — The data element that is uniquely valued in a segment; the data element by which the segment can be identified. A key is normally (but not necessarily) unique. A segment may or may not contain a key.

Level — In a hierarchical structure, the number of parents down a vertical path that a segment has.

Level of Acceptability — The maximum average amount of time in which a transaction can execute and still provide satisfactory user service.

Load Time (Initial Load) — Initial creation of a data base; typically includes overhead not associated with normal usage of the data base.

Logical Access of Data — Retrieval of data down a path other than the physical path.

Logical Parent — Parent of a segment as logically defined to the DBMS.

Logical Relationship — Feature allowing structuring of data to occur on other than the physical structure.

Native Data Organization — The access method of the data.

Network — Terminals or nodes where transactions are input to the DBMS. These terminals are physically attached via communication lines to the computer.

Network Configuration — The definition of how lines and terminals are arranged in the network.

Nine's Complement — Transformation of a numeric field calculated by subtracting its value from a value greater or equal to the field consisting digitally of all nine's.

On-Line — Computer-supported environment in which the end user can actively access data.

Overflow — The part of the data base used when synonym conflicts occur or data base records are inserted where there is not enough space to hold the record in the primary data portion of the data base.

Parent — A segment that can have a dependent segment.

Path, Data Base — Traversal from one segment type to another vertically down a data base (i.e., from parent to child, parent to child, etc.).

Path Length — The number of instructions executed for a given unit (transaction, subroutine, program, etc.).

Peak Period — Time (day, month, etc.) when the system experiences the greatest volume of transactions or activity.

Physical Access of Data — Traversal of data structures along physically directed paths.

Physical Parent — The parent of a segment as physically defined for the DBMS.

Physical Twin Chain — Occurs when the same segment type occurs multiple times beneath the same parent.

Pointers — Addresses to another location.

Pointers, Direct — Pointers referring to the physical location of data.

Pointers, Hierarchical — Pointers used to order segments hierarchically.

Pointers, Physical Child/Physical Twin — Pointers from the physical parent to the first physical child; pointers from a segment to its physical twin.

Pointers, Symbolic — Keyed values that can be hashed or indexed to produce an address (a form of indirection).

Prefix Data — Data in the segment used for system control; usually unavailable to the user.

Process — Work performed by the computer; a transaction or a program.

Processing Relationships — Any relationship between two or more processes (e.g., process A must be run before process B, or transaction A under certain conditions creates transaction B, C, and D).

Processing Requirements — Programming specifications.

Profile, System — An overview of the major processes and data bases of a system.

Profile, Transaction — Usually measured by calls to the data base, length of execution, load module size, and so on.

Programs — Executable code; processes; transactions.

Program Specifications — Documentation of the flow of processing used by the program to create the program.

QBE — Query By Example—a relational query system.

Query Language — A high-level language whose purpose it is to allow users and/or programmers quick access to a data base (bypassing the process of defining, creating, implementing, and testing of transactions).

Random Data Access — Retrieval of data either through an index or a "hashed" value of the key.

Recovery — The action taken to restore the data base to a usable state when it becomes impaired.

Recursive Hierarchy — A hierarchical structure in which a parent and a child represent the same entity: may be logically or physically implemented.

Recursive Relationship — Occurs when the same segment type participates in a parent-child relationship with itself.

Redundancy, Physical — The physical occurrence of the same data value in multiple places in the data base.

Redundancy, Semantic — The multiple occurrence of the definition of the same data element to the data base.

Reorganization — Process of unloading data (in a poorly organized state) and reloading (to a well-organized state). Reorganization in some DBMS is also done to restructure the data base.

Replace Segment — Occurs when a segment is retrieved, nonkey values are changed, and the segment is sent back to the data base.

Response Time (user) — The amount of time the user has to wait from the time a transaction is entered until a response is returned to him or her. Response time is a function of communication line time, processing time, and amount of processing activity.

Root — The first-level segment in a physical hierarchical structure. The root key determines the key for the data base record (root and all dependents).

SCP — System control program: for example, MVS, OS, DOS.

Search Fields — Data elements defined for the DBMS, on which the DBMS can scan for a match for a predetermined value.

Secondary Indexing — Feature allowing alternate entry into a data base on other than the key.

Secondary Indexing, Sparse Indices — Secondary index in which an index may not exist for a given segment, depending on the values in the segment.

Segment — (1) Group of data elements as defined for the DBMS. (2) Fundamental unit of hierarchical structure; data elements are defined to be within a segment; data is stored and transported in units of segments.

Semantic Data Definition — Definition for the DBMS of the type, structuring, and size of the segments in the data base and of certain data elements within a segment.

Sequential Data Access — Traversal of data from one segment to another based upon physical adjacency or physical pointers.

Sibling — Two segment types that exist on the same level.

Single Threading — Inability of a machine to process two transactions concurrently.

Slack Period — Period of time (day, month, year, etc.) when processing requirements are lowest.

Standard Work Unit — Measurement and control of the resources that can be used by a given transaction.

Structure — The static ordering of segments in a data base.

System Availability — (1) The percent of time the on-line system is up and functioning. (2) The ability of the user to easily access data and change the contents and form of data.

System Development Time — Amount of time necessary to build a system (typically from feasibility study to implementation).

System Downtime — Amount of time the on-line system is unavailable to the user. System downtime consists of two types of downtime: planned (PM, etc.) and unplanned (power outage, etc.).

System Flexibility — Ability of a system to change semantically. Typically, the more flexible a system is, the worse performance is and vice versa.

Table Look-ups — Algorithms designed to retrieve specific data from a table or array.

Time-dependent Snapshot — Capturing of the form of data and its values at a given instant. Typically occurs at year end, quarter end, monthly, and so on.

Total — A data base management system (by CINCOM).

Transactions — Response-oriented discrete execution of user-selected code.

Traversing a Structure — Retrieval of data from one segment, then retrieving from another segment.

Twin — Identical segment type existing at the same level under the same parent.

Twin Chain — Linkage of twin segments by pointer, physical position, or other method.

Typical Traversal — Parent to child, sibling to sibling, twin to twin, and so on.

User Data (in a segment) — Portion of a segment not used for data base control and maintenance fields. This space is available for programmer use.

User Function — How much work will be done by the application to make the job of the user easier. Typically, the greater the user function, the more complex and the longer executable path length the transaction and the slower it runs;

and the simpler the user function, the smaller the transaction and the more quickly it runs.

User's Environment — The "real world"; the environment in which the system will operate and will perform a useful function.

User-sequenced Transactions — Transactions run in a set sequence controlled by the user (as opposed to machine-generated and -sequenced transactions).

Variable Length — Segments whose length has not been preset.

Volatility — The propensity for change of the contents of data.

Volume of Transactions — Number of transactions run through a machine over a specified period of time.

VSAM — Virtual Storage Access Method—IBM's access method, designed specifically for keeping the same level of efficiency of retrieval of data after growth.

APPENDIX

VARIABLE FORMAT SEGMENTATION

In an environment where frequent change is a large factor in the design criteria, one alternative may be variable formatting of a segment. In this case only the key of the segment has a fixed format. The DBMS must know where to locate the key within the boundary of the segment and how many bytes the key is so that it remains in a static form. The segment length may be fixed or variable. The remainder of the space inside the segment that is nonkeyed is free to be formatted by the programmer however he or she likes. There are many possibilities—only one will be explored here.

Each data element will have a prefix that describes the data type and tells the length of the element. The actual value of the data element then follows immediately behind the prefix information (see Fig. A.1).

This technique allows new data elements to be added to a segment type with no impact on other programs or disturbance of data that already exists. In an environment where change is constantly happening and will

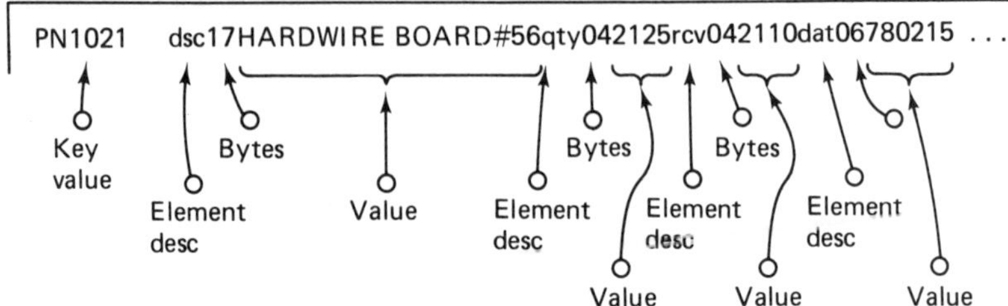

Figure A.1 Variable formatted data.

continue to happen for the predictable future, this technique may warrant close investigation.

There are some serious drawbacks to this technique that must be considered before it is adopted. The data must be encoded upon every insertion, decoded upon every retrieval, and a modification to an element that will change its length requires that the entire record be reformatted. When a data element grows in length, it may even cause a new segment to be created if the existing segment runs out of space. The segments cannot be dumped and examined intelligently without going through the decoding process. The very fact that there is encoding and decoding opens the door to errors that may not otherwise have occurred. The segments cannot be searched on anything but the key field. If an extract of the segments is done, they must be decoded before they can be sorted into a meaningful order. If the encoding/decoding algorithm changes, it must be changed in all programs accessing the data base. By now the reader should be impressed with the fact that variable formatted data is not the panacea for problems of flexibility.

There are some cases where variable formatting of a segment (or some variation thereof) can be quite useful. When the encoding/decoding algorithm is simple and is used for only a few elements within the segment and when change is inevitable and the scope and general nature of the change is predictable, variably formatted segments may prove to be cost-effective. As a general solution to the problem of flexibility, variable formatted segments have severe limitations.

REFERENCES

1. Control of the Data Base Environment, McDonnell Douglas Automation Company, Manual GP 76-6261-2.

2. C. J. DATE, *An Introduction to Data Base Systems* (Reading, MA: Addison-Wesley Publishing Co., 1975).

3. ESTHER L. DECHOW and DON C. LUNDBERG, IMS Data Base (Application Design Review, IBM Manual G 320-6009, 1977).

4. DONALD E. KNUTH, *Art of Computer Programming: Fundamental Algorithms* (Reading, MA: Addison-Wesley Publishing Co., 1968).

5. JAMES MARTIN, *Computer Data Base Organization* (Englewood Cliff, NJ: Prentice-Hall, Inc.).

6. IMS/VS Primer, IBM Manual 5320-5767-02.

7. IMS/VS Version 1, Application Programming Reference Manual, IBM Manual SH20-9026-6.

8. IMS/VS Version 1, System/Application Design Guide, IBM Manual SH20-9025-6.

9. Query-By-Example Program Description/Operations Manual, IBM Manual SH20-2077-0.

10. MICHAEL R. SALLEE, LARRY BRISTOL, HARRY HARTMAN, MIKE McKENNA, Capacity Planning for IMS/VS Systems, Guide 47.0-Chicago, Session 1 M-13.

11. MOSHEM ZLOOF, "Query-by-Example: A Data Base Language," *IBM Systems Journal*, Vol. 16, No. 4, 1977.

INDEX

T

U

V

W